edges

lic

ith black lace

Oyster

from Montparnasse
to Greenwell Point

 This project has been assisted by the Commonwealth Government through the Australia Council, its arts funding and advisory body.

Assistance by staff of The State Library of South Australia is gratefully acknowledged.
'Evening', Anna Akhmatova, translated by Lenore Mayhew, courtesy *FIELD: Contemporary Poetry and Poetics*, no. 39, Fall 1988, © 1988, Oberlin College. Reprinted with permission of Oberlin College Press.

Every effort has been made to locate copyright holders. The publishers would be pleased to hear from any copyright holder that has not been contacted.

HarperCollins*Publishers*

First published in Australia in 2000
by HarperCollins*Publishers* Pty Limited
ABN 36 009 913 517
A member of the HarperCollins*Publishers* (Australia) Pty Limited Group
http://www.harpercollins.com.au

Copyright © Nicolette Stasko 2000

This book is copyright.
Apart from any fair dealing for the purposes of private study, research, criticism or review, as permitted under the Copyright Act, no part may be reproduced by any process without written permission.
Inquiries should be addressed to the publishers.

HarperCollins*Publishers*
25 Ryde Road, Pymble, Sydney, NSW 2073, Australia
31 View Road, Glenfield, Auckland 10, New Zealand
77–85 Fulham Palace Road, London W6 8JB, United Kingdom
Hazelton Lanes, 55 Avenue Road, Suite 2900, Toronto, Ontario M5R 3L2
and 1995 Markham Road, Scarborough, Ontario M1B 5M8, Canada
10 East 53rd Street, New York NY 10022, USA

National Library of Australia Cataloguing-in-Publication data:

Stasko, Nicolette.
　Oyster: From Montparnasse to Greenwell Point.
　Bibliography.
　Includes index.
　ISBN 0 7322 6802 8.
　1. Oysters. 2. Cookery (Oysters). I. Title.
641.694

Cover photography: Sonya Pletes
Maps: The Telltale Art – Trudi Canavan
Cover and internal design by Judi Rowe, HarperCollins Design Studio
Printed in Australia by Australian Print Group on 79gsm Bulky Paperback

6 5 4 3 2 1　　00 01 02 03 04

Oyster

from Montparnasse
to Greenwell Point

nicolette stasko

HarperCollins*Publishers*

This book is dedicated to my mother and father,
Alice and John Stasko, and to all the oyster farmers
who spend their days ensuring that we can still
enjoy the delectable mollusc.

Foreword

IF THERE WERE a Ministry of Food in Australia, its sermons would centre on the land and the sea, and its churches would be erected in all those diverse and precious regions where our food grows. Its enchantments and its hymns of praise would be the poetry of gastronomy. The oyster would serve perfectly as the Ministry's central symbol. After all, it has been said that the best description of an oyster also describes the perfect state: 'clean, fresh, delicious and desirable'. These four words cannot be bettered as a combined focal point for a world in which we might coherently care about what we eat. By coherency, I mean that we must shift our attention from particular public plates to wholesale knowledge, to the getting of wisdom.

To do this is to make every effort possible to understand the whole climate of production. Knowledge is central to our caring about what we eat, and sharing knowledge is central to the future well-being of our table. The more we know about our produce (differences in species, what produces flavour, the time in the year when we might expect a particular food to be available and more, to be at its best, and so on) the more we will ask for it to be 'clean, fresh, delicious and desirable'. Just like the oyster. The more we know about oysters, the more we consumers might ask for them when demand is legitimate, and more, ask for them in the right condition.

I can't pretend to any distance from this book, having accompanied Nicolette Stasko on some of her forays into deep and shallow waters in Tasmania and South Australia in search of everything the oyster would tell her before she ate it.

We were in Cowell, for instance, hundreds of kilometres from Adelaide, on the Eyre Peninsula. A town of 600 just like the other oyster-producing centres we'd been to in South Australia. One of the oyster farmers in Cowell reckons that when a town reaches 600 they just create another. We drank to that on the verandah of the Franklin Harbour Hotel, opening two dozen or two Stansbury Pacifics by necessary candlelight. Stansbury, where we had been before driving on to Cowell, is on the boot-shaped Yorke Peninsula. You learn a lot about the land and the water when you're chauffeur to an oyster lover who is crazy enough about her subject to write a whole book on it.

Out on the leases in dreamy Franklin Harbour, kilometres from the shore, breakfast was extraordinarily plump and clean Pacifics and the wild native oysters which grow on the stakes for the farming baskets. Oh I'd like a lot more of those. The oyster farmers reckon the natives a little bitter but they are my favourites and each to her own taste. We brought dozens of Cowell Pacifics home (this was June, a good month) just as we had brought oysters back from Little Swanport and Freycinet on the east coast of Tasmania last October. You even get better at opening them which is just as well because I don't think I'll ever eat another oyster which has not been opened before me, or by me, and I've Nicolette to thank for that.

Foreword

Citrus australasica F Mueller is a native of our subtropical rainforests. Grafted onto different root stock, it grows well enough in my backyard, in South Australia's McLaren Vale region, to produce the fruit by which it is known, the finger lime, the 'rainforest pearl'.

I slit one finger lime lengthwise like a vanilla pod and scooped out the crisp, caviar-like seeds, opened some *Crassostrea gigas*, and spooned some of the rainforest pearls into each oyster shell. Tipped into the mouth the whole became a succession of sea, cream, lime crunch and again, sea; an exquisite, prolonged sensation, an addition to the short list of what goes with what, like sorrel melting to velvet inside a runny omelette.

In serving oysters naturel, writes Stasko, there are only two rules: 'keep it simple and make sure the oysters are absolutely fresh. Who was it that said "the true art of gastronomy is to respect perfection"?'. 'An oyster,' she writes in her introduction, 'is like a well-written poem, beautifully compact and concise with no extraneous decoration or superfluousness.'

Surely the understanding that a particular kind of perfection exists before cooking is part of the accumulated knowledge which will form the basis of a profound food culture in Australia. *Oyster* will persuade you that all the cookbooks in Australia, although a pretty garnish, will never, even in profusion, amount to a maturing gastronomic culture unless we are as persistently, gloriously curious as its author.

Gay Bilson

contents

Foreword by Gay Bilson 5
Introduction 'A Mollusc Proposal' 11

chapter i

These Breedy Creatures 21

What is an oyster? 25 ❦ A rose by any other name 29
❦ The Rock (Sydney and western) 32 ❦ The Pacific 33
❦ The Native 34 ❦ The politics of reproduction 44
❦ Metamorphosis 50 ❦ Spent 53

chapter ii

Where Have All The Oysters Gone? 55

Wild and free 57 ❦ First attempts 66
❦ Way out west 67 ❦ Farming the sea 70
❦ Poor Britons 72

chapter iii

How to Catch a Good Oyster 75

Sticks, stones and shells 78 ❦ Try try again 80
❦ Waiting for the signals 86
❦ The well-travelled oyster 88 ❦ Set and forget? 93
❦ Between tides 94 ❦ Deep water 96
❦ A matter of life and death 98 ❦ Picked today? 108
❦ The big oyster 110 ❦ By hook or crook 112

chapter iv
Oyster Tales 116
And the winner was 120 ❦ Under the towering cliffs 122 ❦ Echidnas can swim 126 ❦ Oysterless 131 ❦ In the beginning was the spat 133 ❦ To the lovers of oysters 142 ❦ Clean and green 154

chapter v
The Right Time 166
Fattening the good oyster 172 ❦ The oyster opens 176 ❦ Bringing in the catch 183 ❦ The market 185 ❦ The bureaucratic oyster 199

chapter vi
Breaching Those Stony Doors 202
The enclosing shell 204 ❦ Breaking and entering 209 ❦ Shucking/splitting/opening 212 ❦ The secret lever 224 ❦ Those empty shells 230 ❦ A word 233 ❦ Pearl of any price 236

chapter vii
A Gastronomic Nostalgia 241
All the other bits you may have wondered about 247 ❦ Perhaps you might care to try 258 ❦ The way they look 269 ❦ The rituals of dinner 274 ❦ The oyster and a glass 278 ❦ Poverty and oysters 281 ❦ A way of life 287

Bibliography 294

List of Illustrations 297

Index 299

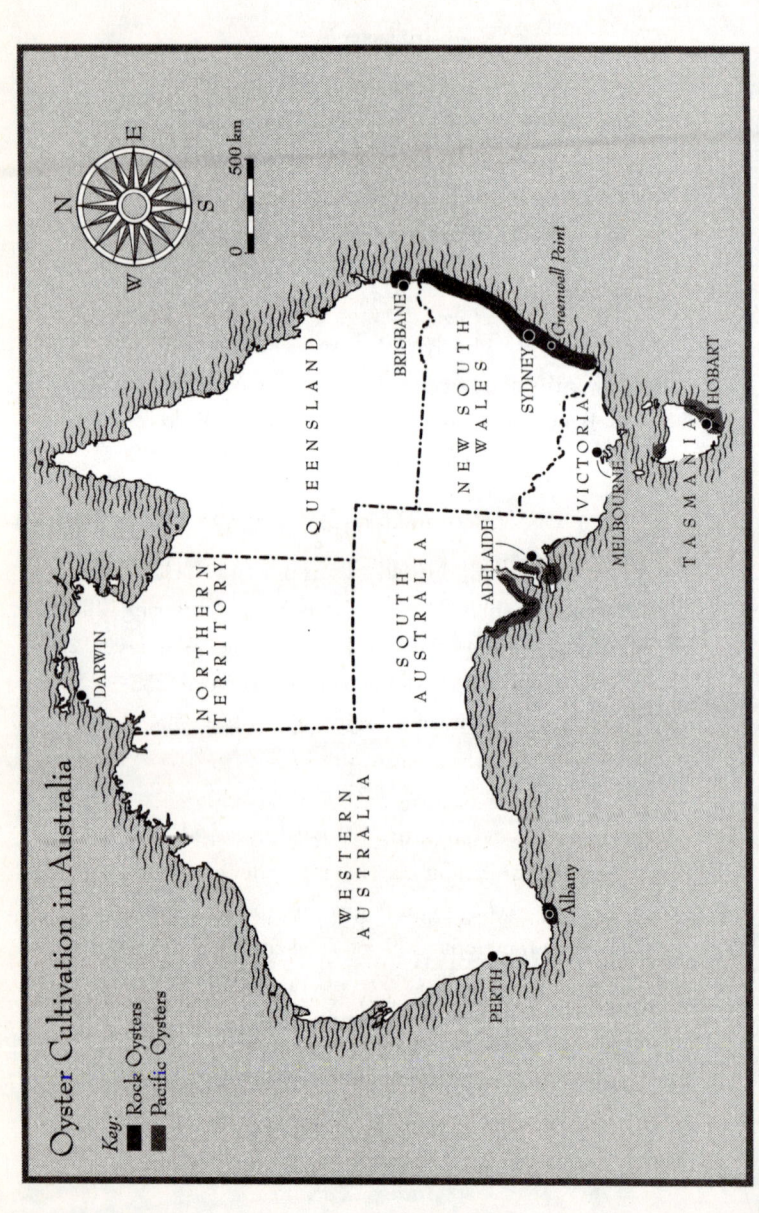

introduction

A Mollusc Proposal

> THE VISIBLE WORLD WOULD BE MORE PERFECT IF SEAS AND CONTINENTS HAD A REGULAR SHAPE.
> —Malebranche *Méditations chrétiennes*

THIS IDEA OF Malebranche's seems incredible, arrogant, and even a little mad. I suspect, however, that many would agree with him and that these opposite ways of thinking probably divide the human race. It's like oysters. You either love them or you don't. Few people are middle of the road about this. And if you do love oysters, it's as much for their crazy irregularity, their strange shapes and colours, their viscous, almost too-natural nature as anything else. For the converted their visible perfection is *because* of their strangeness and differences. Although many species of oyster require deep water to mature and all can swim at an early age, they are not creatures of the open sea. They need an irregular coast, bays, estuaries, coves, all those little imperfections of the continents which so disturbed our Christian meditator.

In spite of what we'd like to believe, we don't own the oyster; it owns us. This mysterious, wilful, eccentric creature is like a movie or pop star—bestowing its bountiful presence only under the most exact circumstances. We have spent the last six thousand years trying to coax them into increased production and further fields. Sometimes it appears we have the most marvellous success, then suddenly the whole scheme falls apart: the oysters won't breed or disappear entirely. The reasons vary. It can be the slightest variation in water temperatures—as in the heating up of the bay caused by the San Francisco earthquake—or the alteration of a coastline (dear Malebranche) through storm or alluvial deposit, or because of some previously unknown, unsuspected disease. The history of oysters is much like the history of human civilisations: decline and fall, vast changes in a blink of the eye, powers and populations growing and failing. And human greed for this mollusc places it, in the realm of edible things, on a par with gold.

A famous story tells of how Louis XIV was offered some of the renowned *huîtres vertes* from Marennes. His mistress, Madame de Maintenon, alarmed by the bright green colour around the edges, thought that the king was being poisoned and had them taken away. We don't need to be concerned with kings, nor with green oysters that are, in fact, a specialty of the famous French basins where the oysters feed on a certain kind of algae—but it is worth noting, not only to illustrate how a little ignorance can rob one of a great pleasure, but also as an example of how oysters 'are what they eat'. This is the *goût de terroir* (the taste of the land—or in this case the water), which oysters take on from wherever they are grown. Like wine, the characteristics of an oyster are largely determined by the conditions it finds itself in rather than parentage. Every bed is affected by the environment that surrounds it—weather, temperature, tide, salinity, mud, in a delicate balance—and every bed will produce an oyster with a unique flavour.

Eleanor Clarke, in her classic book on the French oyster industry of Locmariaquer, writes without equivocation: 'Obviously, if you don't love life you can't enjoy an oyster'. In the Antipodes we love life a great deal and consume large numbers of the delectable shellfish, but we actually know very little about the creature we put into our mouths, raw or cooked.

I have always delighted in oysters—in the whole idea of them, in painting and literature, and especially in eating them. But I must admit that for a long time I, too, knew absolutely nothing about them. Living in Paris a few years ago I had the opportunity of having really fresh oysters, opened on the spot, and attempted in a poem to re-create the sensation. By the time I was again in Paris we had learned how to open our own oysters and, equipped with a French oyster knife, we set about eating as many as we could afford to buy in the Montparnasse markets—including the legendary *huîtres vertes*. To celebrate and remember the experience, my daughter gave me an elegant little volume called *l'Huître* for my birthday. When I began to read it I realised I was as ignorant about oysters as Madame de Maintenon, and with much less excuse. Thus began the long and amazing journey which has culminated in this book.

During the course of it, I have often been asked two questions: have I gotten tired of eating all those oysters, and what is my favourite oyster? The answer to the first one should be fairly obvious. The second is almost impossible to say, for many different reasons, not the least of which has something to do with the place, the situation, the company and the wine with which the oyster is eaten. Other variables, such as which region and lease on the river it comes from are important, as is the season, or the particular year, since oysters like other 'crops' have good years and bad. Probably one of the most significant factors in producing a memorable oyster is how carefully it has been handled, not only in transport and storage, but by the farmer—what is termed 'well-farmed'. Even from the same area and estuary, the oyster will taste differently for better or worse depending on who grew it.

Taking these things as given, I still find it difficult to pick a favourite because I love oysters, all kinds of oyster; and every one, as long as it is fresh and in reasonable condition, is a new and enjoyable experience for me. But if I'm forced, I'd have to say oysters from the Crookhaven for consistent quality and flavour. From Moxhams' on the Hawkesbury, the hessian sackful we shared with friends for weeks. The Tasmanian Pacifics I had once in a restaurant in Launceston (I didn't know enough then to ask where they came from) because they were delicious, delicate and picked up my dejected spirits immensely. And the huge 'boats' I ate straight out of the water in Little Swanport under an imminent sunset; the small Creuses I had for breakfast sitting on the edge of the bay at Cancale in Brittany because they were some of the coldest (by this I mean a kind of 'flintiness' I associate with cold water), freshest tasting oysters I'd ever eaten. And all the flat *Ostrea* I've ever had the fortune to savour both in Australia (especially the time Andrea Cole sent up a box of her extraordinary Freycinet Natives) and Europe, because of their firm texture and sea taste, which remind me not so much of an oyster but a cross between a cherrystone clam on the half shell from the Atlantic *and* an oyster. This may be because my first real experience of eating raw shellfish was not with an oyster but with a clam my father urged me to try when I was around twelve. And I've never looked back since.

Perhaps it might seem unusual for a poet to be interested in oysters. But the truth is an oyster is like a well-written poem—beautifully compact and concise with no extraneous decoration or superfluousness. What may appear simple and closed on the surface, when opened reveals a wonderful complexity and richness. And sometimes, if irritated, both are thought to produce pearls. Every oyster, in a way similar to a poem, is as different as the place it was grown, the food that fed it, the sun that shone on it, as well as the person who nurtured it, the person who opened it and put it before you on the table.

When I began to research the famous mollusc, I found an enormous amount of material containing almost as many misconceptions and as much misinformation as fascinations. In so short a book, it is impossible to cover all that I would have liked to. My intentions are to try to clear up some of this confusion; to give the ordinary reader, the average oyster-eater some basic details, wonderful stories, rules of thumb; and above all to concentrate on our unique Australian oyster.

I am indebted to CM Yonge's invaluable book *Oysters* for basic biological information, and to RM Philpots' *The Oyster and Everything About It* for the quotes and details from the classics. I particularly wish to acknowledge the work of GS Smith whose remarkable *Queensland Oyster Fishery, an Illustrated History*, has supplied numerous fascinating anecdotes and most of the information contained herein about the Queensland oyster industry, and Evelyn Wallace-Carter's *For They Were Fishers* for information on the history of oyster dredging and early cultivation in South Australia.

As always in a book of this type there are many acknowledgments to be made and thanks to be given. The following is just the crown of the oyster bank and I can only hope that anyone I may have inadvertently left out will know who they are and accept my gratitude for their generosity.

Grateful thanks to: Barry, Brian, Ted and the rest of the Allen family (of Greenwell Point) without whose patience and generous help at the very beginning (and until the end), this book would not exist; Jonathan Bilton (Ocean Foods International); Jerry Fraser; Rob and Paul Moxham; The Dyke family, Sue, Colin and Hayden; Andrea Cole and son Joe; Geoff and Janet Turner; Henry, Marie Pope and their son Stephen; Ian and Cheryl Bishop; Bob Arnold (Queensland Oyster Growers' Association); Laurie Larner; Enola Ralston; Terry Lucas; Jim Wild; Peter Clift; Steve Felletti; Roy Mills (NSW Fisheries, Batemans Bay); Ken Burrows; David Willis (SA Oyster Farmers' Association);

Jeremy Pearce; Neil Hickman (Marine and Freshwater Resources Institute, Queenscliff, VIC) for his never-ending patience in answering questions; John Nell, Mike Heasman and Andrew Derwent (NSW Fisheries); Darby Ross and Tony Thomas (TAS Fisheries); Ian Lock (Australian Museum); Barbara Horton (David Jones Archives); Sue Trewartha; Ted Pettafor (OYSA); Dennis Abbot (CSIRO Marine Research); Peter White (University of Sydney Archaeology Department); Peter Rankin; staff of the NSW State Library; staff at the Battye Library of Western Australia; members of the 11th Gastronomic Symposium; particularly Scott Minervini; The NSW Oyster Farmers' Association; Martin Palmer; John Newton; Frank Moorhouse; Inez Baranay; Michael Klausen; staff at the Boathouse Restaurant particularly Robert and Andrew; David Heyden for the title of the introduction; my agent Tim Curnow; and from HarperCollins, Shona Martyn and Helen Littleton, who recognised the book's promise; Rod Morrison; designer Judi Rowe and my intrepid editor, Vanessa Radnidge; John Parkinson; Stephen Hyde; and especially Chris O'Brien and Gay Bilson for their unwavering faith, support and excellent driving skills; for a room to write, Alan and Eva Gold and Geraldine Barnes when the jackhammering was happening. Also many thanks to all the friends who listened to endless talk about oysters and shared the feasts of eating them for research sake. And of course, as always, to David and Jessica.

The Walrus and the Carpenter

The Walrus and the Carpenter
'O Oysters, come and walk with us!'
The Walrus did beseech.
'A pleasant walk, a pleasant talk,
Along a briny beach:
We cannot do with more than four,
To give a hand to each.

The eldest Oyster looked at him,
But never a word he said:
The eldest Oyster winked his eye,
And shook his heavy head—
Meaning to say he did not choose
To leave the oyster-bed.

But four young Oysters hurried up,
All eager for the treat:
Their coats were brushed, their faces washed,
Their shoes were clean and neat—
And this was odd, because you know,
They haven't any feet.

Four other Oysters followed them,
And yet another four;
And thick and fast they came at last,
And more, and more, and more—
All hopping through the frothy waves,
And scrambling to shore.

The Walrus and the Carpenter
Walked on a mile or so,
And then they rested on a rock
Conveniently low;

A Mollusc Proposal

And all the little Oysters stood
And waited in a row.

'The time has come', the Walrus said,
'To talk of many things:
Of shoes—of ships—and sealing wax—
Of cabbages—and kings—
And why the sea is boiling hot—
And whether pigs have wings'.

'But wait a bit', the Oysters cried,
'Before we have our chat;
For some of us are out of breath
And all of us are fat!'
'No hurry!' said the Carpenter.
They thanked him much for that.

'A loaf of bread', the Walrus said,
'Is chiefly what we need:
Pepper and vinegar besides
Are very good indeed—
Now, if you're ready, Oysters dear,
We can begin to feed'.

'But not on us' the Oysters cried,
Turning a little blue.
'After such kindness, that would be
A dismal thing to do!'
'The night is fine', the Walrus said.
'Do you admire the view?'

'It was so kind of you to come!
And you are very nice!'
The Carpenter said nothing but
'Cut us another slice.

I wish you were not quite so deaf—
I've had to ask you twice!'

'It seems a shame', the Walrus said,
'To play them such a trick,
After we've brought them out so far,
And made them trot so quick!'
The Carpenter said nothing but
'The butter's spread too thick!'

'I weep for you', the Walrus said:
'I deeply sympathize'.
With sobs and tears he sorted out
Those of the largest size,
Holding his pocket-handkerchief
Before his streaming eyes.

'O Oysters', said the carpenter
'You've had a pleasant run!
Shall we be trotting home again?'
But answer came there none—
And this was scarcely odd, because
They'd eaten every one.

Lewis Carroll, *Through the Looking Glass*

chapter i

These Breedy Creatures

THIS IS A SMALL BOOK ON A VERY BIG SUBJECT ... THERE IS SO MUCH TO SAY ABOUT OYSTERS. THE MORE ONE STUDIES THEM THE MORE FASCINATED ONE BECOMES ... IN STRUCTURE, TO QUOTE THOMAS HENRY HUXLEY, THEY ARE 'GREATLY MORE COMPLICATED THAN A WATCH' ... PROBABLY NO MARINE ANIMALS—AND CERTAINLY NO MARINE INVERTEBRATES—HAVE BEEN SO INTENSELY STUDIED AND WE ARE NO MORE THAN AT THE BEGINNING OF INTIMATE KNOWLEDGE OF THEM.

C M Yonge, *Oysters*

ONE OF THE greatest problems for the lover of oysters is when to eat them. And sometimes, when to stop. (The Roman Emperor, Aulus Vitellius, whose feats of gluttony have probably never been surpassed, is supposed to have downed a hundred *dozen* oysters at one sitting.) Most of us have heard the general rule (from Samuel Butler's *Dyet's Dry Dinner*, 1599) that 'It is unseasonable and unwholesome in all months that have not an R in their name to eat an oyster': May, June July, August—summer in the Northern

Hemisphere. Logic suggests that this has something to do with high temperatures and the tendency of fragile shellfish to spoil easily in times before refrigeration, especially in transport. But, as MFK Fisher puts it, men's ideas 'continue to run in old channels about oysters as well as God and war and women. Even when they know better they insist the months with R in them are all right, but the oysters in June, July and August will kill you or make you wish they had'.

With today's modern refrigeration and efficient fast transport the problem of spoilage is no longer a great concern. Theoretically, anyone in Perth can enjoy a freshly harvested Sydney Rock oyster in the hottest 45°C weather. Well, yes and no. The part about refrigeration and transport is basically right, although it's not something most of us would ever have had to think about anyway. Even in earlier times, when oysters could be expensive in big inland cities, this was not the real problem and could usually be gotten around, especially by the rich or the resourceful. The Romans carted oysters overland in winter, packed in ice or snow which was regularly replenished at ice houses along the way—a system used in France up to the middle of the nineteenth century. In warm weather they were carried in cisterns full of sea water; and pickled oysters, the invention of Gaulish fishermen, were always available and not to be sniffed at. In the early 1800s in Britain, oysters were in such demand for Christmas that the long-distance stagecoaches were loaded with barrels of them, almost to the total exclusion of passengers. Here in Australia anything from bullock drays to sailing cutters were used to transport oysters. Of course, if you had the good fortune to live near the coast, oysters could be eaten every day by just going down to the tide's edge and collecting them.

The reason for the R rule (or our confusion about it) is amazingly simple: we are, in fact, talking about different species. There are two main types of edible oyster in the world, the Ostreinae and the Crassostreinae. All oysters spawn in warm weather, but one of the major differences between them is that Crassostreinae oysters, including our own Sydney Rock and the imported Pacific, expel their eggs and their sperm, whichever the case may be at that moment, directly into the water, where they then meet by chance. The female European oyster (*Ostrea edulis*), on the other hand, produces eggs which it doesn't expel. Instead, it takes in the sperm with water. It then incubates its spawn until the larval stage, when the tiny oysters have actually developed a shell, at which point they are released into the ocean to fend for themselves. One can imagine how decidedly unpleasant a

mouthful of oyster would be complete with baby shells—like grains of sand or bits of grit surrounded by a greyish or black milky, oily-tasting liquid—referred to as 'greysick' or 'blacksick', and concentrated in the loveliest part. Even for those of us dedicated to not rinsing our oysters, this would certainly put one off!

Australians, as they do so many other things, simply inverted the rule. Translating Northern summer to our Southern Hemisphere, that meant we should avoid oysters in our summer: November, December, January and February. And even when we haven't, there has been a certain unease about it. A good illustration of this was when the Queensland legislature debated the Oyster Act in 1863. Concerned about protecting oysters during the breeding period, it discussed, at some length, inserting a clause about not harvesting oysters during the summer months—in the case of Australia, months *with* an 'R' in them—despite their confusion about whether the months they had chosen (one would assume based on the Australian seasons) were in fact the local oyster breeding period or not. Apparently there was no time to inquire into the matter and the bill was passed without this clause.

Though the presence of larva in *Ostrea* oysters during the summer months in the Northern Hemisphere is the original reason for the 'R' story, it is still a bit more complicated. Europeans usually enjoy their oysters in the winter particularly during the holiday season, Christmas and the New Year—the same as us. But here's where it gets confusing. If the European oyster is at its best, or close to, in the Northern winter or coldest months, then how is it that our oysters are eaten during our hottest months if that's when *all* oysters spawn, even given the business about the larva shell etc.? Can species of edible oysters be *that* different? As in so many situations in Australia, some of these left-over ideas surprisingly make sense, or who would have paid attention to them in the first place?

This seasonal difference is one of the most crucial points about what makes a good oyster, but before exploring it, it may be best to backtrack a little to find out what an oyster actually is.

WHAT IS AN OYSTER?

> Now we are of the opinion that an oyster, only regarded as a thing to be eaten, and having actually a low place in the ascending series of animals, not only demands, but will richly reward, an enlightened examination.
>
> Rev Charles Williams, *Silvershell or the Adventures of an Oyster* (1857)

The most significant fact to appreciate is that an oyster is an animal. It grows and eats; it also breathes and has its means of reproducing. Perhaps many of us assumed it just arrived at the table on a plate of ice *fait accompli*, or, like Aristotle, that it spontaneously generated from slime. Pliny, the next writer we have on the oyster, seemed to agree with the spontaneous-generation theory but felt that oysters came from mud (the more putrid the better) and also from the foam that collected around posts and logs in the sea or around ships that had not sailed for a long time.

If served in a restaurant today, an oyster of 200 million years or more in the past would look perfectly familiar to us, despite having evolved over many millions of years, probably from a form of mollusc with a stocky under-body concentrated in a 'foot', much like a modern snail. The family Ostreidae (edible oysters pretty much as we know them) first made an appearance in upper Triassic deposits, but possibly they occurred even earlier, in late Palaeozoic times.

One of the most important developments along the way was the evolution of the two shells, or 'valves' (hence *bi*valve), held together by an elastic ligament or 'hinge', and the total enclosure of the animal by these. In a real sense, this entailed the loss of the head—all bivalves are essentially 'headless' (*acephalous*). It doesn't seem entirely fair, but, in familiar French, to call someone an 'oyster' (*huître*) is to say they are a fool or a mug. In the *Timaeus*, Plato assigns the state of fish, oysters and other marine animals to ignorant people and those incapable of thought. Shakespeare seems to have agreed.

Another feature of the majority of the single-adductor-muscle bivalves is that they have abandoned a snail-like vertical position for a horizontal one. Most of them prefer to lie on their right side. The oyster, however, for some reason—and this is made a great deal of in all the literature—like a partner of many years in a particular marriage bed, prefers to lie on, or attach itself by, its *left* side. Interestingly though, should the oyster become free for any reason, it will frequently come to lie on its other side.

When you look at an oyster, you might ask who can tell one side from the other and who cares anyway. But the oyster is different from other bivalves in that its two shells are not the same shape or size, so which side it lies on does make a difference to the way the oyster opens and feeds. In our terms, the flat or *right* hand valve (shell) is more or less the top or 'lid' which covers the bottom, deeper and/or cupped *left* hand shell containing the body of the animal so that in its natural state this means the oyster is more or less up-side down. And because it is 'fixed', the oyster does not have to have its body balanced, or bilaterally symmetrical, as say a human with two arms and two legs or a horse with four legs does to enable it to move, and therefore is better fitted for its peculiar immobile way of life.

Oysters are among the most sluggish of all bivalves and require very little oxygen — even compared to their more primitive, though certainly more mobile ancestors — having lost the foot that would have allowed them some possible movement. Although many of the oyster's close cousins have retained them, these feet are not generally used for locomotion: the famous swimming of the scallop (a bivalve who does own a foot but uses it for other things) is actually managed by flapping its valves and expelling water in one direction while moving in the other — a kind of primitive form of jet propulsion!

In the oyster, on the other hand, 'when arrived at full growth, this faculty or inclination [for movement] ceases, and while some of their active relatives are darting around them', according to a *Popular History of the Mollusca* (1851), 'they remain contentedly in their place of abode, surrounded by a numerous and continuously increasing progeny'. Whether this philosophical attitude on the part of the oyster is true or not (Professor Rymer Jones describes

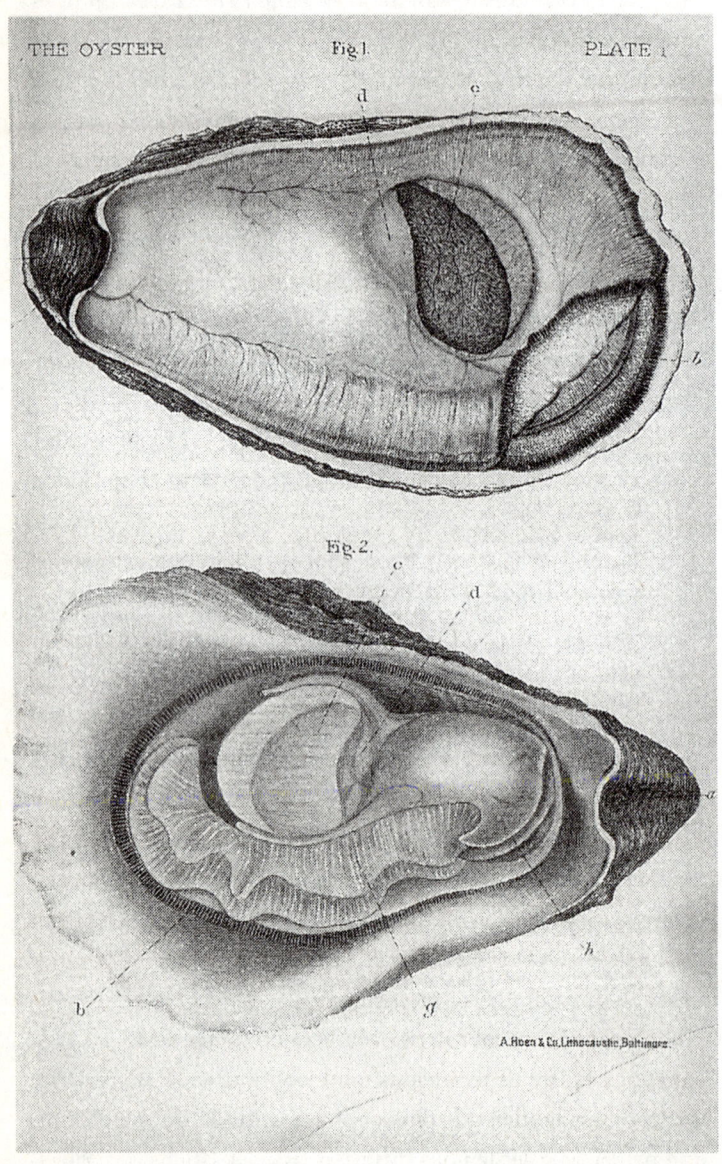

them very differently as 'the helpless inhabitant[s] of these shells!'), their sedentary existence belies the extraordinary amount of activity going on within their closed world.

It is in fact an extremely complex and fascinating system (truly 'more complicated than a watch') but for our purposes it is enough to think of the oyster as a tiny vacuum cleaner suctioning up all that is around it. The main difference is that the usually irritating job of having to empty the bag when it is full is done regularly by the little creature itself as part of the process, with varying degrees of efficiency depending on the species and the conditions that surround it.

A ROSE BY ANY OTHER NAME

The sea is indifferently well stocked with Fish of various sorts—all excellent in their kind. The Shell-fish are Oysters of 3 or 4 sorts, viz Rock Oysters and Mangrove Oysters which are small, Pearl Oysters, and Mud Oysters, these last are the best and largest I ever saw.

Cook, from the *Voyage of the 'Endeavour'* (23 Aug, 1770)

Though there are many groups of bivalve molluscs known as oysters and some even bear a striking resemblance to the one we are so familiar with, *edible*, or what are called 'true' oysters are of the family Ostreidae. (From the Greek *ostreon* [oyster]. The practice of casting votes to send someone into exile in ancient Greece was done by writing the name of the person on the flat shell of an oyster called an *ostrakon* = ostracism). The difference from other bivalves is easy to see by comparing them to something equally familiar, like a mussel. A true oyster has different-sized valves, as we have said. It is attached by the *left* one with a kind of cement and not by a 'byssus'—the thread that some bivalves, like mussels, use to attach themselves. It has completely lost all trace of a 'foot' and therefore any ability to move when an adult. And it has a much more complex gill and a triangle-shaped ligament.

There has been a great deal of discussion as to whether, of the hundreds that exist, certain species are in fact *true* oysters, and there have been calls to further divide the existing classifications. Although such fine hair-splitting is bread and butter to the scientific community, it may seem of little use to those of us who just want to eat them! But remember the Reverend Williams' promise of 'rich reward': it is also worthwhile to keep in mind that besides allowing us to know exactly what we are actually eating, this kind of scientific inquiry leads to development of better means of cultivation, and a better, fresher oyster.

Very simply, the two main subfamilies or groups of edible oyster, Ostreinae and Crassostreinae, live in all the shallow coastal waters of the globe except the polar regions. Generally the species of the Ostreinae family extend into colder waters than do those of the Crassostreinae, which are the dominant oysters in warm, temperate and tropical waters (although there are also exceptions to this rule as well). Again, generally speaking, Crassostreinae prefer the least saline conditions and so will be mostly found in estuaries and the mouths of rivers rather than in the sea; Ostreinae more salty and the third large group found in Australia, Pycnodonteinae (or pearl oyster) the most saline conditions.

In Australia there are three main species cultivated for food: two belonging to the Crassostreinae: *Crassostrea gigas* (the 'Pacific' oyster—imported this century) and *Saccostrea glomerata* (the indigenous 'Sydney Rock'). The other belongs to the Ostreinae, *Ostrea angasi* (the 'Native' or 'mud' oyster). There are also two other indigenous oysters harvested in northern Queensland—the *Saccostrea amasa* ('milky' oyster) and the *Saccostrea echinata* (the 'Blacklip') although these are not readily found outside of the state and have little commercial viability.

It is interesting to note how complicated the business of classification can be by briefly relating the chequered history of the indigenous Sydney Rock oyster, which has had more names than a lost dog. The Rock oyster, which until fairly recently was called *Saccostrea commercialis*, and still is in much of the literature available at the time of this writing, was described variously as *'cuculatta'* *'mordax'* or *'glomerata'* until 1933 when it was renamed *'Ostrea commercialis'* by T Iredale and T C Roughley. Although part of the name stuck, the rest has gone through various transformations, the first of which was when Iredale, only three years later, proposed that the Sydney Rock oyster be placed in a 'separate genera *Saxostrea*' [sic], since 'Rock oysters are distinct in every essential feature'.

Among many others, CM Yonge in 1960 and Peter Korringa in 1976, both well respected in the oyster field, described the Sydney Rock in their books as belonging to the genus *Crassostrea*. This term was also used in Australia until the early 80s, when someone took notice of Iredale's suggestion and began to refer to it as *Saccostrea*. (No wonder we get confused.) Then, in 1994, DNA comparisons showed that the Sydney Rock is identical to the New Zealand rock oyster, *Saccostrea glomerata*, and it is now officially referred to by this name.

Although it is certain the Rock oyster is a distinct genus, different to the *Crassostrea gigas*, it belongs to the same subfamily and, from what I can discover, is the same in all the aspects important for our purposes. Therefore, when *Ostrea* is referred to, it means the oysters of the Ostreinae subfamily, but when I refer to Crassostreinae it includes *both* the *Crassostrea* (*gigas* or Pacific oyster) *and* the *Saccostrea* (*glomerata* or Sydney/Western/New Zealand Rock).

THE ROCK (SYDNEY AND WESTERN)

The natural range of the Rock oyster (*Saccostrea glomerata*) in Australia extends around the northern, eastern, and southeastern seaboard as far as Wingen Inlet in eastern Victoria. On the west coast of Australia, it is found as far south as the 30th parallel (about 95 kilometres north of Perth) and except for some recent artificially planted pockets such as King George Sound (Albany), does not occur on the south coast. Above the Tropic of Capricorn, it is very prolific but the extreme tides and the hot sun cause the shell to be stunted and irregular, and therefore, unless intensively cultivated, of little economic value.

Although there have been experiments with selective breeding of the Sydney Rock oyster to develop disease-resistant and faster-growing strains, the Sydney Rock remains in a sense a 'wild' oyster, having been neither imported or seeded by foreign oysters. Indeed, for the past fifteen years it has managed for the most part to resist attempts to reproduce it successfully in hatchery situations. In a world where the rise and fall of natural beds has been disastrous enough to lead to widespread importation and artificial methods of inducing spawning, the Sydney Rock is fairly unique.

THE PACIFIC

In his then definitive oyster monograph (1925), TC Roughley wrote 'there are several species of oysters found on the Australian coast, but only two are of commercial value, the rock oyster (*Ostrea cucullata* [sic]), and the so-called mud oyster (*Ostrea angasi*)'. He could not know that twenty years later a whole new species would be making its appearance in this country.

The Pacific oyster (*Crassostrea gigas*) was introduced into parts of Australia in order to fill the gap left by the demise of the native wild or 'mud' oyster (*Ostrea angasi*), the other indigenous oyster found in our waters.

As the name *gigas* indicates, the Pacific or 'Japanese' oyster is a relatively large oyster. Originally a native of Japan, it is now the main oyster grown in Tasmania and South Australia but is classed by the New South Wales Department of Fisheries as a noxious pest, required by law to be destroyed everywhere in the state except Port Stephens, where it has been cultivated since 1991. (In 1923, oyster farmers in Brittany, likewise wanting to protect the native *Ostrea edulis*, obtained a decree forbidding the farming of Portuguese oysters [*Crassostrea angulata*] north of La Vilaine.) Victoria also considers the Pacific oyster detrimental to the environment and its cultivation is banned in that state.

In 1940 a trial shipment of *gigas* seed from Japan was condemned on arrival in Sydney by the Fisheries Department and destroyed. But between 1947 and 1952 the Pacific oyster was introduced to the south coast of Western Australia and parts of Tasmania by the Commonwealth Scientific and Industrial Research Organisation (CSIRO), as these areas were considered outside the natural range of the Sydney Rock. The population in Western Australia did not survive the first winter but the oysters in southern Tasmania did well and were transplanted to Port Sorell where they soon colonised the Tamar River. (Interestingly, the latitudes of Japan and Tasmania north and south of the equator are almost exactly the same.) They were also introduced to Mallacoota Inlet (unsuccessfully) in Victoria and to Coffin Bay and Stansbury in South Australia in the 1980s.

There have been a number of attempts to cross-breed various species of Pacific oyster to produce hybrids. The most detailed attempt was in Japan, where different races of oyster from the south (Kumamoto), central (Hiroshima) and north (Miyagi and Hokkaido) were cross-bred to a third generation; most strains of Pacific oyster now cultivated internationally would have been affected by this experiment.

THE NATIVE

As is New Zealand's famous 'Bluff' oyster, the Native or mud oyster (*Ostrea angasi*—named for George French Angas [1822–86], artist, explorer, naturalist and at one time secretary of the Sydney Museum) is a close relative of the European flat oyster (*Ostrea edulis*) and part of the same genus. The habitat of this indigenous Australian oyster ranges from Leeuwin along the whole of the south coast, and up the east coast as far as the Clyde River where by 1922 it was already scarce. North of the Clyde it was by then almost extinct. Once found in great numbers in the upper reaches of Sydney Harbour, quantities of shells indicate that it was also found in all the rivers south of and including the Clarence. By the time of the establishment of the colony in Western Australia, the Native oyster, which by all accounts had once been abundant in the Swan River, was extinct and those found in King George Sound did not last much into the 1920s, both populations apparently being wiped out by massive flooding. At one time it was incredibly prolific in Tasmania, especially on the east coast of the state. Earlier in the twentieth century it thrived in South Australia, especially at Port Lincoln near Adelaide, and was sometimes known as the 'Port Lincoln' oyster. *Ostrea angasi* still survives in small numbers in various areas of Australia but at present is not, on the whole, commercially viable.

Occasionally the term 'Belon' has been used in Australia to describe the Native oyster but is really not much use for our purposes except that Belon refers to the French oyster to which it is related and bears some resemblance. According to Eleanor Clarke, this most expensive of French oysters is the indigenous *Ostrea edulis*, called 'Armoricaine'—from the ancient name for Brittany (*ar-mor-* by the sea). Until the 1890s 'Belon' was only used to indicate oysters which had actually been 'fattened' in the mouth of the Belon River in the Morbihan area of Brittany. The indiscriminate use of the name became the subject of a court case when it was decided to allow the term to refer to all *Ostrea edulis* oysters from the region. Nowadays in France, 'Belon' usually means any flat *Ostrea edulis* oyster, and since almost all of these come from Brittany the name is not entirely incorrect. Locally these prized oysters are often referred to as *les plates*, the flat ones. This term may cause further confusion for the would-be informed oyster lover, as the commercial oyster-growing industry in Australia calls its top grades, or oysters meant for the restaurant/half-shell trade, 'plate' oysters, meaning those destined for the dining plate, not the jar.

A friend, who is a food critic and writer, once said in a fine but all too brief article, that all the oysters in the world were of two kinds—cupped and flat. (The Rock and Pacific, by the way, are 'cupped' and *Ostrea*, the Australian Native is 'flat'.) Basically he is completely correct and many of us won't need to know more, but local conditions can sometimes make this hard to determine and visually confusing, as is the

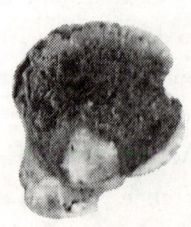

case of the American 'Blue Point' which is round like an *Ostrea* but cupped like a *Crassostrea* and is in fact of the species *Crassostrea viginica*, or the case of the tiny *Ostrea lurida* ('Olympia' oyster) which is actually quite cupped and not flat at all.

An oyster leads a dreadful but exciting life
                              M F K Fisher, *Consider the Oyster*

There are basically two factors which determine a good oyster: where it lives, which will decide what it eats and how it grows, and when (and how well or regularly) it spawns.

If one thinks of the oyster as a little Hoover, vacuuming up the sea around it, or as an extremely efficient filtering plant, then it is easy to see why the first of these factors — where it lives — is so important. Because the adult oyster has attached itself permanently and doesn't move, its food must come to it. By using its adductor muscle (that lovely round chewy morsel near the centre of the shell), it is able to open its valves and take in water through an inhalant chamber by means of cilia.

Cilia are microscopic, hair-like filaments found in their millions within the gills. They function in tandem with other associated organs to bring particles of potential food suspended in the water into the open oyster. After the water has been filtered and sorted through by sieving cilia, it is then flushed out. Some of the particles, if small enough or of nutritional value, are absorbed by the gut while the others are rejected and passed back into the sea through the exhalant chamber. The amount of microscopic plant cells (plankton) in the water the oyster uses for food will vary depending on where it lives and the time of year. If the number of plankton is high, the rate of feeding/pumping will slow down, and if the number of the organisms is low, the oyster's rate of feeding will be faster. A decent-sized oyster (depending on the species) can pump up to 37 litres of water an hour.

Logically, given such a simple system, an oyster will also take in anything else small enough in the water, such as sediment or organic debris, which it can't use. Within the body, the elaborate system of filters and feeding surfaces eventually selects what it can use and rejects what it can't. In the *Ostrea* or 'flat' oyster, this seems to be based almost entirely on the size of the particles. (It may be that the conditions they live in have not caused these species to have to adapt any further as it prefers a hard, rocky or shale bottom.) This simpler feeding process means that the *Ostrea* is more at the mercy of any build-up of silt or changes in coastline such as heavy rain, flooding or storms, since it will more quickly and easily become clogged up and suffocate in its attempt to take in food. Such, indeed, has been the history of the whole European coast, where huge natural beds of *Ostrea edulis* that extended from Scandinavia down the Atlantic and into the Mediterranean as far as Greece, have disappeared through, as the insurance companies would have it, 'acts of God'.

Our Australian *Ostrea* (the Native *angasi*) is often called a 'mud' oyster, but obviously this is a misnomer since all true oysters are filter feeders and cannot survive in muddy or silt conditions. One of its differences to the Rock oyster, besides incubating larvae like all *Ostrea*, is that when the *angasi* oyster attaches itself, it does so with only a very small area from which it continues to grow out, often to a fairly large size (unlike the Rock which enlarges its base as it matures). Because of this, the heavy Native oysters usually drop off their place of settlement and fall into the mud where they are often found—hence the name. If the mud is fairly firm, everything will go well. If it is too soft the oyster will smother. Native *angasi* oysters are rarely found between tide marks but almost always subtidally— that is, in deeper water.

From evidence of scientific studies, it appears that the cupped oysters of the Crassostreinae group—and therefore our own Sydney Rock and the imported Pacific—are much more able to 'sense' and select particles with nutritional value through other means (perhaps chemical) than by just size, like the *Ostrea*. The more sophisticated sieving and feeding system of the Crassostreinae enables them to take advantage of the denser food available in shallow estuaries and rivers, and also to deal more efficiently with the accompanying waste and silt also present in these more turbid waters. This is probably one of the reasons that on the whole, Crassostreinae tend to be more hardy and grow faster and to a larger size than the *Ostrea*.

It is difficult, however, to generalise in any way about oysters: Philpots, for example, commented around 1890 that the Port Lincoln (South Australia) *Ostrea angasi* was one of the largest oysters in the world—as 'big as a dinner plate'. Interestingly, Australia is also credited with having one of the smallest. Discovered in the estuary of the Ord River in Western Australia, the *Ostrea ordensis* was named by the eminent William Saville-Kent (of whom we'll hear quite a bit more later). This 'Pygmy' oyster grows on the leaves, stems, and respiratory shoots, called 'cobbler's pegs', of the white mangrove. Though possibly mistaken for the offspring of a normal-sized oyster, they are in fact quite mature at less than 10 mm—fifty of these oysters can fit on a leaf only 70 mm long without crowding.

Having literally 'taken over', because of their extraordinary survival and reproductive skills, *Crassostrea* oysters are the main species now grown all over the world. Yet in some areas of Australia the Pacific oyster is considered a pest, the 'marine rabbit'. *Crassostrea gigas* seems to have the supreme ability to live in even the muddiest conditions, much more so than the Rock. If, for example, it drops off a stick into the soft tidal flat it grows rapidly and in an elongated fashion toward the surface so that it can still open, feed and manage not to smother. I have seen feral Pacifics at Greenwell Point the shape and size of a man's shoe! Even an average market-sized Pacific can pump out millions of eggs and a very much greater number of sperm. A few unchecked Pacifics could one day completely take over and wipe out the native (in this case Rock) population in New South Wales as it has done to similar populations in some parts of Japan and elsewhere. As well, in certain favourable circumstances, *if uncontrolled*, the Pacific oyster can make foreshores unusable for recreation and more seriously, utterly change the ecosystem of a river or estuary.

All members of the Crassostreinae share another advantage over the flat Native oyster. Given the manner in which oysters filter feed, obviously the ability to remove accumulated build-up from within is extremely important. In a smooth-running process under normal conditions, the oyster expels or exhales what it doesn't want or can't use in a constant rhythm during the feeding process, which goes on more or less all the time it is submerged and undisturbed. This occurs through an exhalant chamber by way of the action of the gills and movement of other cilia. Where the *Ostrea* (in our case, the Native *Ostrea angasi*) has one of these chambers, the Crassostreinae (Pacific and Rock) have two and therefore a far greater capacity to expel waste.

Clearly, what makes a good oyster is *exactly* what goes in and what it can manage to filter out with the most efficiency in order to produce maximum growth. This is where the *goût de terroir* comes in — the fact that every oyster not only develops according to its surrounding conditions, therefore assuming a local shape, colour and texture of its shell, but it also takes on a distinctive flavour, colour, and texture of its *inside* as well.

You may remember the story of King Louis and the green oysters — the *huîtres vertes* which develop their beautiful, vivid blue-green gill colour and a creamy consistency due to the time spent in the *claires* or shallow ponds (many of which once served as *salines* for the production of sea salt) in the Marennes of France. These ponds, constructed in such a way as to let in sea water only during high tide, develop conditions of high salinity and temperature which produce abundant food, and sometimes, though not always—it seems this is purely a matter of chance from season to season—of a type (diatom *Navicula*) with green pigment called *marennine* that the oyster feeds on. This also naturally occurs in some creeks and waterways elsewhere, for example, the River Crouch in Essex. A similar phenomenon happens in the Pelican River and various other areas of Freycinet, Tasmania, where, again depending on a random coincidence of weather factors and temperatures, an occasional seasonal increase in algae known as *naricule bleu*, will cause oysters to develop a striking green gill colour and very salty flavour. However, there is also a pathological condition that can develop in oysters which is not natural and is due to their tendency to accumulate copper in certain waters. Unlike a *huître verte* in which only the edges take on colour and the middle remains white, in this case the whole oyster is an unpleasant green. This is *not* a good oyster and should be thrown away.

As well as the type of food or other elements, such as lime present in the water (for shell growth), interrelated factors of temperature and how salt the water is, all determine a good oyster. Generally speaking, Crassostreinae can withstand greater changes in salinity so that they are able to tolerate not only very salt water during low tide or periods of dry weather, but also the influx of fresh water due to rain and the natural movement of rivers. Although any extremes in these areas can cause the oyster, and the oyster farmer, much heartache and sometimes disaster, on the whole it is these conditions—a mixture of fresh and salt water, warm temperatures and tidal change—which produce the rich nutrients and the delicate, unique flavour of Australian oysters.

There has been a great deal of research into what exactly the oyster likes to eat and when. Depending on the species, oysters feed at different temperatures so that, again, if the temperature goes below a certain level, such as in winter, the oysters don't feed and therefore, by many of our growers, are not considered 'in condition' or 'fat' enough to be harvested. (Curiously, there is also a combination of environmental factors called 'eutrophication' that affects the growth and health of oysters, when there is *too much* food in the water.) What Australian growers consider 'condition' does not seem to be a concern in Europe, where on the whole the oysters are usually much larger than our Sydney Rock. Oysters there are just as relished in the cold months when they are in reasonable condition—that is, lean and with a firmer texture but not 'fat'—and can be seen piled high on *plateaux de fruits de mer* at outdoor cafes being devoured by people in scarves and overcoats. This is also the time of year when the native European *Ostrea edulis* can be guaranteed not to contain larvae.

However it is not only the food supply that determines an oyster's 'condition'. Temperature plays a large part in other aspects of the oyster's functioning such as opening and closing its valves, its heartbeat and respiration. Most importantly for the purposes of discovering the good oyster, the temperature determines when and *if* it spawns.

THE POLITICS OF REPRODUCTION

Perhaps no other creature's sex life has been so carefully scrutinised as that of the oyster. As late as 1925 at least, the Sydney Rock had managed to keep some of its secrets hidden. For even then it was believed that our *Saccostrea glomerata* (thought at that time to be *Crassostrea cuculatta*) was either a male or female and remained that way for all of its life. More was known about the flat *Ostrea*, because, as pointed out earlier, this species incubates its larvae (is 'larviparous') and therefore the females can easily be identified when opened. Not so the Crassostreinae. Close study is difficult because when an oyster is opened for examination much of the tissue is destroyed, especially the small and delicate tissues of the reproductive organs. Some observations have been made through the transparent shells of larvae but obviously not of the sexual inclinations of the adult. Eventually, it was observed in Europe that *Ostrea edulis* oysters which had produced eggs and incubated them one year were then seen to produce sperm in the next. Clearly something odd was going on. It seemed the *Ostrea* was actually hermaphrodite — changing throughout its lifetime from male to female and female to male with no apparent alteration of its appearance. From this knowledge and by lengthy observation, it was worked out that Crassostreinae also change sex, usually spawning first as a male and later as a female. (There is normally a higher percentage of females among older oysters during the active breeding season; this then drops in autumn to a large proportion of androgynous individuals.) Crassostreinae have also been observed, though rarely, to be both male and female at the same time.

What a surprise! Not that it makes all that much difference to your average oyster lover, but you can imagine the consternation in an industry that was working more and more toward the cultivation or farming of the oyster as a *domesticated* animal, in a way similar to that of sheep or chickens, with which such basics could be counted on. People who had been tending oysters for decades probably shrugged their shoulders, 'so what else is new?' But, in effect, it makes no difference; the process of spawning continues, as it has for millennia, regardless. The crucial variable is whether the oysters *choose* to or not, and this is where temperature comes in again.

All species of oyster, regardless of their normal optimum growing temperatures, spawn at a relatively higher one, and this, of course, occurs during the summer months. (Back to the 'R' rule!) Oysters of the Crassostreinae group need fairly high water temperatures, over 20°C; *Ostrea* only 16°C. Oysters generally begin to develop eggs or sperm, apparently by converting their winter stores of glycogen, when water temperatures begin to rise in spring—in Australian waters, usually around September. As the water warms each oyster in a male phase produces its sperm while those in a female phase produce their eggs. If they are opened at this time they will have the appearance of being opaque, 'fat' and creamy, sometimes with a milky substance around the margin. At a certain signal (this varies with the place—the right temperature *exactly* coupled with the amount of light or cloud cover, the phase of the moon, the type and amount of food present and, in the case of rivers and estuaries, the input of fresh water brought on by rain) the oyster will release this 'spawn' into the water, which itself will take on a milky appearance as well if the spawn is in high enough concentration. (Roughley, in a 1933 study, suggested 'spawning may be triggered on the ebb tide following a high spring [new moon] tide'.) But there are other mysterious factors. Barry Allen of Shoalhaven Oyster Service tells a story about a very busy holiday season (early March) when they needed to bring in more harvest. They had some trays showing a good crop, 'nice and fat', which they took back to be processed (purified) in the shed. For three tense nights of full moon they prayed the oysters wouldn't spawn. All was going well until one night there was 'a huge clap of thunder and all the oysters went off at the same time! Nothing to do then but return them to the leases.'

All oysters spawn by much the same methods as they use to take in water and flush it out: sperm from an oyster in the male phase is expelled by cilia through the normal exhalant chamber. In the female phase the process is sometimes a bit more complicated, but let it suffice to say that it is accomplished by a strong contraction of the adductor 'quick' muscle. This causes a sudden clapping together of its valves, which forces accumulated eggs or larvae out in a stream from the *inhalant* chamber, the exhalant chamber meanwhile being deliberately closed off. Apparently eggs must be expelled with greater force and distance (as far as 30 centimetres has been observed) than the more mobile sperm.

It also seems that oysters are extremely gregarious and like to be in company when they reproduce. Besides the natural signals such as temperature and rainfall, there is also evidence in the Crassostreinae that there must be some kind of biochemical substance released, probably by some of the males, that cause the others to expel sperm, and then the females their eggs. According to Barry Allen, 'there might have been only one oyster spawned in a row and the tide or the current might have taken the spawn through the others [to a row 50 metres away] and they all got the signal and that's it ... boom, boom, boom'.

A story, reported by the *Daily Telegraph* in 1840 may serve to illustrate the true nature of these 'breedy creatures'. The 'Whistling Oyster' was the name of a London 'oyster and refreshment room' frequented by many writers and artists of the day. Apparently one evening, the landlord, a Mr Pearkes, thought he heard a strange sound coming from a tub in which oysters 'lay piled in layers, one over the other placidly fattening upon oatmeal [this is how oysters were usually stored at the time] and awaiting the inevitable advent of the remorseless knife'. He went closer to investigate and, sure enough, he could hear a distinct whistling! It didn't take long to separate the talented mollusc from its fellows, and it was put alone in a separate tub with as much oatmeal and bran as it could possibly want. Here it kept up its performance for a few weeks, much to the delight of the patrons of the inn and its proprietor, who probably sold more oysters and much more ale on account of it. Its fame spread so far that even the respected novelist Thackeray went out of his way to see it.

The story is probably more the ingenuous wish of the landlord to make good the name of his establishment — or the overactive imagination and high spirits of the writers who drank there — than true. Nevertheless it is also a sad tale since it shows how clearly the oyster is misunderstood. No doubt the good Mr Pearkes wished to single this diva out and preserve it from its impending fate, but the oyster had probably been whistling merrily out of pure happiness for being so close to its friends, neighbours and relatives, singing for the joy of being in a crowd. Hearing the oyster go through its performance, a visiting American said that 'it was nothing to an oyster he knew in Massachusetts which whistled Yankee Doodle right through and followed its master around the house like a dog'. Putting it in a tub all alone certainly would have changed an oyster's tune to one of panic and distress. No wonder it gave up whistling after a while. Paul Moxham, an oyster farmer on the Hawkesbury, swears that oysters do make sounds, maybe not so much a distinct whistling, but they certainly appear to be communicating with each other by all kinds of rustlings, clicks, fizzes and sighs.

As well as its many other talents, the *Ostrea* — of which our whistling oyster would have been one — normally alternates its sex on a regular basis. Crassostreinae are a little less showy; their sex reversal, when it happens, takes place during the winter, never during the spawning period when they remain the same sex the whole time. Nor do they always change their sex the following winter — this seems to be determined by the amount of food available. A higher metabolic rate induced by good feeding (remember, this is also relative to temperature) seems to favour the development of ovaries, while lower metabolism seems to be connected with development of the male condition. Especially in warmer climates like Australia's, the Crassostreinae oyster starts out as male and then changes to female, which it will remain for the rest of its life unless some drastic change in conditions occurs. Most of the time approximately 75 per cent of prime eating Sydney Rock oysters are female, though oddly, oyster farmers generally refer to oysters as 'he' and 'him'. Of course in French they are feminine, while, for some reason, an oyster bank or bed is masculine.

The number of times an oyster will spawn in a season depends on its health, the temperature of the water, and food supply. In Britain, the *Ostrea* usually spawn twice in a season—once as each sex—but in warmer waters several spawnings may occur in an extended breeding period. The breeding season of the Crassostreinae in Australia is of a much longer duration than that of the same species in Europe and North America so that Pacific oysters here generally spawn at least twice a year and this, depending on weather conditions, is also the case with Sydney Rocks.

The American researcher William Brooks once estimated that 'if all the oysters were to be fertilised and were to live and grow to maturity they would fill up an entire bay in a single season, while the fifth generation of descendants from a single female would make more than eight worlds as large as the earth, even if each female spawned only once'. Crassostreinae have been recorded as shedding up to 100 million eggs in a season.

Metamorphosis

The sperm of the oyster (as well as the eggs of the Crassostreinae) are at the mercy of currents and tides but, given the right conditions, a certain proportion of eggs and sperm will eventually come together. In the *Ostrea* this takes place within the female who incubates the larva until they develop shells, at which point they are expelled into the open ocean. Crassostreinae seem to have no such maternal feelings and do not incubate their larva. Therefore, it may be remembered, there is no problem with the unpleasant gritty mess ('greysick' or 'blacksick') in our oysters during breeding season in the summer months.

Floating in the sea, the tiny Crassostreinae oyster larva or 'spat' (apparently this name came about because it was believed female oysters spat out their young) quickly begins to grow a shell—usually within 24 to 48 hours of fertilisation. In both species it has the ability to swim Mary-Poppins-style by use of the *velum*, a tuft of cilia positioned like a tiny umbrella at the top, which has not yet been enclosed by the valves. The survival rate during this period is pitifully low: less than 0.1 per cent, as the brave little creature swim-drifts until it finds an appropriate hard surface. Then, retracting the velum, it uses its 'foot' to move over this surface until it finds exactly the right spot. Here it rocks backwards and forwards ('curiously reminiscent of a dog preparing its bed', according to one observer) to produce a cement by which it then attaches its left valve. It was once thought that the weight of the developing shell actually caused the larva to sink, with no choice in the matter at all; recent research, however,

These Breedy Creatures 51

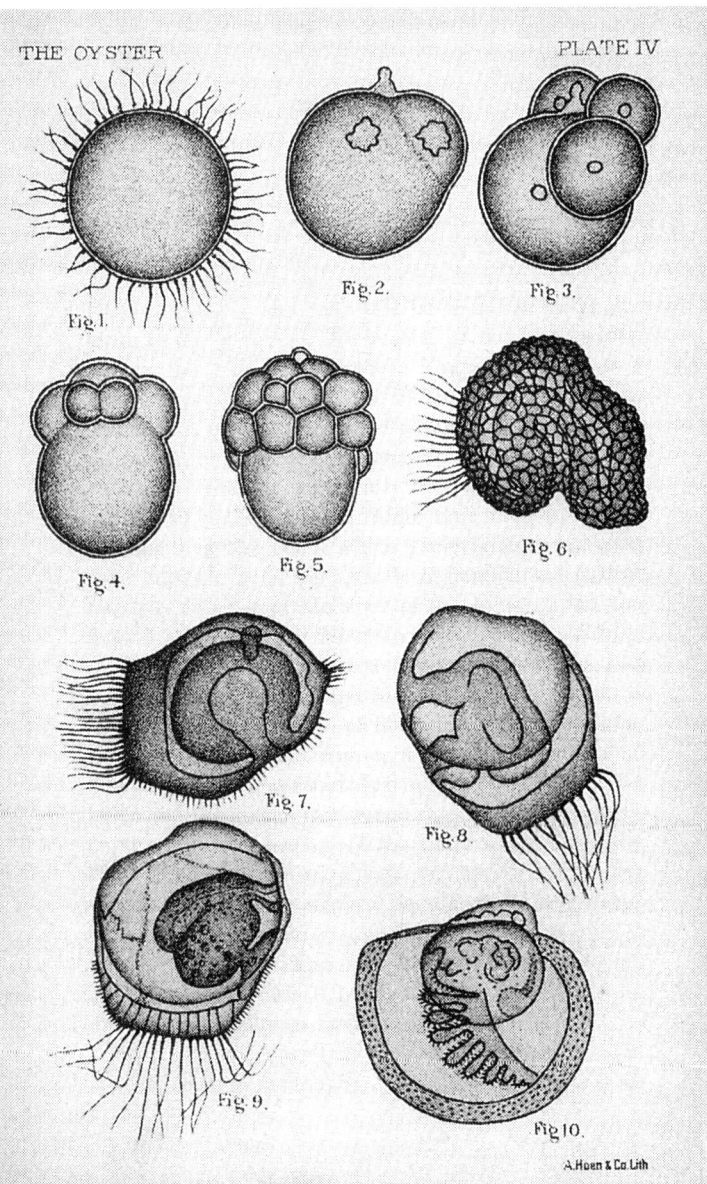

suggests that the larva may possess some kind of sensing ability which allows it to actually 'feel' whether the surface is suitable or not before settling.

At this stage the oyster is between two to three weeks old. Within a few hours of settling it enlarges and flattens its shell, and the exterior velum/cilia and foot disappear, so that it is now permanently fixed to its new home which it will never leave unless knocked off for some reason (or transported by an oyster farmer). At this point it is no bigger than a pinhead, fairly transparent and almost impossible to see, but it is a complete animal with all the organs necessary to breathe and eat.

The larval oyster begins feeding the moment it has developed a semblance of a mouth and quickly grows under good conditions by putting out shoots or 'frills', which it will continue to do for the rest of its life. This fragile, transparent shell material looks, in an oyster that has not been harvested, like the delicate petals of an aquatic flower. These harden to enlarge the shell, or are broken off on the way to market, so it's not often that you see them. Like most animals, oysters grow rapidly when young, and slow down as they get older. Growth almost ceases when an oyster is four to five years old. They are considered to be fully mature at about three to four years although they have been recorded as living for up to ten years by some, and one writer, Toussaint-Samat, claims that if no accident befalls them and they are not eaten, they can live for up to fifty years. Some old-time oyster men say you can tell how old an oyster is by counting the ridges in its shell, similar to counting the rings of a tree.

Spent

In Australia then, from the point of view of the oyster lover (and the oyster suppliers), good oysters can be had all year round because there are no incubated larvae in the species of Crassostreinae, to which our Sydney Rock and Pacific belong, and therefore no need for the 'R' rule.

Well ... once again yes and no.

Under normal conditions, the oyster will be fully 'ripe' by the end of December or thereabouts, depending on the area. Spawning can occur anytime between late December and early March, but will usually take place in January or February. If growing side by side, as say in Tasmania or the Bassin d' Arcachon, Crassostreinae tend to spawn later than Ostreinae because they need warmer water temperatures.

Regardless of the species, however, an oyster puts an enormous amount of effort into the production of eggs or sperm and the process of expelling them. They also don't feed during this time. The oyster is considered by most oyster farmers in Australia to be 'fat' or in 'the condition' just prior to spawning. Just after spawning, however, it is nearly transparent, thin, watery, and thought by most to be insipid and even sour and unpleasant tasting. When opened, they look much like a piece of wet tissue lying at the bottom of the shell and taking up very little of it. The oyster's condition at this time is at its lowest level of the year. But then the spent oyster begins to build up again during late summer or early autumn, more or less reversing the proportions of its chemical make-up to the point where it has a great deal less protein and less fat but almost a doubling of carbohydrates and glycogen. By May its winter condition has usually been established and will greatly influence how well it will survive the colder temperatures. This, along with the availability of nutrients, will determine its ability to gain full condition again in spring. Inevitably, oysters gain greater condition in the spring than in the autumn because in this season the combination of variables is best for producing the most abundant food. In winter the demand for food is less and feeding is reduced (oysters grow best in early summer when the sun beats down to the bottom, according to Pliny 'those beyond its rays eating little for sadness'). Like many other creatures, the metabolic system of the oyster slows down dramatically in cold temperatures.

Growth is mainly a matter of accumulating carbohydrate and glycogen, which is the major food reserve needed for reproduction and the maintenance of health. The success with which the oyster grows depends largely on the amount of food available. However, where oyster larvae settle is not always the place where there is the most planktonic life needed for fattening. It may also be conversely true that the best areas for fattening, or where an adult oyster can gain the most condition, do not always have high enough salinity, or temperature, for it to spawn or for the larvae to survive. Herein lies the problem the oyster farmer spends a lifetime solving.

chapter ii

Where Have All The Oysters Gone?

To feed rock oysters :

PUT THEM INTO WATER AND WASH THEM WITH A BIRCH-BESOM TILL QUITE CLEAN, THEN LAY THEM BOTTOM-DOWNWARDS INTO A PAN, SPRINKLE WITH FLOUR OR OATMEAL AND SALT, AND COVER WITH WATER. DO THE SAME EVERY DAY, AND THEY WILL FATTEN. THE WATER SHOULD BE PRETTY SALT.

Mrs Rundell, *Domestic Cookery for the Use of Private Families by a Lady* (19th Century Australian)

THIS MAY SEEM an unusual way to get your oysters but it was obviously believed and practised, as evidenced by the number of times the suggestion comes up in the literature of the nineteenth century. I asked some oyster farmers what they thought about oatmeal and they were dubious as to whether an oyster would extract any nourishment from it, since they feed mainly on microscopic plant life. On the other hand, because oysters are omnivorous and will take in anything small enough suspended in the water, 'they might fatten, but taste like porridge'.

The apparent widespread popularity of Mrs Rundell's method may be due to that frustrating reality that the place where an oyster will fatten is not necessarily where it will spawn or survive as larva. Besides the temperature and salinity of the water, there are many other crucial variables: strength of tides, soil erosion and run-off, silt build-up, hardness of the bottom, suitable surfaces to attach to, protection from predators and storms, heat and sunlight, pollution, diseases. Oyster farmers must take into account all of these, and it's easy to understand why they might get a little cross when the naive oyster-eater asks whether the oysters they're selling have 'just been picked today?'

Although a cultivation of sorts has been going on in Australia since around 1870—by gathering small, slow-growing oysters from mangroves or from rocks along the foreshore, and then moving them to areas where they would grow faster and fatter—we still like to consider Sydney Rock a 'wild' oyster and this may partly account for our affection for it. Once we found one growing on the underside of a dead branch fairly high up from the tidal mark (probably the only reason it had somehow been overlooked in the landscape of empty shells) at Berrara Creek on the south coast of New South Wales, which like many places in Australia, was obviously once abundant with Rock oysters. It was quite large, but somewhat distorted, and opening it was almost impossible. The meat sucked from the broken shell was delicious and one would have been hard pressed to tell the difference from a locally farmed oyster had they been served together. This was certainly not the same with the wild Pacifics I had from Port Sorell in Tasmania which are very different from cultivated ones.

WILD AND FREE

Oysters were always a staple food of coastal Aboriginals, as can be seen by the number of 'middens', or mounds of shells, which look to an untrained eye like hills or natural cliff ledges since they are often covered with vegetation. Some of these middens consist of layer upon layer of compacted shell which have been carbon-dated to at least 6000 BC, although digging through such mounds (as T C Roughley in 1925 describes doing) is now illegal. The largest, he claims, was probably one on the north arm of the Richmond River:

> This mound extends for hundreds of yards, and is several feet in width and depth. Thousands of tons of shells have been used to top-dress the mud flats [for oyster cultivation] which in their original condition were too soft to support the oysters it was desired to mature there. Large quantities have also been used to form the footpaths of Ballina. And still many thousands of tons remain.

> Fossicking amongst such heaps one frequently comes upon the stone implements used by the aborigines for cutting the muscles of the oysters when removing them from the shells. These primitive knives vary from three-quarters of an inch to two inches in length, and are fairly constant in shape [slightly rounded]. They were obtained by knocking smaller pieces of water-worn stones in such a way that at least one edge would be reasonably sharp.

Captain Cook records in the journal of his voyage to Australia that 'on the Sand and Mud banks [of Botany Bay] are Oysters, Muscles, Cockles & Ca which I believe are the chief support of the inhabitants, who go into shoald water with their little Canoes and pick them out of the sand and Mud with their hands and sometimes roast and eat them in the canoe, having a fire for that purpose as I suppose, for I know no other it can be for' (4 May, 1770). Apparently some tribes broke oyster-encrusted branches off coastal mangroves and carried them inland so they could have them fresh even at considerable distances from the sea.

There is also evidence to suggest that Aboriginal tribes were already engaged in oyster cultivation. Oral history of the Quandamooka people of Southern Queensland indicates that oyster-farming techniques which form the basis for present-day practices of some members of the community have been handed down by their ancestors. In Moreton Bay, around North Stradbroke Island, artificial reefs have been built up over hundreds of generations by the dumping of shells on naturally occurring high points. These have been constructed at the appropriate depth below the surface of the water to encourage spat to settle. The Quandamooka farmers then break off the small oysters and move them to deeper water to fatten.

Clearly oysters were extraordinarily abundant in Australia before its white occupation. George Vancouver recorded the following observations in his ship's log of October 1791:

> In our way out of this harbour, the boats grounded on a bank we had not before perceived; this covered with oysters of a most delicious flavour, on which we sumptuously regaled; and loading in about half an hour, the boats for our friends on board, we commemorated the discovery by calling it OYSTER HARBOUR [Albany, WA].
>
> ... having by the morning replenished our water, and taken on a supply of firewood, Messers Puget and Whidbey went to Oyster Harbour, with three boats, for the purpose of hauling the seine, and obtaining a quantity of those shell fish, previously to our preceding the following morning to sea.
>
> The gale moderating the next morning, the boats returned, not having been very successful with the seine, but bringing a sufficient supply of oysters, not only for our convalescents, but for the affording also of two or three excellent meals for all hands.
>
> from *Voyage of Discovery to the North Pacific Ocean and Round the World*

From December 1816 until December 1821 (when perhaps it was no longer felt necessary, as the 'enemy' had been sufficiently subdued), Governor Macquarie held an annual 'feast day' with Aboriginals near Parramatta to which he supplied large quantities of food and drink. No doubt the invaders served the guests their own oysters, as these would have been growing in great profusion on the nearby shores.

Even as late as 1840 the explorer Edward John Eyre could still write:

> The oysters [these would have been the flat natives *O. angasi*] were procured from the most southerly bight of Streaky Bay [South Australia] on some mud banks about two to three hundred yards below low-water mark where, they were found in immense numbers of different sizes. The flavour of these was excellent, and the smaller ones were of great delicacy. The men were in the habit of taking the cart down to the beach frequently, where, by wading up to their knees in the sea at low water, they were able to fill it. This supply lasted for two or three days. Many drays might occasionally be loaded, one after the other from these beds.
>
> (*Journal*, 3 Nov, 1840)

Strangely enough, he concludes: 'The native of the district do not appear to eat them, for I could never find a single shell at any of their encampments'.

Such was the greed and lack of conservation of the settlers, however, that, by 1870, after thousands of years of prolific natural abundance, the beds on the coast of New South Wales, and those of most of the other colonies, were decimated. W K Brooks puts it succinctly: 'In all waters where oysters are found they are usually found in abundance, and in all of these places the residents supposed that their natural beds were inexhaustible until they suddenly found they were exhausted'. The *Sydney Illustrated News* in 1872 reprinted the contents of a pamphlet on oyster fishing in Tasmania, 'as it may contain hints useful to our readers'. The author, J E Calder, having visited 'those places where our chief supplies were then derived—namely Southport and Recherche Bay', was of the opinion that 'the deterioration of the beds arose solely from the manner in which the fish [oysters] were wilfully wasted (so to speak) by the fishermen themselves' as well as by 'lately unsuspected enemies both living and inanimate'. Because of these lax practices, already there were 'no oysters young or old to be found in the Tamar', though 'some persons in Launceston are bestirring themselves to plant oyster-farms in the shallows'.

Calder's original letter to the government (dated 1867 and also reprinted in the *News*) reports the practices of Tasmanian oyster dredgers, who worked the natural beds from a month *before* the official season commenced on 1 April, until the last day of October—a period that practically extends over eight months would have severely depleted the breeding population (these would have also been *Ostrea angasi*)—and then left the beds idle during the rest of the year. He compares this to the men of Whitstable, England, who worked their ground all year removing pests, raking, culling etc., and remarks that 'far more seems to be done with private farms [there] than with public beds'. As a result, Calder calculated the waste in Tasmania was up into the thousands of pounds, in spite of the high profits made by the dredgers, of whom he clearly thought little. He grimly concluded:

> ... it is hard to believe, considering the carelessness of the class of persons employed in this trade, and who have no interest in any particular bed, that the same waste is not going on at every place that contributes to the oyster supply of the colony.

'Dredging' (or 'fishing') is the term used to describe one of the oldest means of harvesting oysters in deep water. A dredge, sometimes called an oyster guillotine, is a kind of triangular trap or net, open at one end, made out of wire mesh and steel bars, that is dragged by a boat—and, in the past, smaller wood and leather ones by a person walking waist-deep. It dislodges the oysters and anything else, scraping them into the opening. It is then hauled onto the deck, emptied and sorted. The dredge has proved useful for finding and controlling pests and can have the added advantage of moving young oysters from beneath smothering silt. But it has also been blamed for the destruction of natural beds in many countries. When a natural bed is depleted to below a certain critical point, the oysters apparently stop breeding and the bed will eventually disappear. This has happened over and over again around the world, including parts of America. The famously prolific Chesapeake Bay, having produced over 400 million bushels of oysters, was perilously close to being dredged out, with a harvest of fewer than 100 000 bushels in 1993. In some American states, only tonging—the use of very long tongs to pick up the oysters, which is considered ecologically more friendly—is now allowed in public oyster beds. (In South Australia at the turn of the century these implements could have handles of 12 metres or more in length.)

Where Have All The Oysters Gone?

Dredging was a feature of early oyster farming in Australia, especially in Queensland, South Australia and in New South Wales on the Georges and the Clyde rivers, playing a large part in the depletion of the natural beds. One theory to explain how this may have occurred is that a natural bank of oysters is built up of layer upon layer of the shells of the dead—the younger, live ones survive by resting on the others, which keeps them out of the mud. When a bank is heavily dredged, this 'crown' of live oysters—which more or less holds the structure together—is removed and the bed begins to compact and spread out to level bottom. It takes many generations for the oysters to build back up again, if they can do so at all. A few dredge beds in the Manning and Hastings rivers are still operational but account for less than half of a per cent of the oysters produced in New South Wales.

It should be no surprise that the decimation of the natural oyster beds in Australia was not due entirely to the white man's uncontrolled appetite, but also to his never-ending thirst for 'progress'. Lime, made from the ashes of oyster shells, was an important ingredient used for mortar in the buildings of the new and burgeoning colony, especially government offices and churches, as well as for private residences. Aboriginal middens were quickly exploited as they were a readily available supply. But it was soon discovered that the lime provided by *live* oysters was far superior (giving the lime more 'body') to that manufactured from empty shells—so much so that it became normal practice to stipulate in contracts for only live oysters to be used. This, and the growing population's penchant for gorging themselves on the hapless mollusc, meant that the natural beds were soon depleted. Legislation was passed in 1868 in New South Wales prohibiting the burning of live oysters for lime, but the damage by then had been done. Ironically, according to Roughley, the need to find new means to provide lime meant that the lime-burners began casting about for artificial means to grow oysters.

But accounts differ. According to Nell (1993) the 'Commercial production of Sydney rock oysters (*Saccostrea* [*glomerata*]) in Australia began simultaneously in New South Wales and Southern Queensland around 1870 with the exploitation of dredge beds, intertidal oyster beds, and with the placement of a range of catching and growing substrates such as sticks, slabs of rocks, and shell placed on intertidal mud flats.' (Would it perhaps put the cat among the pigeons to cite another source, who claims the Kominos family

pioneered oyster farming in New South Wales and also accords the same honour to the Greeks in Western Australia, where, says Michael Symons, 'Athanasios Augoustis was one of the first to set up oyster beds ...'?)

'As dredge beds were depleted and problems with accumulation of silt and mudworm increased,' continues Nell, 'the industry progressively adopted stick and tray culture on intertidal racks.' As early as 1890, a Mr T Whitlegge had already written an apparently definitive study on the mudworm pest.

C M Yonge also stresses the introduction of mudworm from New Zealand as the main cause for the reduction in deep-water dredge supply, with the 'happy consequences' that this crisis, in New South Wales at least, stimulated cultivation and resulted in renewed interest in the area 'between tide marks and under conditions where oysters could not be affected by these worms'. One thing everyone seems to agree upon is that the demand of the colonies for oysters very quickly outstripped the supply.

First attempts

Between 1866 and 1868, during an art-collecting trip to Europe, the Honourable Thomas Holt visited France and made it his business to study the various methods of oyster culture used there. Holt was a member of the New South Wales legislature, and a wealthy entrepreneur, financier and grazier who had dabbled in timber-getting and coalmining and, among other ventures, sheep and cattle raising on pastures sown with imported grass. Back in Australia, around 1870, he had the first 'claires' dug on the banks of Gwawley Bay, Georges River. These were six and a half metres wide and deep enough to retain a metre or so of water at low tide. The inlet and outflow of water was regulated by flood gates and dams which had already proved so successful in France (and still is). According to Roughley, 'Oysters from Port Hacking, Cowan, Brisbane Waters and Pittwater were brought in to stock them, while over two hundred men were employed and thousands of pounds spent on the project'. The British expert, William Saville-Kent, puts the figure at about £10 000.

It was a complete failure. Holt had been criticised before for ideas that were 'considered somewhat unsound' and he had not counted on the fierceness of the Australian sun, which heated up the still water to the point where the oysters cooked. Others were suffocated by deposits of silt. After a few years of trial the whole thing was abandoned.

Although a Royal Commission was appointed in 1876 'to inquire into and report the best mode of cultivating the oyster, of utilising, improving, and maintaining the natural beds of the colony, and also enact the legislation necessary to carry out these objects', the writing was on the wall, and, it seems, very little happened after that. Unfortunately, the ambitious failure at Gwawley Bay provided both the public and the oystermen with an excuse to persist in their bad habits. Letters written by a leading oyster merchant appeared in the *Sydney Morning Herald* as late as 1890, condemning wholesale the French methods ('a dead failure in Europe'—which, as we will see, was not true) and all other methods likewise. Saville-Kent felt it necessary at the time to publicly expose these widely read missives as 'calculated to mislead the Australian mind concerning the achievements and capabilities of scientific oyster-culture' and, probably, an attempt to keep 'certain existing monopolies' in business. Ordinary farmers, however, continued to move oysters somewhat haphazardly from one area of growth to a better one for the next twenty or more years. This continued to be much the case for the short history of the oyster industry in Queensland which relied heavily on dredging and harvesting natural beds until well into the last century. Supposedly, it was not until around 1896 that fairly systematic cultivation began in New South Wales.

WAY OUT WEST

During this period, the colony on the west coast was experiencing a similar scenario. In 1893 however, Saville-Kent, now the first Commissioner of Fisheries of Western Australia (and formerly of Queensland and Tasmania), began to actively investigate the possibility of oyster cultivation in that state. On more than one occasion he delivered speeches on the subject to the Premier and Treasurer, which were reported verbatim in the *West Australian* newspaper. His first, made 'as a result of Saturday's cruise in the Government launch', concerned the 'possibility of establishing oyster fisheries' in the Swan estuary:

> That the so-called 'mud-oyster' *ostrea edulis* (var. *angasi*) abounded in the river to such an extent that, if now living, they would represent a most valuable commercial asset, is a matter of common knowledge.

The oysters, he went on to theorise, had probably been destroyed by an extraordinary flood which caused the 'sudden and complete alteration of the estuary character'. The subsequent silting up of the river mouth and retention of fresh water would have killed all the oysters, and, as these conditions were not likely to change in the near future, there was little hope of reviving the natural beds. Saville-Kent concluded, however, with a fairly detailed plan for using the lower part of the estuary where, according to local fishermen, there were very deep holes which retained their salt water throughout the duration of the annual flooding. By bringing in the eastern Rock oyster (then known as *Ostrea glomerata*) which thrived in less saline water, or the far northern *Ostrea mordax*, already imported for food from Shark Bay, these areas could be successfully planted. (Remember, until the twentieth century *all* edible oysters were classified *Ostrea*.) As well, the new Fremantle breakwater just being completed at the time would allow freer access of the sea and alleviate some of the problem of fresh water. The breakwater structure, Saville-Kent thought, would also make a 'magnificent planting ground' in itself.

The first phase of Saville-Kent's plan was accomplished by April 1894, in the vicinity of the breakwater, using a small number of Rock oysters from Shark Bay. The possible extension of the experiment to the foreshores of Garden and Rottnest Islands was later mooted. Although the earliest records of the State Fisheries Department indicate that in 1900, an R Gee and D Angels separately applied 'to erect an oyster crate' near Fremantle Bridge, it is doubtful the government's venture was successful. No large oyster industry has ever been recorded for the area.

It was, however, for King George Sound in Albany that Saville-Kent's expectations were highest. He had been credited with the miraculous 'resuscitation of the practically extinct oyster fisheries of Spring Bay in Tasmania', where the supply of oysters went from nonexistent to such a glut that vendors in Hobart were forced to reduce their prices by 50 per cent! No one doubted he could do it again in Western Australia—for a proposed maximum government expenditure of £300.

Meanwhile what 'turned the tide', so to speak, in New South Wales? Probably nothing more than, after staring glumly into their own progressively barren rivers and estuaries, and reflecting on the failure at Gwawley, oystermen finally began to realise that what worked in France wouldn't work here. The native oyster, the Sydney Rock, was clearly a different kind of creature and required treatment tailored to the harsh conditions of Australia. Still,

the experiment might provide some direction and, just as settlers had been forced to adapt in every way imaginable to what seemed an inhospitable land, oyster farmers would have to adapt in this as well. And what better adviser to point the way than the local oyster itself?

Farming the Sea

Of course, oyster cultivation had been going on for centuries and human beings had long faced the same problems. We know that the Chinese and the Japanese were probably cultivating these molluscs long before the birth of Christ, and that the ancient Britons and the Greeks enjoyed them; Aristotle reported that fishermen at Rhodes threw shards of pottery into the sea to encourage oyster growth by providing settling surfaces. There is also some evidence that American Indian tribes had elaborate and extensive means of cultivation. The discovery under the centre of the city of Boston in the early 1940s of a 'fishweir' (a large permanent trap consisting of an arrangement of wattles) in the midst of the remains of an ancient oyster bed, is believed by some anthropologists to have actually been a spat collector.

The first definite accounts of *ostriaria* we have are from the Romans, who began to fatten oysters, probably on stakes, and later on hanging sticks, in Lago Lucrino, a small lake, near Naples, connected to the Mediterranean by a narrow channel. Apparently Sergius Orata, who is credited with this brainchild, made a fortune from the venture. He even gave his oysters a special name: *calliblephara*, meaning 'beautiful eyebrows', which had to do with a fine purple thread that ran around the edge of the body and was thought to indicate a superior mollusc.

It was not by accident then that the distinguished French embryologist, Jean Jacques Marie Cyprien Victor Coste, visited Lago Fusaro (also near Naples), convincing Napoleon III in 1857 that he had discovered some means of saving the ailing—almost dead—French oyster industry where eighteen out of twenty-three natural beds were reported in 1858 as completely destroyed. It should be noted though, that while Coste carefully studied the Italian methods, he did not attempt to copy them in France, where the conditions at Saint-Brieuc in Brittany were very different, but adapted them as was needed. Figures from French government statistics show how successful Coste's innovations actually were: in 1873 the official value of the revived industry was an enviable £99 000. By 1874 it had grown to £528 050 from the 335 774 070 oysters produced. So much for 'dead failure'. This area (probably the one Holt visited) continues to produce a large percentage of all the oysters eaten in France.

Little is known about the famous Coste, more or less the founder of modern oyster culture, except that he was born in l'Herault not far from Montpellier where he studied medicine and published a small paper on the ovology of the kangaroo. Only a short drive southwest are the oyster-growing towns of Bouzique and Mèze—the centre of the *coquillage* industry on the shores of the Bassin du Thau, where the hanging stick/rope method of culture employed nearly thirty centuries ago at Lago Lucrino is still being used. And in the local vineyards the distinctive sticks— with flat depressions gouged into them, each with its own little dab of cement to hold an oyster—can be found propping up the vines.

POOR BRITONS

CM Yonge provides a fascinating picture of the oyster industry as it developed in England. ('Poor Britons', wrote Sallust in 50 BC, 'there is some good in them after all—they produce an oyster'.) As early as 1189, the Corporation of Colchester was given a charter by Richard I, confirming the rights to oyster fishery in the Colne and its creeks, enjoyed during the two preceding reigns and 'from time immemorial beyond that'. By 1577, oyster dredging in the Thames estuary was prohibited during the breeding season 'between Easter and Lammas' (a harvest festival held on 1 August). Cultivation increased as the beds were carefully tended and greater areas of surface were provided for settling of spat. According to contemporary reports, as quoted in Yonge (who got it from Philpots):

> In the Month of *May*, the Dredgers (by law of the Admiralty Court) have liberty to catch all manner of

Oysters, of what size soever [with detailed instructions as to the removal and return of spat in order 'to preserve the ground for the future']. 'But after the Month of May [remember the stipulation of months with an 'R' in them] it is a Felony to carry away the Cultch, and punishable to take any other *Oysters*, unless it be the size (that is to say) about the bigness of an half Crown piece, or when the two shells being shut, a fair shilling will rattle between them'. ... This brood and other *Oysters* are then carried to creeks and thrown on to 'their Beds or Layers, where they grow and fatten'. There were penalties for 'those that destroy the Cultch', or 'take any *Oysters* that are not of size, or that do not tread under their feet, or throw upon the shore, a Fish which they call a *Five Finger* [star fish] ... because that fish gets into oysters when they gape, and sucks them out'. The penalty for destroying the cultch was because 'if that be taken away the Ouse [mud] will increase and then the *Mussels* and *Cockles* will breed there and destroy the *Oysters*, they having not whereon to stick their Spat'.

Bishop Sprat, *The History of the Royal Society of London*, (1667)

In spite of such careful regulations to conserve the bountiful resources, the demands of the burgeoning population and, later, the importation of many highly successful pests (including the slipper limpet from America and the acorn barnacle from Australia—the colonies did eventually get their own back!), caused depletion of the beds. Oyster production in Britain eventually came a cropper in the same way as so many others, and has never really recovered. So much so that during the late nineteenth century Tasmania enjoyed a lucrative dredging

industry for Native oysters which were shucked, pickled in barrels and shipped by the tons to the UK.

Although dredging or 'fishing' has been used as long as human beings can remember when natural beds were plentiful and cultivation unnecessary, the real challenge came when oyster farmers realised that it was up to them to husband the oyster into greater production and away from depletion and destruction.

Roughley defines the *artificial* culture of oysters as 'the laying out of suitable material in positions where free swimming larvae abound in order that they may have an opportunity of attaching themselves, and the transference of these attached larvae, or spat ... to a faster growing ground if the one where they were caught is not conducive to rapid growth'. Somehow the addition of 'artificial' seems redundant, although by now it should be obvious that there are two operative words that define oyster cultivation: *catching* and *transferring*. Korringa, in his 1976 comparative study, makes the distinction of a 'semi-culture' being one in which 'larval development and the provision of food for all oysters is left entirely to nature'. Australian oyster culture, with some exceptions, generally fits into this category.

chapter iii

How to Catch a Good Oyster

> OYSTERS CAN LIVE, AND INDEED THRIVE, WHEN
> SUBJECTED TO SHORT PERIODS OF IMMERSION ...
> IN SALT AND FRESHWATER, AS IN THE MOUTHS
> OF CREEKS AND RIVULETS ... [THIS EXPOSURE]
> IS WELL KNOWN TO BE PARTICULARLY FAVOURABLE
> TO THE GROWTH OF OYSTERS.
>
> W. Saville-Kent, *Reports on Tasmanian Oyster Fisheries* (1880–1890s)

EXCEPT FOR THE momentary enthusiasm over French methods in the 1870s, oyster cultivation in Australia remained, for many years, a simple and fairly haphazard affair of providing hard surfaces for optimum catching—rocks or rock slabs, sometimes logs, sticks, or even just empty shell spread over the mud.

Since then the industry has become, and is considered, 'well organized' in Professor Yonge's learned opinion. Writing in 1960, he adds that it is carried on largely in estuaries or inlets such as the mouths of the Georges, Hunter, and Hawkesbury where

> spat is collected on a variety of surfaces such as sticks of mangrove or other woods (the former for preference

because it is heavier than water and so does not float away), bundles of brushwood, stones and cement blocks and even rusted bars' ... later grown on racks or trays raised above the surface of extensive estuarine *mud flats on which oysters would never live* [my emphasis].

But let us go back to catching.

Roughley's description of the 'early free-swimming stages of the oyster's life' is so wonderfully melodramatic it's worth quoting in its entirety:

> ... its most hazardous period ... that when an oyster spawns, the eggs from the female and the sperms from the male are cast direct into the water after the manner of most fishes. They are at once at the mercy of wind and tide, they provide food for a host of other animals, and many adverse conditions may work for their destruction. Mullet are often attracted to the region of spawning oysters, and the eggs and embryos are strained from the water and freely devoured. The number thus consumed, if allowed to develop to maturity would probably have been sufficient to stock the whole river with a prolific crop. The survivors soon begin to swim, but their movements are very feeble, and are carried about by currents which may take them out to sea or leave them stranded on the foreshore with each receding tide. Sudden changes of temperature and salinity kill off large numbers, and everywhere are the gaping mouths of molluscs, crustaceans, and numberless other animals waiting to absorb them. Daily their numbers diminish as the dwindling army battles on to that critical stage when the individuals must cease to roam, they must find some clean stable object in the water to which they may cement

their shells or perish. They cannot swim powerfully enough to search for such objects, but must trust to the fortunate course of the current to carry them to their vicinity. At this period the death-rate must be very high; large numbers settle on to mud and are quickly smothered, others are carried backwards and forwards with the tide and never encounter any surface suitable for their future sedentary life.

The oyster cultivator now begins to take a hand ...

The first objective of the oyster farmer then is to lay out suitable material to which the maximum number of larvae will attach, in places that the oyster is expected to spawn, at the time the larva is expected to settle — that is during the warmer months, or what was known in France as *lorsque la vigne a flueri* (when the vines are in flower).

The best spat-catching (called 'recruitment' in the latest international speak) is generally found at or near the mouths of rivers, where the water is clear and the salinity high. This is because oyster larvae prefer surfaces that are not 'fouled' (that is, colonised by other marine life — barnacles, sea squirts or algae for example), and these conditions mean the catching surfaces tend to remain relatively clean. However, it is also true that oyster larvae do not like a surface that is *too* clean and their gregarious nature tends to motivate them to places where others have already settled. Finding the optimum catching material has been of major importance for most growers. While methods vary from place to place all over the world, all catching material tends to have certain characteristics in common: a smooth, hard surface; the ability to remain in the water for at least three years (until the oyster is ready to be harvested) without decaying; and a consistency which allows the oysters to be removed without their shells breaking.

STICKS, STONES AND SHELLS

Stone of all kinds was used as catching surfaces in areas where it was naturally found: slate, in Australia sandstone, and often the blocks used as ballast from ships if none other was available. These were built into various edifices, from pyramids to mounds and clumps. In some places they were laid flat or stuck vertically in the mud. In others, slabs of rock were leant against each other in such a way as to make tent shapes, providing the optimum amount of catching surface. 'Stones laid in heaps' was a method used at the entrance of Port Macquarie and on the Brunswick River. On the Georges River 'on one lease alone', Roughley estimated in 1925, were 'upwards of over half a million such slabs under cultivation'.

One of the most ingenious methods, called 'pegstone', was introduced to the Clyde River by J F Brassington in

the 1930s. Stone gathered from Runnyford Creek was laid flat on top of three wooden pegs pushed down into the mud. Because oyster larvae tend to attach to the underside of surfaces for protection and shade, spat was caught on the bottom of the stone. Twelve months later the stones were turned over to expose the maturing oysters to the light and stronger currents, while leaving a fresh underside for a new catch. When the oysters were ready for market, the top side would be 'worked' and then turned over again. It was a simple and efficient method, so much so that 20 000 pegstones was considered enough of a living for one man.

Shells of all kinds have also been, and are, used to collect spat. They can be pushed through a loosely twined rope suspended in the water, or strung like beads by punching, with specially designed machines, a hole in them through which line is threaded, a practice highly developed in France and in Japan (where systematic cultivation of *Crassostrea* was recorded as early as the seventeenth century). Ted Allen of Greenwell Point remembers farmers hanging ropes of oyster shells from mangroves in the early days of cultivation in New South Wales. In the warm waters of Pendral Sound, British Columbia, spat-falls are collected on shells suspended on wires, a form of floating cultch. The important oyster-growing region of the Louisiana Delta uses a particular species of clam shell, which because of its small size collects usually only one spat per shell, which means the maturing oysters can be more easily prevented from growing into clumps. In New Jersey, Brooks reported that the oystermen of the East

River, having discovered that spat settled on shells scattered over beds during the spawning season, had already 'started the practice of shelling the beds in order to increase the supply and in 1855, three years before Coste represented to the French Emperor the importance of similar experiments, the State of New York enacted a law to secure to private farmers the fruits of their labour'. This is still done in some places on the American east coast by taking out large quantities of clean shell from a company stockpile in boats to deeper water (they call it 'sailing out the shell').

But it is not all sticks, shells and stones. New and more efficient collectors were, and are, continually tried: different shapes such as cylinders or plates; different coating mixtures and materials. In parts of eastern France scrap iron (box springs included), iron bars, or finely grooved plastic tubing cut in lengths and plastic 'Netlon' discs are used. Along the middle eastern seaboard of the United States, wire-netting bags full of clean shell, cardboard egg cartons covered with lime, twigs or brushwood, even paper tubes dipped in cement have been used with success.

TRY TRY AGAIN

In the famous French oyster area of Morbihan, Eleanor Clarke recounts seeing in 1959 millions of tiles covered with a lime slurry gleaming in the spring sunlight, awaiting the signal from the *Docteure-ès-Sciences*, when they are moved in barge loads into the open water between Saint Philibert and Quiberon to set *le naissain*,

> each boat towing its ghostly load of ten or twelve thousand tiles at the end of an immense length of cable. People far inland are awakened by the roar of the motors, and those near the shore run out to watch ... It is more as if the souls of all the dead and living, all forgiven and packaged alike in white, were about to be peacefully dumped somewhere up the coast.

Leaving aside these romantic visions for a moment, all in all the spat-catching business is not easy: *exact* timing is of the utmost importance. As Barry Allen explains, 'We know they're going to spawn when the first rains come and fresh water comes down into the estuary; when the mullet begin worrying the oysters on the sticks'. Apparently the fish sense the imminent spawning long before anyone else. 'You have to be *ready*, the bundles [of sticks] cleaned and freshly tarred.'

Depending on weather conditions—particularly temperature, which affects the growth of plankton available—the larvae or 'swarm', although actually present in the water, may take a long time to settle. If collectors have been put out at the first sign, they may become fouled and the young oysters 'will simply perish for lack of a place to attach themselves'. Too late, on the other hand, 'and the larvae will be lying dead on the beach, a barely visible jelly being dissolved into the sand by the tides'. The oyster farmer has therefore gone to a great deal of effort and expense for nothing, on top of which the whole process, using *clean* collectors, must be gone through in another couple of months, or even postponed to the following season. This means the farmer has no seed with which to plant his or her leases, unless spat or young oysters can be gotten from somewhere else—as was the case in areas on the Clyde River in New South Wales, where seed from Port Stephens was used. The Hawkesbury is an important source of spat for New South Wales growers, as are Camden Haven and Manning River.

Generally, until the widespread advent of hatcheries, in oyster-growing areas all over the world larvae development was left in the hands of nature. This is still the case in New South Wales. Whether a catch is good or bad can vary greatly from year to year, sometimes alarmingly so, even if the number of breeding oysters and the number of spawn produced is exactly the same. Pioneer farmers in Queensland considered the presence of a certain species of whelks a good sign; the more whelks an area or lease had, the more oysters they believed they would eventually harvest. This was because spat often settled on whelks and was carried about by the living creature over the mudflats in search of food—which of course also benefited the oyster—until they got so big their weight stopped the whelk from moving and it eventually died, leaving the oysters nicely planted out and much of the work done for the grower.

By the turn of the century Australian oyster farmers had begun to leave shell and stone methods of catching spat behind. Shell was too labour intensive for the limited return, and stone, though very durable, was difficult to transport. Since earliest times, bundles of twigs or faggots have also been employed for spat-catching, as indicated by the practice of the Chinese, Japanese and east-coast

How to Catch a Good Oyster

American Indians. The use of these by the Romans has also been documented. Coste used chained *fascines* made of boughs in his experiments at Saint-Brieuc. In Norway, spat is collected on birch branches interlaced in squares of wire netting suspended in the water of specially constructed 'polls' or ponds. In Australia, the observation that wild oysters grew naturally and profusely on the limbs and roots of mangroves encouraged farmers to progress rapidly to a widespread stick culture. The discovery and development of this method proved to be significant and highly successful, particularly on the east coast.

Initially mangrove sticks were set up in bunches like a teepee, laid in bundles along the shore, or stuck vertically in the mud. It soon became evident, however, that there were more oysters on a certain *part* of the vertical sticks and that those oysters grew faster than those below and above them. Growers eventually came to a sophisticated arrangement of sticks laid out horizontally at the appropriate level on intertidal racks. This provided more efficient and intensive cultivation since the new method meant that the sticks could be laid at a height where maximum crops would be obtained at the most rapid rate. It also meant the entire length of the valuable, fast-disappearing mangrove wood could be used.

Sticks have an advantage over rocks in that they are easier to handle and lighter to transport. Moreover, the kinds of hardwood that were available in Australia are extremely sympathetic to this method, being especially durable and resistant to decay: black or red mangrove, swamp oak, and white honeysuckle have all been employed. Now mainly blue gum, blackbutt, brush box and turpentine are used. These can withstand attacks of marine borers ('shipworm' or 'cobra') for at least six to eight years, are fairly long-lasting in the water when tarred, and can be easily supplied by sawmills in standard lengths and widths as waste wood. In Western Australia and in parts of Tasmania, growers use treated pine which they say is less trouble and will easily last ten years in the water, as long as it is regularly removed and dried out.

Because the Crassostreinae (Sydney Rock and Pacific) can grow both between tide levels and submerged in water up to depths of 15 metres or more, methods of cultivation will vary according to conditions. In spite of some of the disadvantages of having to work with (or against) the tide, a difficulty overcome by deep-water cultivation, one of the distinct advantages of intertidal cultivation is that the tides regularly uncover the leases and make checking, maintenance and removal or placement of sticks, frames and racks much easier. Being out of water so regularly also discourages predators, fouling and mudworm.

How to Catch a Good Oyster

Waiting for the Signals

They move their black stick bundles
across the river, put stakes
aside for fresh water, making racks
to drench in tar; oyster-farmers
who strive for an order
of their own, gardening their shells
bunching-up smoked mullet
assorting old bleached branches
along a ragged shore—

Robert Adamson, from 'Farming the Oysters'

While waiting for the all-important signals—temperature, rainfall, the interested nosing of mullet—the farmer isn't just sitting around counting his proverbial oysters. Hardwood 'catching' sticks which are new or scraped clean are made into frames or lattices that consist usually of approximately 22 sticks (25 mm x 25 mm x 1.8 m) nailed parallel to each other at 100 mm intervals. Some farmers dip individual frames in cold liquid tar and allow them to dry before wiring into the blocks (or batteries, or crates, depending on who you're talking to) of five to six frames. In some areas, like the Hawkesbury, a cement/lime coating, which the oyster spat seem to prefer over straight tar, is also applied to the sticks.

The design of the battery is extremely clever. It is loose enough to allow an easy flow through of water, but will also provide some shelter for the baby oysters and keep out fish, which can do a great deal of damage to a new spat-fall. Fish are one of the main predators in Australia, which does

not suffer quite as much as other places from borers, crabs, rays and starfish, since these prefer more saline waters and much of our cultivation is carried out further upstream in brackish areas. Generally the spat settles on the clean undersurface of the sticks, so the batteries are often unwired at intervals and replaced in such a way that all the spat are facing inwards before rewiring. Once the oysters have matured somewhat and developed a harder shell, predation is less of a problem.

The batteries are placed on racks made of tarred hardwood posts and rails sunk into the mud at about 300 mm height, the mid-tide or 'catching level' of an area, usually at the mouth of the river/estuary where a good spat-fall can be fairly assured. This occurs, depending on the locality, from the last month of summer (February) until the last month of autumn (May). Again, depending on the area, the racks are set at such a height that the frames will spend up to 70 per cent of the time under water.

THE WELL-TRAVELLED OYSTER

After the perilous adventures experienced by the oyster larvae in their effort to find a home, you might think that they then lead a completely peaceful and sedentary life stuck in one place, never to see any more of the world. Not so for a thoroughly modern oyster in a highly evolved farming system.

At about four to six months, once the spat are fully settled, the batteries are moved upstream to more sheltered and brackish waters, where growth is accelerated due to increased food supplies. This ensures that all the oysters in the crop are about the same age and also helps to avoid the problem of 'overcatch'—a second spat-fall. Most areas of oyster cultivation in Australia are in such warm waters that lack of spat is rarely a problem; in many regions, the opposite problem of overcatch is more likely to be a concern. Overcatch is when later spawn is released into the water and the new larvae settle on the shells of the still-immature oysters. As a result, the growing crop can suffer deformations, competition for food and even suffocation and death. (This can also be caused by a spat-fall of mussels.) It is a particularly difficult problem if there are breeding Pacific oysters present in the same area as Sydney Rocks. In the warm waters of Port Stephens, for example, leases that are too difficult to control have been given up and, in some cases, farmers have gone out of business.

Overcatch creates an enormous amount of work for the grower who must remove it manually by 'culling'. With mature oysters, farmers may leave the racks out of water to

How to Catch a Good Oyster

'dry' in much the same way as they do for mudworm; or, they are dipped into tanks of boiling water for a few seconds, killing the unwanted overcatch, but not harming the adult oysters which can then be put back on the leases to continue growing. But dipping is not so foolproof or simple as it sounds: the water temperature must be exactly right—hot enough to kill the unwanted overcatch but not so hot as to harm the oyster crop. (At least one farmer on the Clyde, I'm told, found out the hard way and boiled his oysters.)

The frames of young oysters are left in the blocks, which are now called 'depots', until the following winter to protect them from the ever hungry fish. Racks in maturing areas are slightly lower, so that the top frame of the block is out of the water at about the same time as sticks set at the optimum growing level. This period can be thought of as the nursery stage and the depots the baby oysters' cots.

It is important to remember that this is only a very generalised account of the stick and tray culture, which varies according to the river, the position on the coast, and is often as individual in method as the oyster growers themselves. In most areas of Tasmania and South Australia, where spat is now produced in hatcheries and placed directly into trays, larvae survival is not an issue and methods of cultivation are slightly different. There may not, for example, be a depot stage.

At about a year to eighteen months old, the young oysters are 'laid out' from their protecting depots, sometimes in another place, often further upstream. Laying out usually begins in June or July or even as early as May in some locations, depending on the weather, and may continue until late August. In laying out, the blocks of frames or depots are dismantled. The individual frames are nailed or wired horizontally onto the racks with all the oysters facing upwards. Racks are set apart at varying distances depending on the capacity of the area — from between only 5 m in an area with good feed and currents, to 10 m or 15 m apart in a poor one. When exposed by low tide, racks look something like sections of railroad tracks and need to be as level and precise. They are built quickly on days of unusual calm and low tide, when the water itself can be used as a handy spirit level.

The young oysters, at this stage, can also be removed from the sticks and placed in tarred wooden trays with a wire-mesh bottom. These trays are normally divided into three sections and sometimes covered with wire netting or hessian — which protects against both predators and being washed off the racks. (Hessian also prevents sunburn.) Trays are often used to 'finish' oysters, since this method tends to produce a more uniform shape, important for the plate trade; oysters cultivated on sticks sometimes develop a groove where they have grown around them. (Next time you eat an oyster turn it over and look at the shell. It will tell you a fair bit about what method was used to grow it.) This habit of growing to match the contours of the surface is called 'xenomorphism' and results in the strange and wonderful variations of oyster shells that delight some and so dismay others.

In some rivers, fencing is erected around the newly laid out sticks to minimise potentially destructive wave action or further protect against predators. At one time, fish caused so much damage in Port Stephens that the Melbourne Oyster Company was forced to enclose over a hundred acres of their 'paddocks' with 2.5 metre high fencing — about 250 kilometres of hardwood battens and supporting posts. They claimed it would have stretched 'almost from Melbourne to Adelaide'.

In either case — tray or stick — at this stage the maturing oysters are spread out in a single layer. Many farmers are now also using plastic-mesh pillows, cylinders or baskets. The main thing is that the oysters have plenty of elbow room in which to grow without stunting or distortion, and are free to feed and enjoy the 'kiss of the sun'.

Oysters are usually left at this point, until they reach marketable size. Then they are loaded into punts and taken back to the shed or 'shore depot' where, if necessary, clumps of oysters are knocked off the sticks with a sharp whack of an iron tool (often handmade) and then separated manually, cleaned and sorted. From catching to harvest takes around three to four years, though it may be as little as eighteen months for Pacifics. For the Sydney Rock grower this represents a cultivation period far longer than most other food crops—between an average of 1100 to 1200 days. (No wonder most are so passionate about their final product.)

By this stage the 'sedentary' oyster has probably travelled a fair distance up and down the river, and until recently, some may have travelled even farther than this. Before quarantine restrictions implemented in 1985, to stop the spread of the Pacific oyster in New South Wales, a whole culture of 'highway' oyster production had sprung up. Taking advantage of new efficient road transport, these mobile farmers would move partially grown oysters by truck from one estuary to another to use the best characteristics of each area. Nearly mature oysters would be taken on trays to another estuary to

'fatten' for six to eight months until ready for market. The relatively recent restrictions on movement, which have limited transport between certain zones subject to inspection, have meant that many of our oysters aren't quite so well travelled as they might have been, but are certainly safer.

SET AND FORGET?

Stick and tray culture has been referred to by some as a 'set and forget' system, apparently because, before the problem with Pacific-oyster overcatch, Sydney Rock oysters nailed out on single frames 'required little attention for approximately two years until they were harvested' (Nell and Holliday, 1993). Although stick and tray may require less capital and labour, problems with the available supply of hardwood and, more recently, successful cultivation with single-seed culture, have challenged the efficiency of this method.

Single-seed culture—a catchphrase amongst growers and researchers for a few years now—is a method in which separate spat are grown in a hatchery, or removed from the collectors (usually by scraping) soon after settlement, when the oysters are still only 3–8 mm in diameter, and grown in fine mesh frames and then trays, baskets or cylinders. A recent innovation in this method has been the Stanway cylinder—developed and patented by farmers from the Hawkesbury. Made of plastic and mesh, these cylinders allow single-seed culture with less difficulty in handling as they can easily be moved or rotated to keep the young oysters from growing together and free of silt. They also have the advantage of protecting the young oysters from predation, but they are useful only up to a certain age and size of oyster (40 mm). Because the cylinders rotate almost continuously in the force of water currents, the oysters grind against each other, more or less as in a gem-polisher, and the new growth shoots are knocked off. As a result the oysters can be small, distorted and rounded like a marble. Plastic net baskets or 'pillows' have similar advantages to the cylinder without the problems, and many farmers are more and more using them.

There is still some disagreement as to the efficacy of single-seed as opposed to stick and tray culture. Proponents claim that growing single oysters from the start produce more uniform 'teardrop' shaped shells with no culling necessary. On the other hand, the amount of handling and increased cost of the method, which is very labour intensive, can be prohibitive. In New South Wales at least, many growers have remained with stick and tray, maintaining that in the end, it is a more efficient and suitable method. Steve Felletti, a successful farmer on the Clyde, feels that in his specialised 'boutique' oyster-supply business, single-seed culture produces oysters with little character; and character is something the more enlightened restaurateur and diner actually appreciate.

BETWEEN TIDES

The use of rock, and later the stick and/or tray culture in Australia, is an example of *intertidal* culture (or, as some would have it, a 'horizontal' method), because the racks with sticks or trays are set up at the point which, while not actually on the foreshore, is not in water so deep that they would always be submerged and never exposed. The advantage of this intertidal position is that the oysters are covered with water a good part of the day but exposed to the air long enough to prevent or prohibit mudworm infestation. It also means that natural fouling is kept at a minimum. Exposure at low tides gives the farmers fairly easy access to their leases, so they can inspect their crops, hosing off accumulated silt if necessary. The disadvantage is that the oysters—whose job it is to grow as fast and as fat as possible—cannot feed when out of the water. Instead they close their valves hermetically and switch from their usual aerobic life to an anaerobic metabolism—a kind of suspended state.

But interestingly, there is a benefit to this. It is during this time out of the water that the oysters learn, as the French would say, 'to close their mouths' (known as the *trompage* stage). In this process, the oyster is actually forced to exercise, and therefore strengthen, its adductor muscle. As a result, it develops in a sense its own self-packaging, which means it will survive for a longer time when exposed to the air during harvesting and transport. This technique is used in Japan, where shell strings covered with maturing spat are laid out on wooden grids fairly high above the tide mark so that the young oysters are out of the water a large part of their lives. Only the most vigorous oysters survive this period of hardening, stunted, but with the margins of their valves thickened and fitting tightly together, ready for export as brood stock.

The Sydney Rock, grown mainly intertidally, is naturally well acclimatised and can live out of water for up to three weeks. Pacifics fare less well, although there is some debate on this and advice about storage varies. Generally it is recommended they should be kept one or two days at most. On the other hand, storage time may depend on whether the Pacific oyster is grown intertidally or *subtidally* (see below). If grown intertidally, a properly refrigerated Pacific can live for up to five days, but more on this later.

DEEP WATER

The other kind of oyster culture practised around the world—and, until recently, to a lesser extent in Australia—is deep-water, known as *subtidal* culture (a 'vertical' method). Theoretically, the advantage of this method is that the oysters are continually submerged and therefore have more time to feed, so that they grow faster and improve their condition more quickly than oysters grown intertidally. It allows farmers to work their leases regardless of the tides. On the other hand, it is more difficult to get to the oysters or inspect them, and the amount of fouling is significantly increased, so that farmers must usually remove the oysters and all the gear from the water every six weeks or so for at least ten days. Oysters grown subtidally are less susceptible to heat kill but more susceptible to the effects of flooding, mudworm and predators such as starfish, which prefer the deeper, more saline water. Though the quality of the meat is often considered better and the shell more uniform, these oysters do not travel as well, as they are less tolerant of being exposed to air. The way around this is if before going to market, they are 'hardened' or *taught* to shut their mouths by being taken out of the water on a regular basis before harvesting.

The two main means by which oysters are grown subtidally are by using a long line anchored to the seabed and floated by buoys, or with rafts. The rafts, with stacks of trays suspended beneath them, are used in Tasmania and in some rivers in New South Wales and in Moreton Bay, Queensland. Pontoons made from plastic pipes are also used in pairs to support single layers of sticks or trays. In 'bottom culture', stacks of tray are placed on small platforms on the floor of the estuary.

Ocean Foods International has a great deal of stock growing subtidally in Oyster Harbour (Albany, Western Australia) but is developing intertidal leases. In spite of all the theory, the Western Rocks aren't growing as fast as they should in deep water. Manager Jonathan Bilton (echoing Saville-Kent) thinks this is because the oysters are not as happy as when covered and uncovered by the tides, probably because of the nature of the organism that has evolved to cope with such conditions and therefore actually prefers them.

Regardless of what method is employed, it should be clear that the second most important part of the process of growing a good oyster, after catching (or hatching) the often-elusive spawn, is the *transferring* of the young, immature oysters to an area where, watched over by the farmer, they can grow and mature in relative peace and quiet.

A MATTER OF LIFE AND DEATH

> I was too busy with shark and cray fishing to put in the time. The oysters bloody carked it from borers or something, or bastards pinched them.
>
> ex-oyster farmer, Kangaroo Island, South Australia

A 'set and forget' notion about *any* method used to raise oysters may seem incredible to anyone with even a smattering of knowledge about the business. The problems the oyster and the oyster grower face are truly matters of life and death. And they are numerous: protection of the oysters at all stages of their life from different predators; and competitors—the feral Pacific, the aggressive mussel which some farmers say 'push off' the oysters; pests and parasites such as the mudworm, which, in the early days of the colony, virtually wiped out most of the natural beds; and environmental extremes.

Many diseases which affect oysters are a result of uncontrolled or careless movement of stock. A typical scenario was when imported New Zealand oysters were temporarily relaid in the Hunter River in the early 1900s, to await a rise in prices during a summer glut in Sydney. It is thought that this was the likely source for mudworm infection which spread north and eventually helped to destroy the industry in Queensland. Many countries including Australia have since implemented strict quarantines and other regulations to prevent this kind of contamination, although in many places it appears the remedy has come too late.

Mudworm (*Polydora websteri*) is a marine parasite that lives inside the oyster shell but maintains a tube to the outside through which it siphons in mud—the element in which it needs to live—filling ugly blisters which are foul-smelling if broken. The oyster itself may appear normal, but will reveal red stringy worms underneath when lifted from the shell, much to the horror and disgust of the diner. Mudworm can cause very high losses especially in subtidal leases where the build-up of silt is greater and the oysters are not out of water at any time. Some farmers use heavy spraying equipment to keep the oysters free of mud and therefore infection. Oysters that have become infested are sometimes left out of the water for ten days to kill the worms before being returned to their beds, hopefully free of their tormentors.

Another problem for growers is winter mortality (once called 'opening disease' because its most obvious sign is the high numbers of 'grinning' or gaping shells). It tends to occur in the southern or cooler half of the Sydney Rocks range, from Port Stephens to the Victorian border. Death can occur in winter, but mostly the oysters die at the onset of the warmer spring weather of September or October. Ted Allen tells of a time when a particularly bad outbreak of winter mortality occurred on the Crookhaven. A good crop was nearly ready for market. He remembers coming around the bend of the river, fearing the worst when he could 'smell 'em', the dead and rotting oysters, well before he could see them. Characteristically though, with a shrug of his shoulders and a laugh he adds, 'A fortune made was lost that day'.

The severity of the kill can vary markedly between areas, estuaries, and even leases. You may find that this is the cause of the disappearance or sudden increase in prices of your favourite kind of oyster. It is also likely that oysters you do get from the affected area will be smaller and poorer, because it is the larger, older oysters which are most susceptible and this may point to a connection between the disease and eutrophication, or the presence of too much nutrient in the water. And for some reason, it appears that oysters grown on sticks seem to be less vulnerable to the disease than those grown in trays.

Dry autumns resulting in high salinities and early winters increase the severity of loss. Good rains in autumn and late winter appear to prevent the disease. Research and experience indicate that farmers can avoid these losses by increasing the growing height of the oysters to 150 mm over the normal so they receive a change of water only every second tide, or by moving the oysters to leases further upstream before autumn, or simply by selling the oysters (though they may not be as big as the farmer would like) before winter starts.

The mysterious QX disease (*Marteilia sydneyi*) appears to be exacerbated by environmental degradation. Little is known about it except that it seems to prefer low salinities and high water temperatures (almost the opposite of winter mortality) and is more likely after a 'fresh'—a heavy rain—in March and April, early autumn. It is possible that another host carries a parasite between oysters but research as yet has not been able to establish this. QX is thought to have been responsible for the decline of the industry in Queensland and northern New South Wales in the 1970s. It is probable that similar strains like the European 'Abers Disease' have caused complete devastation of oyster beds in other parts of the world, including ones recorded in the 1800s or earlier that we can now only speculate about. To minimise the effects of QX, the northern New South Wales and southern Queensland oyster farmers have resorted to importing half-grown oysters from non-infested areas for short-term growing, and harvesting them in summer before the main risk period.

In the early 1980s, I R Smith, a biologist at the Brackish Water Fish Culture Research Station (Port Stephens) wrote that QX 'is the least economically important of the problems at the moment but it poses the greatest threat to the industry as a whole'. In his 1993 review, Nell stated that 'the range of the disease [had] extended as far south as the Macleay River (31° S)'. Only three years later the QX virus had virtually wiped out one of the largest, most productive oyster-growing areas in Australia—Botany Bay and the Georges River—where once a major industry had produced more than 3.5 million dozen oysters per year. Between 1998 and 1999, the total production for the Georges was 28 100 dozen and 189 432 for Botany Bay. At the time of writing there is still some production around Quibray, possibly due to the protection afforded by the Towra Point Aquatic Reserve. And very recently this insidious disease has been detected in the Brunswick River.

In 1991 another parasite, only lately identified by science, was discovered in Australia during studies of *angasi* aquaculture in Victoria by the Marine and Freshwater Resources Institute, Queenscliff. 'Bonamia' has been known in the rest of the world (including New Zealand), and is another contender as the cause of the devastating losses of natural beds in the 1800s. The disease results in the oyster suffering damage to blood cells and tissue lesions from which it eventually dies. *Bonamiasis* is host-specific, meaning it affects only mature Native oysters (usually over two years old and sexually reproductive), but not the Rock or Pacific oyster, and is not known to cause harm to humans. It seems to occur episodically but the factors which control outbreaks have not been discovered. Stress is a possible factor but it is not known if the higher summer temperatures resulting from global warming are also involved.

Those of us who may have wondered why there is no real production of the prized Natives in Australia, especially as *the* commercial industry in otherwise 'oysterless' Victoria, may be interested to know that Bonamia is the reason. So far the disease has proved a major stumbling block to successful production of *Ostrea* oysters internationally, with the French spending millions of francs on research to control or cure it, by breeding disease-resistant strains of oysters, which they have done with some small success. Developing a genetically engineered Bonamia-resistant oyster is proving more difficult.

Research on *Ostrea angasi* aquaculture in the late 80s and early 90s in Port Phillip Bay, Victoria, suggested that cultivation of flat oysters at normal high densities may, at times of low food availability, result in stress of the animals. However, a method developed by Victorian researchers of attaching them separately to lines called 'droppers', similar to those described on page 72 and then growing them subtidally provided faster and more steady growth. This was because the oysters were not crowded into baskets and had access to good water flow, which provided more food. It appears that if a marketable-sized oyster can be cultivated before it reaches sexual maturity and begins to spawn regularly, usually at two years, then the disease-caused mortality can be avoided. This may be because the condition is related to the *Ostrea* oysters' distinctive mode of reproduction, which as you may remember is incubatory, unlike the Rock and Pacific, and could explain why those species of oysters are not affected.

Other oyster disasters can be caused by environmental factors, such as the effects of summer heat, when temperatures rise to 30–40°C. 'Heat kill' can devastate exposed intertidal leases, especially when low tide coincides with strong sun and the hottest part of the day. The oysters literally cook. Farmers now use irrigation sprinkler systems to help protect the crop, as well as shadecloth. Brian Allen remembers being at a meeting of the Oyster Farmers' Association of New South Wales when the news of a heatwave came through. Apparently the growers practically knocked each other down to get out and check on their leases.

'Blooms', as they are called, are caused by an organism which in one form or another is a natural part of every marine ecosystem on the earth. But, as explained by the Canadian biologist Dan Quayle, 'it is only when the right combination of light, temperature, salinity, nutrients, minerals and vitamins are present that the bloom may occur. In a broad sense these conditions may occur fairly frequently but the specific combination only rarely', causing either marine or freshwater phytoplankton to grow excessively. When this is due to nutrients and the waters go green, it is 'eutrophication' which the public knows generally as a 'blue-green algae bloom'. Most blooms are harmless. The problem arises when a certain species of algae which can produce a range of toxins becomes dominant. These do not have to 'bloom' in the sense of eutrophication, but their numbers do have to increase significantly. Because oysters are filter-feeders they take in these algae and can retain the toxins in their tissues for some time. As prevention, all commercial shellfish in Australia are checked regularly and the areas in which they are grown are routinely monitored to comply with a shellfish sanitation program.

Floods, too, can be a major problem, causing damage to leases by washing down large trees, branches and other debris, destroying racks and trays. Run-off, similarly, can bury the oysters in silt; and freshets—streams of fresh water entering the river or estuary after heavy rain—can lower salinity, sometimes even to the point where the water becomes fresh enough to drink. Although oysters are capable of closing up tightly for sustained periods during these emergencies, they cannot survive this condition for too long: according to Roughley, by 1925 'practically all the oysters on the Richmond, Clarence and Macleay had been wiped out at intervals because of freshets'. This is a good example of the importance of balance in oyster culture. Oysters generally benefit from an influx of fresh water and usually grow rapidly upstream in more brackish areas. But, as they say, too much of a good thing ...

To prevent possible health problems, areas of rivers with oyster leases are closed for a few weeks after a heavy rainfall (more than 25 mm in 24 hours) which may result in any potentially dangerous run-off—that is, rainwater which may be carrying sewage, chemicals, fertilisers or other effluents from the land—and are carefully tested before being reopened. Farmers are not allowed to harvest oysters during the closed period, although they may still be selling oysters brought in *before* the rains and closure. Oysters do not necessarily die during heavy freshes, although there can be severe losses, and will soon recover and clean themselves out once the river returns to normal.

Finally, in the twenty-first century the oyster and its dedicated minder face their biggest challenge—that of pollution. As human habitation encroaches on formerly fairly empty regions and the demand for recreational waters increases, pressure is being put on the rivers, lakes and estuaries that they are often unable to sustain. Waste being emptied into the water, sewage seepage, agricultural run-off (especially from dairy farms), chemical effluent, acidic water due to excavation of acid sulphate soils, emptied ship-ballast, and even the use of anti-fouling paint on pleasure boats (now outlawed in Australia) are all taking their toll on the once pristine waters where leases are situated. The occurrence at Wallis Lake in February 1997, when sewage got into the water, is a recent example. The problem of who, precisely, is responsible for clean water became painfully apparent when government agencies—from the Federal to the State to local councils—began to run for cover in the wake of the disaster.

There is good reason to call the sensitive oyster 'the canary of the water'—an allusion to an old practice of taking a caged canary down into the mines so the miners would know, when it stopped singing, that the oxygen was running out. (Remember, water in, particles sifted and consumed, water out.) And it is of paramount importance for our environmental health, even for those who do not like to eat oysters, that the industry be held up as an example and supported in its battle against water pollution. Every oyster farmer I have met has had to become their own environmental watchdog and spends a great deal of time in surveillance, guarding against and reporting this problem, and making governments and local communities deal with its causes. The oyster farmers on the south coast of New South Wales are a good example: in the last few years they have forced at least one major chemical polluter to change its method of waste disposal, cooperated with the

How to Catch a Good Oyster

local council to engineer a new environmental sewerage system in the area, and worked out ways with the local dairy farmers to recycle agricultural run-off and effluent by re-irrigating their land with it.

In Tasmania, the shellfish industry prides itself on its 'clean waters' policy, a quality-assurance program introduced by the State Government in 1981 and now 80 per cent funded by the industry. The program ensures that shellfish are grown in unpolluted waters and therefore do not have to be purified prior to consumption. Areas of cultivation are carefully monitored and given a category status, which can be raised if problems are cleaned up, or downgraded if they become endemic. A similar program operates in South Australia and will soon be instituted in Queensland.

Of course, the pollution crisis is not confined to Australia by any means, nor has it yet reached the epidemic proportions faced by other countries. In an important study published in 1891, W K Brooks predicted the devastation of the mighty Chesapeake Bay system. This, when it occurred, was the result of a complicated set of interrelated factors: the dredging of the natural beds, for example, resulted in the loss of a vast filtration system which had once cleaned the water, and so further exacerbated problems caused by industry and population density. Unfortunately it has come hideously true less than a century later. In 1995, a little further down the coast, I sat in the Oyster Factory restaurant on the fairly isolated island of Hilton Head, South Carolina (where an international conference was recently held on these issues) eating freshly shucked local oysters that had been grown in the same leases (a total of 1700 acres at one time) and worked by the same company since before the turn of the century. They were delicious and cost only ten cents apiece! When I returned in 1998, the oysters were gone, not only from the restaurant but from the entire area. That part of Broad Creek had been closed due to the pollution resulting from overdevelopment as more and more people have crowded onto the island to enjoy its beaches, its beauty, its wildlife, and its oysters, the very things which inadvertently they are helping to destroy. The crucial question is, will the story have the same sad ending in Australia?

Picked today?

A man ... who is willing with his family to live in solitude amongst the islands of the Bay, and personally supervise the working of his banks, has a chance of making a fairly comfortable living.

C S Fison, 'Report on the Oyster Fisheries of Moreton Bay' (1887)

Unlike in *Through the Looking Glass* where the Walrus and the Carpenter had but to entice the young oysters to follow them along the beach before snaffling them up, the lot of the grower is hard work. The typical yearly schedule of an oyster farmer would be one like the following drawn up by the Allens at Greenwell Point, who practise the so-called 'set and forget' oyster culture on their large leases in the Crookhaven River:

January	harvesting and selling oysters
February	harvesting and selling oysters, laying sticks out to catch spat
March	harvesting and selling oysters
April	harvesting and selling oysters
May	selling oysters, laying out sticks from depots
June	laying out sticks from depot
July	culling oysters for harvesting and selling next year
August	culling oysters for harvesting and selling next year
September	culling oysters, depoting catching sticks
October	culling oysters, depoting catching sticks, nailing up new sticks for catching in February
November	harvesting and selling oysters
December	harvesting and selling oysters

This describes a 'normal' year, without any unusual weather occurrences or catastrophes. Nor does it mention the constant demands of routine maintenance, business meetings, deliveries, cleaning up leases (say, of feral Pacifics), dealing with government regulations and taxes, making or repairing tools, bagging and shipping, 'depuration' (which is the purification process required by law in New South Wales), or the hours spent transferring oysters from place to place in the river or to the shore depot. Oysters are in constant rotation, new larvae being caught, depoted, moved to fattening areas, while the oldest ones, mature and those that are in 'condition' are being harvested and sold. And much like the dairy farmer, an oyster grower can rarely take the time off to have a holiday.

THE BIG OYSTER

One of the fascinating things about the cultivation of oysters is the combination of the primitive and the modern, the high tech in tandem with age-old knowledge and traditions passed from generation to generation. There is still much about oyster farming that has not changed in centuries, despite continued calls from within the industry for modernisation, profitability, 'attractive presentation and vigorous promotion'—not all of them of so dubious a nature as the one reported in the 1988 *Australian Oyster*:

> The Manning River Branch of the OFA has given its unqualified support to a proposal for a tourist development near Taree which will have the theme of THE BIG OYSTER. The greater Taree Council has adopted the proposal, which is intended to rival the Big Merino at Goulburn or the Big Banana at Coffs Harbour. The Big Oyster is intended to be the centrepiece of a $7 million development on the Pacific Hwy designed to make Taree a more attractive tourist stop.

Now, it seems, we not only have the Big Oyster but the possible commercial viability of a genetically engineered

oyster called a 'triploid'. This oyster has three chromosomes instead of two and therefore cannot reproduce; instead it grows bigger and bigger, and, theoretically is in condition all year round. Other advances have long been accepted: growers are used to high-powered engines to propel the new aluminium boats and flat-bottomed punts, hydraulic winches, depuration tanks with ultraviolet light, high-pressure water pumps and irrigation sprinklers, conveyor belts, laser levellers, cellular phones and computers. But there is no getting around the long hours, back-breaking work, often in a cold sea, the ever present crushed shell, grit and mud, the persistent fish smell, heavy rubber boots and aprons, hand-forged iron tools, tarred sticks and scarred hands. Oyster farmers, like all farmers, are tied to the earth, in this case the oceans and rivers. They know their leases intimately, every kind of fish and bend and tree—the beds 'as carefully prepared and maintained though always underwater, as if they were flower-beds on land' (Collard, 1902). They work with the tides and the weather, and every oysterman and oysterwoman is a marine biologist, an engineer, a meteorologist, and often a poet as well. The season dictates what work needs to be done. Where oysters are cultivated can be some of the most beautiful, wildest and loneliest places on earth, and the oyster farmer will spend hours in isolation out in his or her punt with little but the sound of waves and cries of seagulls. In spite of all the innovation and new technology, there's not much of the gleaming stainless steel and glass we associate with the production of twenty-first century food; the sheds where they work when not out on the water—making and repairing equipment, culling, or waiting for the right tide or weather conditions—can be huge freezing barns in winter and stiflingly hot in summer. And yet the oyster is a delicacy, one of the most elegant and luxurious of foods. Much of its continuous appeal has been because it has not yet reached the stage of industrial production but retains the character and flavour of local produce. Its farmers, in many ways, lead a very hard life and few have the stamina to stay in it. If they do it is because they love it with an uncommon passion. Oyster-growing families seem to have salt water running in their veins.

By hook or crook

There are hundreds of examples of the strange marriage between nature and technology. One of the most bizarre, I think, is Roughley's account of diving for oysters. Diving suits were mainly used on the Clyde River, but 'for a considerable time South Sea Islanders were employed on the George's [sic] River to gather oysters without the aid of a suit'.

How to Catch a Good Oyster

Rather than dredging the deep-water leases, a man in full Jules Verne regalia, including a large round helmet with glass inset, screwed down onto the suit at the shoulders with big bolts, and weighted shoes, would descend a ladder into the water where a bucket would be lowered to him. He would proceed to 'gather the marketable oysters which are either growing naturally or have been dumped on the bottom to mature' and then the bucket would be winched up and emptied. It took three people to man a diving punt: one to operate the pump, another to cull the gathered oysters and look after the diver, and of course the diver himself. Apparently the diver was paid double time. It couldn't have been a very lucrative way to go about harvesting, although recently I discovered flat Native oysters are being gathered by divers at St Helens, Tasmania, and the business seems to be doing very well, so much so that the suppliers can't keep up with demand.

In the 1930s, at the annual Oyster Farmers' Association of New South Wales conferences—which began in the 1920s when a few oyster farmers gathered around a keg once a year, 'swapped yarns' and ate oysters in Fred Selmon's boatshed on the Georges River (they became known as the Knights of the Round Keg)—prizes were awarded for oysters grown on all kinds of assorted iron mongery, for example an iron bedhead and a pram. There seems to be no end to the inventiveness of oyster farmers who have managed to coax the little creatures, by hook or by crook, into growing fat and reproducing in any place and on any surface imaginable.

One of the most impressive is the account Yonge gives of the Norwegians growing *Ostrea edulis* in fjords. At the heads of these are pools having only narrow and shallow connection to the sea; fresh water at near-freezing temperatures flows from the mountains over the surface of these 'polls' into the fjords beyond. The polls develop different layers of water: on the bottom it is very saline with no circulation and no oxygen; the middle layers are also saline but less so and contain oxygen, producing abundant amounts of phytoplankton in the surprisingly warm temperatures. This is because the top layer, which is fresh water from snow melt, acts like the glass in a greenhouse. The oysters cannot live in either the bottom or top layers but thrive in the *middle* layers, suspended from a float in wire cages. Amazingly they grow and fatten happily!

Probably my favourite though, is the story told by G S Smith about Power Irving Nelson Dickson, known as 'Bonty', a part-time Queensland oyster farmer who came up with the idea of an oyster apartment building. In 1952 he bought a derelict 70 m dredge, the *Hercules*, from the Queensland Cement and Lime Company and then sank her over his lease at the 'One Mile' off Dunwich. His plan was to use the lower decks for growing oysters and the upper ones for workshops and living quarters for the crew — a kind of island oyster farm right out over the natural bank. Holes were cut in the sides of the hull to allow water to pass through, but the oysters, as we'd now suspect, weren't happy in their closed, dark quarters and didn't thrive. Regretfully, Smith tells us, the project was abandoned after eighteen months.

chapter iv

Oyster Tales

Test, trial, carry on, survive
Allen Brothers

EARLY IN THE twentieth century Queensland led Australia in oyster production. Its prolific natural beds were mostly found in the south of the state, around Moreton Bay and Great Sandy Strait, with lesser activity in Tin Can, Rodd's and Keppel bays. There was an excellent demand for these oysters—marketed as 'Queensland' or 'Moreton Bay' Rock—and between 1870 and 1920, about two thirds of the annual harvest was exported, mainly to Melbourne, but also to Sydney and even as far as Perth.

It was a boom time. At its height (1901–1910), two hundred men were officially employed and over 21 000 sacks of oysters worth around £29 000 were marketed to the southern states, which had come to rely on Queensland for oysters because of the decline in their own beds. But in a remarkably short amount of time the situation had reversed.

To a certain extent, this may have been because the natural banks of oysters were so large, so abundant and so easy to harvest that, as elsewhere, few fishermen concerned themselves with cultivation, which generally only went as far as breaking-up clumps and moving oysters from spat-catching areas around Sandy Strait (later Keppel Bay and Rodd Harbour) to the fattening areas in Moreton Bay. 'Reefers', as the wild oysters were called, were usually stunted due to the crowded conditions, but quickly grew to marketable size once they were separated. Because of the nature of the coast and the great distances, often impossible to cross by land, boats—small sailing cutters in the early days and eventually steam and marine-engined vessels—were an important feature of the industry, which relied heavily on transporting oysters from one ground to another or dredging natural banks in deep water.

According to a local historian, Thomas Welsby (1918), oysters were known to the Aboriginals in the Brisbane area as 'Kin Yingga' and further north as 'Ningi-Ningi', and were so abundant in Pumicestone Passage that both Toorbul Point and the tribe that lived there were generally referred to as 'Ningi-Ningi'. In 1865, Alexander Archer recorded that 'a reef of rock about three feet out of the water and 300 yards long' was spotted while passing through the Passage. 'On pulling up to see what it was we found it to be a huge and apparently solid bed of oysters, big enough to load several large ships.'

Often this was the way new banks came into production in Queensland—by accident—and they would then undergo a time of popularity and prosperity before needing to be closed to recover. Besides the public beds created in 1868, where anyone could get a feed of oysters provided they ate them on the spot and did not try to take any away, government leases were auctioned on a regular basis—the first in 1874 when 35 dredge sections went under the hammer in Brisbane. Certain beds, sometimes newly 'discovered', became well known for their productivity—so that, for example, at an auction of 1889 the rental fee per annum for No. 3 at Southport Broadwater went for £1000, while another at Russell Island went for only £6. These leases lasted fourteen years but were often 'worked out' long before the time was up.

Queensland attempted to control the over-harvesting of oysters and the burning of live oysters for lime by passing legislation in 1863, followed by a much more comprehensive law in 1874, but in spite of this by the early 1920s the industry was in serious decline. The introduction of mudworm, which had indirectly proved beneficial to New South Wales by encouraging oyster fishermen to discover methods of cultivating oysters in ways resistant to the pest, did not have the same effect in Queensland. Some attempts at stick and tray culture were introduced but, on the whole, oystermen counted on the beds recovering naturally, which eventually they ceased to do. The combined effect of the destruction caused by mudworm, competition from cheap New Zealand Stewart Island oysters and the growing New South Wales industry, aggravated by the shipping difficulties caused by World War I simply proved too much. A final attempt was made to save the industry in 1914 with the 'Fish and Oyster Act' (a provision of which was stiffer penalties for 'oyster thieving', claimed to 'be rampant in some areas') but it was too late. The last dredge section in Queensland on the Maroochy River was forfeited in 1947.

As in the story of South Australia, however, some people never gave up. Cecil Prior and Brian Cheras began cultivation after World War II at Moreton Island and Dunwich and there are today some 130 oyster-growing areas in the state with leases averaging between three to five hectares. In 1998–99 approximately forty of these produced 156 000 dozen Rock oysters (Pacifics being banned in Queensland waters). Most of this activity centres around Moreton Bay, particularly on North and South Stradbroke Islands and to a lesser extent in Bribie Passage and near Moreton Island. (There are no leases located on the mainland.) These farms have the advantage, and the attendant restrictions, of being located in significant areas of wildlife preservation—marine and national parks which afford the growers a guarantee of excellent water quality, although this has also meant that many leases have now been closed or are not to be reissued which may limit future production.

Compared to the past, the Queensland industry is relatively small, producing an annual harvest worth around $500 000. Oyster growers who generally rely on stick and tray methods have their fair share of difficulties, including serious levels of fouling and overcatch due to the warm water temperatures year round. Many are adopting new methods, for example, the B.S.T. system, and at the moment, can hardly keep up with the demand for their oysters in the state. Sydney Rocks imported from New South Wales are also fattened in the passage and Broadwater between April and November to avoid QX disease. Some 'milky' (*Saccostrea amasa*) and 'Blacklip' (*Saccostrea echinata*) oysters are still harvested, though they are mainly enjoyed by locals and do not often find their way out of the state, probably because of their 'strong' wild flavour, but perhaps also because they are thick-shelled and difficult to open.

And the winner was

Clearly oysters could be big business. This fact was obviously not lost on the farmers further south in New South Wales, who quickly began to overtake their northern neighbours in production of oysters through a combination of luck, perseverance, ingenuity and the right circumstance. New South Wales soon became the major centre for oyster production in Australia and remains the centre for cultivation of the indigenous Sydney Rock, despite some environmental difficulties in the last few years. As of 1998, 383 active farmers were working an area covering 3200 hectares in 41 estuaries between Eden in the

Oyster Tales

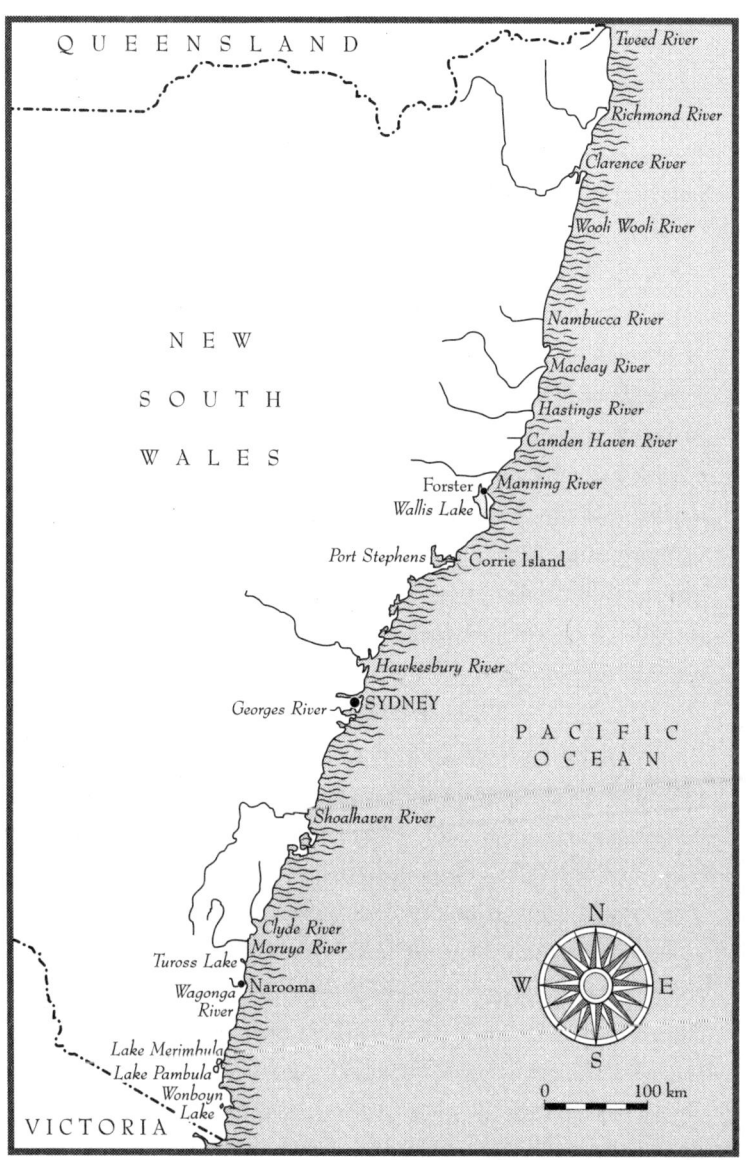

south and the Tweed River in the north. These include the ten major growing areas (by order of the amount of production): Wallis Lake, the Hawkesbury River, Brisbane Waters, Port Stephens, Clyde River, Wagonga Inlet, Lake Merimbula, Georges River/Botany Bay, Crookhaven River, and the Manning River.

It would take nearly a lifetime just to visit all of the areas in New South Wales where cultivation of oysters is carried out let alone gain an intimate knowledge of them. Every estuary is unique in terms of growing conditions and every farmer responds to these conditions with different methods of cultivation (this certainly applies to the other oyster growing states as well). As it is only practical to describe a small number of the possibilities, the oyster growing regions of the Hawkesbury and the Clyde rivers are fairly representative of the state's industry in terms of size of the operations, the kind of cultivation methods used and the personalities of the farmers themselves. They are also some of the oldest and most distinctive areas in New South Wales and are good examples of the traditions and techniques described in earlier chapters.

UNDER THE TOWERING CLIFFS

The Hawkesbury is one of the biggest river systems as well as one of the oldest oyster farming areas in Australia, and the farmers who grow oysters in its waters are justly proud. Rob Moxham is one farmer who is unequivocal in his view that successful oyster farming will continue on the Hawkesbury despite some murmurings I had heard about its imminent demise.

Although stick and tray cultivation was not invented on the Hawkesbury, it was certainly developed and fine-tuned there in the early part of the twentieth century, and is today still the main method used by most of the river's farmers. Talking to Rob and his brother Paul at their shore depot on Brooklyn Road was fascinating, especially since it was punctuated with fresh fat oysters offered on the flat shell, often spiced with a little Hawkesbury mud. They're both passionate about what they do and about what they produce — Rob quietly confident, Paul waxing lyrical about the beauty of their oysters while he culled the huge piles on the bench in front of him. At the time they were having some trouble with an overcatch of small black mussels. This made the culling more difficult, but they remained philosophical since 'there's not much you can do about it'. It seems the mussels are another mysterious element of the river, sometimes a nuisance, sometimes not there at all, with little rhyme or reason to it except for the subtle unpredictable combinations of environmental factors (and lack of predatory, but in this case beneficial, fish), like the algae blooms that sometimes trouble the water.

Because the Hawkesbury is so large, many of the farmers have to cover considerable distances. Most of the shore depots and sheds are located at Brooklyn or Mooney Mooney, but the leases are often miles upriver and the catching area down near the mouth. A day speeding up and down the river in a big aluminum punt (the Moxhams' is said to be the fastest on the river), covering the 15 km or so between leases, is a normal if often tooth-jarring experience for most of the Hawkesbury oyster farmers.

Heading upriver with Rob to inspect depot and fattening leases, you pass all the different aspects of life on the river: the houses, weekend cottages, boat ramps, marinas—one large houseboat catering for a wedding. The sight of a smiling bride in white gown and veil, groom and attendants in tuxedos seemed an appropriate symbol of the coexistence between the people who live on the river and have lived there since early days of the colony—fishermen and oyster farmers, holiday-makers and shopkeepers, boat enthusiasts and locals.

Probably the most extraordinary sight travelling this water system is the steep sandstone cliffs and rock formations which line the river and are a clear testament to its age and size. They also explain why the area has not been as overpopulated as other places so near Sydney: getting down to the water's edge is not easy, there are few roads and in most cases everything must be brought in and out by boat. Much of the area is also National Park with strict controls on development along the river shore and for some distance inland from it. This and the size of the river explain as well why the farmers there generally don't have the same problems with pollution as those, say, in the Georges or Botany. The tides flush the system twice a day, due also to the enormous river mouth; and the catchment area, protected by national park, is free of much of the agricultural and other run-off that can affect other estuaries. Stopping at one of the Moxham leases at 'The Wreck' (marked by a half of the World War I ship, *Parramatta*) Rob pointed out, towering above it, one of the awesome cliffs covered with ferns, studded with small trees and multicoloured as if painted, textured as if sculpted. Clearly, working in such a place was one of the daily joys of his business.

Of course what I now know about oyster farming tells me this may be one of the perks, but it certainly is not the whole story. Toward the end of the day we headed back down toward the mouth of the river to have a look at the catching area. By then the swell had come up and a cold wind was blowing hard—a reminder of how big the river is and how difficult the job. Luckily for us it was too rough to continue out into the huge mouth, which was almost like the open sea. When asked whether the catch this season was any good, Rob's reply was what I've found to be characteristic of the oyster business: 'no use worrying' as nothing could be done about it anyway. Generally the Hawkesbury has been prolific in its spat-falls, so I guess he can afford to be optimistic.

Up at the top of the river we approached an area of racks with trays, partly fenced off to protect the fattening oysters from unwanted waves and swell. Here is probably 'one of the best growing areas in New South Wales' where the Moxhams are fortunate enough to be able to produce oysters in good condition all year round—doubtless part of the secret to their success. Even though it was midwinter, the oysters Rob fished out for us to eat dripping directly from the river were very fine, relatively fat and quite delicious with only a slight hint of salt. When I questioned him about *why* the area was so good, the grin returned. 'If I knew the answer to that,' he said, 'I'd be a millionaire. It's good ground, that's all.' Leases just metres away from each other can produce completely different oysters in completely different condition.

At that moment his crew had just brought up a punt full of oysters ready for their turn at this aquatic country club. They looked like piles of rocks or coal. The crew shovelled them into the trays with big flat shovels (apparently these wear out continuously); it was reminiscent of the backbreaking work of stevedores—except for the fact that the punt kept floating away from the racks and had to be continuously pulled back in. But we weren't in a hellish boiler room. Here the sun was shining brilliantly and the end product will be beautiful Hawkesbury oysters.

Echidnas can swim

The Clyde River, which runs through the town of Batemans Bay on the south coast of New South Wales, originates at the base of the Clyde Mountain in the mountains behind Braidwood and empties into the Pacific at the Tollgate Islands. Massive floods can be one of the chief problems faced by oyster growers in this area, although farmers there tell me that floods—the last big one was in 1976—are now a problem only if they occur during a low tide, and that this is a fairly rare coincidence. One of the great fortunes of the Clyde River growers, like those on the Hawkesbury, is position—their leases are upriver from the town and surrounded almost entirely by forest and National Park so that the nightmare of pollution common to many areas on the east coast is something they don't (as yet) have to worry about. Wildlife abounds, much to the oyster farmer's delight and dismay: herons and other water birds, but also the stingray which can get through nets into the trays to build spacious temporary 'nests' by thrashing around amongst the oysters, causing a great deal of damage and eating their fill. One grower tells of seeing an echidna swimming across to a lease off Budd Island—to have an oyster dinner?

According to an article by an oyster farmer, the late Tim Wray, oysters have been taken commercially from the Clyde since 1870 or even earlier. Before the granting of leases, oysters were gathered on Crown land and a percentage royalty per bag paid to the Fisheries Department. In deep water, usually around the steep foreshores, dredging was done with a hand windlass in the boat. A rope was tied to a tree on the shore, the boat rowed backwards to the selected spot and the dredge was dropped over the stern. The boat was then winched back to the shore and the dredge emptied. Early on, the Lattas (one of the founding oyster-farming families of the area) had a number of tonging boats. Two men usually worked a boat,

one using a long pair of tongs or 'nippers' to gather the oysters, the other grading them as they were picked up into the boat. This system worked well for water 3–4 metres deep. Fifty or so years later oysters were gathered by divers (as described earlier), mainly in the winter when the water was the most clear.

Until the 1890s, as in the rest of Australia, little farming was done on the Clyde. But because each leasee had a set area to work by law, they soon began to realise that to maximise their investment, some sort of cultivation would be necessary. Thus began the process of experimentation seen elsewhere in New South Wales, at first with shell beds or stone supported by poles, then, in the 1930s, with the pegstone method unique to the Clyde (see page 78).

Tray cultivation was used in combination with pegstone until the 1950s when some stick cultivation was attempted, but most oysters still came from stone until the mid-1960s. At this time a number of Greek families moved into the area (the story has it that their forefathers had originally jumped ship at Sydney or Melbourne) bringing with them a great deal of innovation. Gradually stick and tray cultivation became the most common means of growing oysters on the Clyde, and remains so today. Because the water temperature is relatively cold and there is a large influx of fresh, larvae settlement is not generally successful, even when there is a normal spawning. Although some spat were caught locally, at one time 'caught sticks' were often brought down from Port Stephens. Now most growers use seed oysters from various areas and some bags of 'all ins spat' (which means the baby oysters have not been graded by size or age).

Today about thirty-five farmers are clustered in a cheerful, sprawling kind of oyster shantytown of sheds on Latta's Point and Budd Island, pretty much out of sight but just around the bend from the Princes Highway bridge. Although I'd been going to Batemans Bay for over ten years, I had never known it existed—I guess not noticing, or not knowing what to look for. Perhaps it's because, while the area is only a stone's throw from the centre of town, without a boat one has to take a 10 kilometre, unposted, winding dirt track to get there. We drove for what seemed ages through undisturbed forest and it was not until we saw a pile of oyster shells in the middle of the road—probably fallen from the back of a truck—that we knew that we were finally getting close.

Although production of oysters on the Clyde had stabilised in 1982 at between 5000 and 7000 bags annually, it later fell into decline, and the industry has had to undergo a great deal of change since. And as elsewhere in New South Wales, there's also been some confusion and political factionalism in the form of the Oyster Farmers' Association versus the New South Wales Farmers' Oyster Section. In spite of this, production doubled between 1996 and 1998 but has fallen slightly to 6333 bags or 728 471 dozen in 1998–1999. (About a fifth of these are plate grade.) Initiatives like that of the Fellettis, whose company, Oysterage, specialises in growing 'boutique' oysters and supplies directly to the upper-end restaurants of Melbourne and Sydney, have helped to invigorate the climate, as has the formation by a number of growers of Clyde River Oyster Marketing, a group which attempted

to standardise grading and weight (once aided by an ancient machine, which looks something like a *Dr Who* dalek, imported from France). Mark and Enola Ralston of The Oyster Shed are now running guided tours where they explain the ins and outs of oyster farming and even open your oysters for you.

Batemans Bay and the Clyde River Valley may have changed dramatically since the 1980s but some things retain their original flavour—like the oysters. (Farmers on the Clyde tell me their oysters—'Clearwaters'—come into condition around the end of December until May or even June depending on the rain. They are usually at their peak from late January through early February.) You can still hire a boat from The Oyster Shed (address: Last shed, Wray Street) or Harry's Bait & Tackle and follow the river with directions like: 1. Small tin shed, 2. Green-roofed house above shed, 3. Red marker buoy, 4. May's Wharf/windmill, 5. Landing with green shed past oyster leases between Snapper Point and 'mud', up to Chinaman's

Point and Big Island, and afterwards retire to the Bay View Hotel, advertised twenty years ago as 'the BEST spot in town' where 'oyster farmers still only drink' and 'hangovers are installed and serviced'. And it's still possible to have a cold beer among the fishermen there.

OYSTERLESS

In the early days of the colony, huge quantities of the flat or Native mud oysters (*Ostrea angasi*) were taken from Western Port Bay [sic], Port Albert, and Corner Inlet. But, as in much of the rest of Australia, insatiable greed and over-dredging reduced them to the verge of extinction, so that by 1890 Victoria depended upon New South Wales, Queensland, South Australia and New Zealand for oyster supplies. To rectify the situation, Saville-Kent, who had been called in as a consultant, advised the government that reserves should be set up in these areas (especially those at Western Port Bay and Port Albert) and planted with oysters. Apparently this was done with a very small stock found at Port Albert, but, the 'periodical skilled supervision of the beds necessary for their survival' was never provided and they quickly dwindled into decay.

By the evidence of the shells on the shore, and later experimental dredging, Saville-Kent found that Ninety Mile Beach and other areas of the coast also had beds of *angasi*. It was hoped that these naturally occurring oysters, which were themselves actually of fairly poor quality and not profitable to harvest and sell, could be used to restock further beds. Clearly, given the non-existence of an oyster industry in Victoria today, nothing ever came of this, nor of

Saville-Kent's recommendation that a system of leaseholding similar to that of New South Wales and Queensland be set up. Today Victoria, especially the Melbourne market, imports all its oysters from other states—a situation not unlike the one a hundred years ago.

Given the historical and environmental precedents for a viable industry in Victoria based on the Native *angasi*, it is encouraging to think that the successful operation of an experimental hatchery between 1987 to 1991, as well as other research conducted at Port Phillip Bay by the Queenscliff Victorian Fisheries Research Institute (now the Marine and Freshwater Resources Institute) in conjunction with the Australian Flat Oyster Company, may eventually lead to commercial production. According to one of the Victorian researchers, Neil Hickman, evidence suggests that by producing spat early in the growing season combined with mid-water long-line cultivation, it is possible to grow a marketable Native *angasi* oyster in two years—a way of avoiding the problem of Bonamia—until some way of controlling or curing the disease can be found. Recently New South Wales oyster growers, with the support of New South Wales Fisheries, have run a workshop on the production and marketing of flat oysters. Using the past research from Victoria, farmers in various areas of the state have been experimenting with Native-oyster cultivation and so far their trials have not yet suffered from any disease outbreaks and are ongoing. One can only hope.

At the time of this writing, cultivation of the Pacific oyster remains banned in coastal Victorian waters. No commercial oyster industry exists in the state, although limited Pacific-oyster cultivation was allowed at Cheetham Salt Works (at Lara near Geelong). Because all sea water entering the works went to evaporation ponds to produce salt, the company was able to demonstrate that none of their sea water could flow back into the bay. Cheetham was given permission to grow out juvenile Pacific oysters regularly imported from Tasmania, which the company did until 1998, when the aquaculture division was discontinued.

IN THE BEGINNING WAS THE SPAT

Surprisingly, although Perth seems surrounded by water, it is not known for its oysters. Several fairly recent attempts at farming in various northern areas of the state, such as Shark Bay and the Dampier Archipelago, have failed. This seems to have been for varied and complicated reasons, not the least of which are the strong Leeuwin currents sweeping the coast, and the lack of brackish river mouths and sheltered shallow bays. One of my friends, who has lived in and around Perth all her life, agrees with Jeremy Pearce, managing director of Larner's Oyster Supply, that Western Australians are not really 'used to' oysters in the way people on the east coast are—for holidays and celebrations cray and crab would be more likely to have been piled on their childhood tables. Generally their experience has been limited and based on Sydney Rock oysters shipped overland by truck or train from New South Wales. Nowadays Larner's (originally founded by Laurie Larner at the Oyster Beds in Fremantle—beneath which oysters from the east were once left to fatten) supplies a great deal of Pacifics, especially from South Australia. They 'look better', according to Pearce, and people prefer the white flesh. I had a dozen at the Roma Restaurant opened that morning by one of Larner's twelve or so full-time staff (some only shuck and rinse, and some only turn-over—more on this later). They were fresh and pretty and white as chalk but in my opinion without much taste—like eating a drop of water minus the sea.

However, things are changing. Ocean Foods International, the only oyster farm in Western Australia, situated at Emu Point, Albany, in the south, is licensed to grow oysters and mussels—including the Native *angasi* or 'flat' oyster, the abundance of which was recorded by Vancouver on his voyage into Oyster Harbour in 1791. In 1995 when we ate these oysters in Perth and heard of this venture, my interest was sparked. The idea of cultivating an almost lost indigenous oyster is an exciting one, and I made a point, on my next visit to Western Australia, to get down to Albany and see what had been happening in the two years past.

Though they still supply a limited amount to markets overseas and one Perth restaurant, Jonathan Bilton, Manager of Ocean Foods, was a little sad that this area of the venture had not come up to expectations. The *Ostrea angasi*, like its European relative *Ostrea edulis*, is less hardy than the Crassostreinae species; it has a high percentage of mortality and requires a great deal more handling. Perhaps, given what Jeremy Pearce had to say, the Perth market was not quite ready for such a different oyster.

Besides mussels—for which they have been well known—Ocean Foods is now concentrating on growing a Rock oyster (*Saccostrea glomerata*) which is the same species as the Sydney Rock but of a different population. They call it a 'Western' or 'Albany' Rock, and while it bears many similarities to its eastern cousin, its flavour is quite distinct.

Logically, given what has happened in much of the rest of Australia, I asked Jonathan why Ocean Foods was not cultivating the Pacific. As always, there was an official and unofficial answer.

Western Australia Fisheries have a strict policy of not allowing any exotic species into the state without vigorous prior assessment. In light of the outcome of the parliamentary enquiry into cultivating the Pacific in Victoria, Ocean Foods felt it unlikely that they would be given permission. However, it is interesting to remember that in 1948 the CSIRO attempted to introduce the Pacific into the state but was unsuccessful. Many years ago Jonathan met a local who had been indirectly involved in this venture. He maintains 'the only reason they didn't survive' was because it was common knowledge where the oysters were planted and too many of those in the know simply went and helped themselves too often. A clear case of overfishing that, perhaps, in hindsight, we should be glad of.

We were able to taste some of the Albany Rocks, and compare them with the Natives, both of which had just been pulled out of the sea-water holding tanks, opened (or 'massacred', as he says) on the spot by Jonathan and presented dripping on the half shell. In many ways this is the ultimate oyster experience—standing in a shed, near the place where the oyster was grown, and without any of the accompaniments (or distractions) of lemon or ice or wine or even table and chairs!

Both kinds of oyster, though not in their peak condition (it was the wrong time of year) were unique and delicious, each with a strong flavour and firm texture, their colours tending toward pinky-beige or mushroom with dark beards. This may be a bit much for the accustomed palate of people in the wildflower state (a situation which is certainly changing), but those who haven't tried them are really missing something. When in Perth it is essential to stop in at the oyster bar at Mead's, Mosman Bay, to taste these oysters and others through the deft skill of Jerry Fraser, who is probably one of the fastest, smoothest openers I've ever seen. In Sydney, Western Rock oysters are sometimes available at Martin Seafoods.

The set-up at Ocean Foods International is very different from anything I had seen so far in the oyster business. It is a good example of modern-culture based on hatchery stock and single seed, similar to that practised in South Australia and Tasmania. (There is also a commercial hatchery located at Brooms Head, northern New South Wales, which operated in the late 80s until early 90s and was reopened in 1998 by Pisces Marine Aquaculture.)

It's a fair drive from Emu Point, around King George Sound to Frenchman Bay where the hatchery is situated, skirting Oyster Harbour and Princess Royal Harbour. The closer we came to Frenchman Bay, the wilder the scenery, the more turbulent the sea. Greeted at first by a couple of dogs, we were invited by Jonathan into the hatchery—one of seven in Australia. It was sometimes hard to hear what he was saying for the noise of the water bubbling and motors and electricity but was nonetheless impressive. I followed him between small tanks that reminded me of deli freezers and the much larger ones he and a colleague used ladders to get up to. These are filled with pristine water pumped up from Frenchman Bay—the reason the hatchery is located so far away from the main business and shore depot—and contain larvae in different stages of growth. Jonathan was taking samples, using a microscope to measure them, and grading them while running back to the tanks as he talked. We followed him through water that was continually being flushed away through grating in the floor.

The reason for the hatchery in the first place is that the water in Oyster Harbour is too cold for Rock oysters to spawn naturally. (Remember Crassostreinae need at least 20°C and the Sound can get as cold as 15°C but rarely warmer than 22°C. The species *Ostrea* spawns at around 16°C, which indicates the potential for growing the flat oyster in the area.) So, as always in a commercial world, the oyster needs a hand.

But what seems a problem could also be a blessing. The low water temperatures and lack of natural triggers (though a sudden fresh could change this) means that the oysters don't spawn, but are in fairly good condition all year round, peaking in the summer months when food is abundant. By reabsorbing their unexpelled spawn at the onset of cooler temperatures, these oysters retain their opaque, fat appearance but, rather than being creamy, will be firm in texture. And although some can be thin in mid and late winter, you won't get that 'sour' taste that occurs when an oyster has recently released its sexual contents. This is a similar situation to much of Northern France and other European countries which are now growing Pacific oysters in cold waters.

At the Frenchman Bay hatchery, brood oysters, taken from the leases in Oyster Harbour, are induced to spawn in temperature-controlled tanks. Apparently they do so very readily. The fertilised eggs (or larvae) are collected and raised until a few weeks old, continuously sieved for size by the use of graduated fine-mesh screens. The baby oysters, no bigger than a full stop (they are around 0.3 mm when they 'set'), are fed on bacteria-free algae solution similar, although not identical, to what they would eat naturally. This is concocted in a special fluorescently lit lab that reminded me of a Frankenstein movie set. There were shelf after shelf of glass tubes and beakers, eventually graduating to 15 litre Aqua Nuovo water bottles, and thimbleful amounts of natural algae from CSIRO Hobart, Tasmania. In concentrated form the algae soup contains 5.6 million cells to the millilitre, and a thimbleful costs more than a week's groceries!

The oyster larvae, when it's time, have to have some place on which to settle. In hatchery conditions this occurs in large (0.9 m diameter) screens sitting in shallow troughs. Water and food (algae) are pumped in through a spray bar over the screen so the water 'downwells', pushing the swimming larvae down toward the settling material—a thin layer of powdered shell (either oyster or scallop) which has been put through a hammer mill several times and then sieved to produce particles very close to the size of the ready-to-set larvae. The idea is to get only one of the larva to settle on each of the shell particles. (They will also settle on the sides of the setting screen and the mesh as well, but can be removed early on by brushing them off with a good quality paintbrush or scraping with a razor.) The vast majority of larvae are then single seed and not doubles or triples. About a week after they have set, the spat, as they are now known, are transferred to 'upwellers' initially in the hatchery in warm water, and after two to three weeks there, on to the nursery upwellers using the water pumped in from their future home at Oyster Harbour.

It was fascinating to look into the microscope and be able to see larvae which were ready to set—that is, to lose their swimming velum and their feet and to complete their shells, which were still only pairs of tiny valves magically transparent—as well as still-swimming larvae madly beating their velum and moving up and down.

At about six weeks (although Ocean Foods, like growers in South Australia, generally considers the *size* of the oyster rather than its actual age) the set spat is taken on the long ride around the Sound to Emu Point. It's here that Ocean Foods International begins to look much like all the other sheds and leases I had visited—grit, rubber boots, gloves and aprons, smashed shell everywhere, bales of wire and mesh, sticks and racks, strange tools and contraptions, many of them obviously handmade—but on a slightly larger scale.

Once at Oyster House on Roe Parade, the baby oysters are enclosed between two fine layers of mesh held in a treated pine frame, and then transported by boat out to the centre of Oyster Harbour. Working from a large punt moored more or less permanently on the lease, a crew then winches the metal holding racks which they call 'coathangers' up onto the deck, where they are cleaned of barnacles, sea squirts and other fouling. The frames of young oysters are inserted alternately to allow maximum current flow. The coathanger is then gently lowered back into the water where it is suspended from a black barrel-shaped plastic float. This stage of the *élevage* is completely subtidal.

Eventually, as in all oyster culture, the maturing oysters are transferred and spread out, in this case onto trays made of pine and plastic mesh, and either placed back into the coathanger or taken to a newly acquired intertidal lease near the mouth of the Kalgan River. This area has a normal tidal difference of only one metre (as compared, for example, to the northern coast of Brittany where the variation can be as much as six). At low tide the oysters are completely exposed and the farmers are able to walk among them on 'solid' ground. The oysters are approximately a year old when they are set out on racks made of wire coated with plastic (like clothesline) and strung with tensioning clips between well-dug posts. The trays are held on by large rubber bands. This long-line arrangement, developed in South Australia, called the B.S.T. system, is particularly useful in areas of shallow water and high temperatures, or in areas of possible flooding such as this one, because it can easily be removed or quickly height-adjusted, unlike traditional tarred wooden racks. Two people can raise or lower a hundred metres in around 15 minutes. In time, the older, larger oysters are placed in baskets made of wire mesh threaded on sticks and again set out on the long-line wires until they are considered of marketable quality.

In spite of the fact that Ocean Foods International's leases are very much in evidence in the sheltered Oyster Harbour, fishermen are free to work among the racks and lines. Because oysters and mussels are filter feeders, they clean up the water, and at least one fisherman has reported that his catch has doubled since the leases have been there. Standing on the mussel punt the evidence of this was clear as swarms of fish fought to get the crushed mussels that were being swept overboard. It seems that, unlike other places, where fish are the most serious predators, here Jonathan Bilton's major concern is having the new leases wiped out by a sudden flooding of the otherwise bountiful river.

To the lovers of oysters

In 1853, four years before South Australia had a parliament, the first Oyster Fisheries Act was passed in the colony. This legislation sought to encourage cultivation where no oyster beds naturally occurred. But while the government was also concerned to protect these new beds, it did not (as in the worst tradition of the other colonies) consider that the native beds might need the same protection. Oysters by the tonnes, according to Evelyn Wallace-Carter's *For They Were Fishers*, were originally supplied for market from large natural beds at Clinton and Mangrove Point on the Yorke Peninsula and also from the waters off Kangaroo Island—these areas being most accessible to the cutter fleet. Clearly they were an important commodity. An advertisement from the *Adelaide Times* for February 1849 would warm any oyster fancier's heart today:

> To the lovers of oysters. Those who are admirers of this favourite shellfish can procure the best specimens of 'natives' at one shilling per dozen (if used on the premises) by applying at the establishment of the undersigned. If carried off the premises the price will be one shilling and sixpence per dozen. Good refreshments at Adelaide prices.
>
> Charles Osborne, Glenelg Hotel, Holdfast Bay

These 'natives' were of course the indigenous flat or mud oyster (*Ostrea angasi*) which, before the turn of the century, was so prolific in Australia's southern waters where temperatures are generally too cold for the Rock (*Saccostrea*

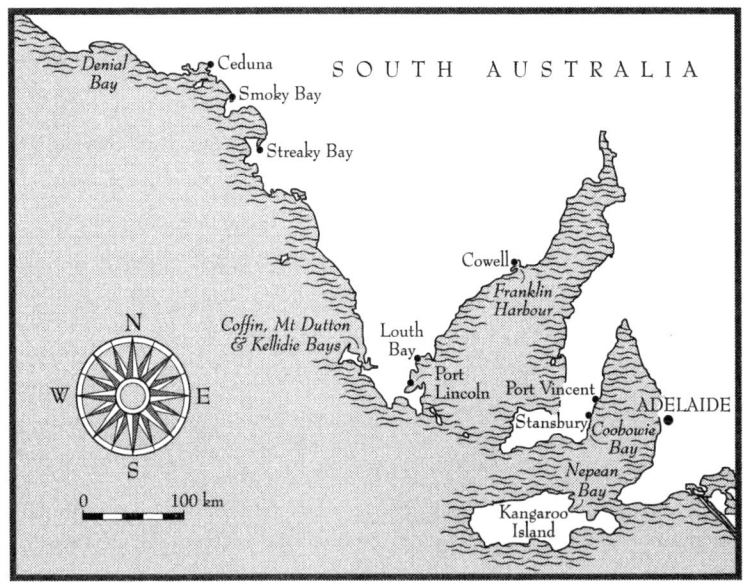

glomerata) to spawn naturally and survive. Port Lincoln and Coffin Bay soon became centres for the dredging industry and by 1870 thirty boats were working for a huge annual catch of around 700 000 oysters! So great were the natural supplies that on the shores of what is now Kellidie Bay, near where the fleet anchored, a settlement known as Oyster Town grew up with the construction of huts for the families of oyster fishers complete with all their domestic necessities. Local Aboriginal tribes also collected oysters there, apparently in relative harmony with the squatters. Dredged oysters were stored in the shallows after being sorted and then, each fortnight, bagged and delivered by bullock dray to Port Lincoln and then by boat to Glenelg or Port Adelaide.

Even if the famous oysters weren't exported very far, the stories certainly were. In 1890 the British writer Philpots enthused:

> [T]he oysters of Port Lincoln, in South Australia ... are indeed the biggest oysters in the world. They are as large as a dinner plate, and the same shape. They are sometimes more than a foot across the shell, and the oyster fits his shell so well that he does not leave much margin. It is a new sensation, when a friend asks you to lunch at Adelaide, to have one oyster set before you fried in butter, or eggs and breadcrumbs. But it is a very pleasant sensation, for the flavour and delicacy of the Port Lincoln mammoths are proverbial in that land of luxuries.

Unfortunately, in spite of what Wallace-Carter terms Coffin Bay's 'oyster el Dorado', the history of South Australia's oyster production is similar to the rest of the

country's. As the more accessible beds were depleted completely or closed for recovery, oyster dredgers had to venture further and further to come up with a catch. The wind could be so strong that the fleet was often forced to run for cover and more than one boat with its crew was lost to violent storms. And, as long as they were still under sail, a calm day could be just as disastrous as a gale for a man trying to support his family. It was difficult and dangerous work with the dredgers living for sometimes up to a week on their boats, some with no shelter and only a container of earth and a small supply of mallee root to build a fire and cook provisions they had brought from home. In a situation not unlike today, a visitor from Adelaide writing about his holidays at this time comments that:

> [i]f the oyster eaters in restaurants could only see these men sailing up and down over the grounds, the stronger the breeze the better, guiding those dredgenets made of iron and wirenetting with their hands, getting their arms nearly dislocated, they would not growl at 2/- a dozen. It's hard work and only the strongest men can stand it.

The 1873 Oyster Fisheries Act and its subsequent amendments attempted to preserve the natural beds by giving two-year exclusive rights to persons discovering a new bed, and twenty-one-year rights to those forming artificial beds. (It may be remembered, as Calder observed of the Tasmanian dredgers, that only those who had specific rights to natural or cultivated beds would take responsibility for preserving them.) The Act also introduced a closed season—one similar to that which had been observed in Europe for decades. A daily newspaper in 1875 reported with some amusement: 'the closed season for oysters commenced on September 1st so that lovers of this molluscan delicacy, after finishing the stock on hand, will have to forego for the next few months the luxury of devouring natives and washing them down with stout'.

Though there were occasional reprieves for the industry when new grounds were discovered or old ones sufficiently recovered, by the 1920–30s oystermen were forced to take up scale fishing during the summer months and dredge oysters in the winter in order to make a living. Often only six to seven oysters would come up with each dredge load, and, eventually a single fisherman might only fill a bag and a half after winching the dredge up 70–100 times in the day. While some oystermen by this time had fitted engines to their boats, many still worked alone under sail. As one told the Royal Commission of 1935: 'I'm pretty tired by the time I get a bagful.' It took thirty-three to thirty-five dozen oysters to fill a bag as the oysters were becoming smaller as well as scarcer.

Various attempts were made to conserve the Native oyster and to plant others (one attempt to collect spat in Proper Bay used malee boughs and a variety of hard rubbish such as pots and pans!) but to no avail, and by 1945, according to Wallace-Carter, there are no records of local oysters being marketed in South Australia. Apparently the last oysterman to dredge for Native *angasi* in the state left around that time for Adelaide to take up taxi driving.

As early as 1885, and again in 1934, attempts had been made to plant the Sydney Rock oyster on various parts of the South Australian coast, but without success because of the high salinity of the water. (Remember, Rock oysters prefer estuarine conditions of low salt mixed with fresh and this would later present similar problems for South Australian oyster farmers attempting to grow the Pacific.) As late as 1969, trials with the cultivation of the Native *Ostrea angasi* were still going on, although again these were not successful. A good quantity of *angasi* spat eventually caught in 1964 at Stansbury proved it could be done, but while the oysters initially did well they did not survive past two years of age (perhaps Bonamia?).

Finally, a company calling themselves Oyster Farmers Coffin Bay was formed to research the possibility of cultivating the Pacific oyster (*Crassostrea gigas*). In 1969 with the permission of the South Australian government, the first fifty bags of Pacific spat arrived from Tasmania and were divided between a farm at Coffin Bay and one at Stansbury. Although there was much trial and error—mainly problems of getting spat regularly and reliably from Tasmania and sometimes having (at great expense) to fly it down from Japan—the first Pacific oysters grown in South Australia were sold by the Dalyrymple Oyster Company from the farm gate and the Stansbury Hotel to tourists in 1972. The rest, as they say, is history.

Because of the problems with local spat-falls and low spat survival due to the cold temperatures and high salinity of the waters, South Australian Pacific oyster cultivation until recently has been inextricably linked to that of the Tasmanian industry. (The failure of the initially promising hatchery program in the state run by ICI and then

Cheetham at their saltworks during the 1970s and early 80s was a serious setback.) But once Tasmanian farmers had guaranteed spat production with successful hatcheries, oyster farmers in South Australia could also be guaranteed stocks. So by the mid-1980s farming the Pacific in South Australia was no longer experimental but a viable industry in terms of sustained production and further possible sites for cultivation were identified. One of these was Cowell on the Eyre Peninsula.

It was a long long drive from the Yorke Peninsula to the Eyre after a brief visit to some new oyster farmers in Stansbury and I have to admit that I had never heard of Cowell in spite of the fact that it produces 46 per cent of the state's oysters. Perhaps Franklin Harbour—the name of the bay the average 10-hectare leases are actually situated in—would be more familiar to oyster-lovers. Coming into the town late in the afternoon was not promising. It had started to rain and as it turned out, due to crossed wires in communication, all of the farmers in the area (there are eleven in Cowell) were elsewhere attending a Quality Assurance Program meeting. We found the place just as they were leaving and as luck would have it, I managed to snag Geoff Turner, whose name I had been given, as he was loading chairs into the back of his ute ready to return to the shore depot. When we arrived at Turner Aquaculture I realised I had discovered oyster-pay dirt—in a town of only 600 population, it was one among an impressive line of huge new sheds and big boats along a road aptly named, Oyster Drive.

Oyster Tales

Geoff and Janet Turner (and son Simon, the farm manager) are typical of the new generation of South Australian oyster farmers. Once wheat and sheep farmers, they began to see the possibilities for oyster cultivation in the state in the late 1980s. But as Geoff says, since he became an oyster farmer, it seems he has mainly spent his time inventing new techniques and tools to cope with the different conditions presented by the area which do not easily lend themselves to traditional stick and tray techniques. One of these innovations has been the Adjustable Longline System or 'B.S.T.' as it is usually called (the Turners happen to be the T of this well-known trademark).

The system, which is the same one adopted by Ocean Foods in Western Australia, allows the grower to raise and lower the oysters on hooks at 10 cm intervals, in the Turner's case in baskets clipped to the lines, to obtain maximum or minimum exposure, with very little effort or

expense. This means that the oysters can be grown to a good size quickly by being placed below the tide mark and therefore submerged for longer periods. They can also be kept free of fouling (and hardened) by being lifted higher and regularly exposed for longer periods to the air and sun. Franklin Harbour oysters are at their peak from March to November, but, by manipulating the heights at which some of his oysters are grown in order to get them to spawn earlier, Geoff is working on extending this season. Being in the sun-warmed water at the surface and then washed by an incoming cold tide seems to do the trick. Once the oysters spawn he can move them to a subtidal lease where they can get maximum food and return quickly to condition.

Raising and lowering oysters can also control shell growth (after all the farmer doesn't want his oysters to put all their energy into growing valves but wants them to concentrate on their meat). These are excellent advantages in a bay which is not only rough but fairly weedy. The hanging baskets also allow for a rumbling action which keeps the oysters clean and free of growths. And without a doubt, the Turners' oysters are some of the most sculpted and beautiful-looking I have seen.

Franklin Harbour is a fairly large, enclosed bay or 'gulf' and like many other growing areas in South Australia has a fairly high tidal change (an average of 1.8–2 metres) providing plenty of food for the oysters. But this means the leases have to be some distance out, in this case through a wide natural channel lined with mangroves and around and past a large sand spit. The need for the powerful boats soon became obvious. Farmers sometimes have to go as far as 15 km out just to get to their leases. In Cowell they've dug their own connecting channel and built a wharf (much of the breakwater and fill is constructed of overburden from the local black jade mine!) to facilitate the process. Like most other areas in South Australia, few rivers empty into the bay, which is therefore fairly salt and has very different growing conditions from those Rock oysters require and find in New South Wales or Pacific oysters experience in Tasmania.

The morning we went out to see the leases fate continued to smile. It was a perfect day, the water like glass, dolphins playing out past fish farms full of snapper. After a brisk ten-minute ride we were suddenly alongside 100 metres of posts strung with line and clipped with plastic mesh baskets—the same lease I had been looking at on an OYSA poster for the past two years or so, longing to take a dip in the crystal clear water. And here I was ready to eat oysters (and, as it turned out, Razor Fish and Native *angasi*) for breakfast on this sunny June morning. It looked like a picture, but as we were warned, hiding in that lovely green weed were catfish that could easily puncture a heavy boot and send a person to hospital with serious poisoning.

As in the Garden of Eden, all is never absolutely perfect.

Pacific oysters now make up the oyster industry in South Australia (ironically, cultivation of Sydney Rock is banned in order to prevent the importation of pests and diseases like winter mortality and QX). (The first major harvest in 1993 produced 1.4 million oysters. The estimated harvest for 2000 is 35 million!) Much of this success is due to the cooperative efforts of the farmers in the South Australian Oyster Farmers' Association and the marketing work of OYSA (similar to TAS Sea in Tasmania), but, much is also due to the clean waters and relatively unpopulated growing areas.

Today, all the spat for Pacific oysters grown in South Australia is produced in hatcheries; around 40 per cent from the recently completed hatchery at Louth Bay near Lincoln Point, the other 60 per cent from the five hatcheries operating in Tasmania. In a process similar to the one used at Albany, Western Australia, once brood oysters have spawned in the hatcheries the larvae attach themselves to finely ground scallop shell and are fed with an algae solution. When the baby oysters reach 1–2 mm, they are transferred to a nursery where they are raised until they are 4 to 10 mm in size (aged between six weeks to eight months). Those grown in Tasmania are air-freighted to South Australia. The farmers then place them on fine-mesh trays and onto the leases until they reach about 15–20 mm. From here the young oysters are graded and put into plastic-mesh baskets and later graded again and moved to baskets with larger mesh. This grading may occur between six and eight times before the oysters are harvested and sold. At the outset there will be about 500 oysters per basket. At full adult size there may be only 40–60. A South Australian Pacific oyster is considered to have reached maturity at around 70–90 mm in length (from lip to hinge) or approximately two years old.

Over 1100 hectares have been designated for intertidal oyster cultivation, and 500 hectares for subtidal in the main growing areas around the Yorke Peninsula at Stansbury, Point Vincent, Cabowie, Point Pierce; and besides Cowell, around Eyre Peninsula at Streaky Bay, Smoky Bay, Louth Bay, Denial Bay and Coffin Bay, and at Kangaroo Island. Oyster farming is now an important, thriving South Australian industry. If you happen to be around Ceduna on the long weekend in October you might stop in for the annual 'Oyster Fest' or visit the 'oyster-oriented tourist centre' at the mouth of the Cygnet River on Kangaroo Island. In Adelaide the Oyster Bar in East Terrace opens fresh oysters from around the state twice a day, to the delight and good fortune of its customers.

Things have changed a great deal since the early dredging days in South Australia. At Turner Aquaculture, a windmill pumps water up from the bay which is filtered into reticulated tanks where harvested oysters can remain completely fresh while awaiting sale (there is no need for depuration in the state). Conveyor belts haul the oysters in from the boats and more belts are used to fill the endless number of baskets. But one thing remains the same. As Geoff tells the story of his immediate fascination the first time he ever saw oyster leases and farmers in Port Stephens on his honeymoon, his face goes all dreamy. 'Who would have thought twenty years later I would be doing it.

There's something mystical about oysters ...'

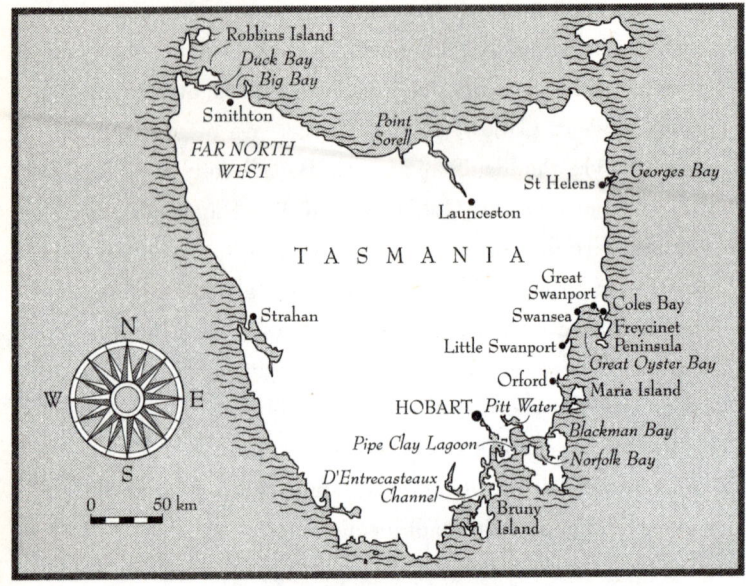

Clean and green

The Dyke family's Oyster Bay Oysters Pty Ltd as it is known (particularly in Melbourne where, except for a few fortunate local restaurants, most of their oysters are sold), has 17 hectares of water under intertidal cultivation at Little Swanport. Like the majority of recent pioneers of the Pacific-oyster industry in Tasmania, they employ stick and tray methods similar to those used in New South Wales.

There are many accounts (both official and unofficial) of the introduction of the Pacific oyster into Australia in the late 1940s, but one thing they all agree on is the reason for the drastic step of bringing in a foreign species in the first place: the demise of the Native oyster was a significant loss to the environment because the oyster, being a filter feeder, has an important niche in the ecosystem of any river, estuary or bay. There is ample evidence to suggest that the re-introduction of oysters to an area improves the quality of the water and encourages fish and other marine life.

An *unofficial* version of the introduction of the Pacific oyster into Tasmania is told by a marine biologist who in the 1940s was concerned to restore the eco-balance and was therefore studying the possibilities of an organism to replace the Native oyster. The story goes that after World War II, as reparation, a devastated Japan proposed a shipment of *Crassostrea gigas* to Australia. Tasmania, being outside the natural range of the Sydney Rock, was offered the oysters. There wasn't much time to think about it because, it seems, the oysters had already come down from Hiroshima by ship (it would have been the first spat-fall after the atomic bomb) and were waiting in Sydney in a none-too-good state, since after the war, due to the disruption of shipping, it had taken twenty or more days to cross the tropics to Australia, instead of the two weeks it would have taken previously.

Our marine biologist and his offsider waited at Hobart airport for the DC3 to arrive with the precious cargo — which it did in the middle of the night. Apparently two pilots staggered off gagging and one demanded they 'get this shit off [the] plane'! They hurriedly unloaded the crates and the aircraft took off again into the darkness. The two men put the oysters onto a ute and drove to the nearest body of water — which happened to be Pittwater near the railway viaduct — where they threw the oysters in. Then they went home and spent the next few hours showering and scrubbing, more than likely their wives threatening to burn their stinking clothes. The next day or so they returned to the river and raked the oysters out. Obviously, enough survived to begin a breeding population. (The official version as told by J M Thompson of the CSIRO's Division of Fisheries and Oceanography is certainly less entertaining and describes a more scientific and organised process.)

The first question anyone who hears this story asks is whether the oysters had been irradiated or were full of nuclear contamination. According to the DNA tests that have been carried out, the genetic make-up of Tasmanian Pacifics is identical to the original unradiated stocks, with no sign of any genetic mutations. The official records state that the first shipment actually came from Sendai (a big oyster-producing area about 160 kilometres north of Tokyo) in 1947, along with a few cases from Kumamoto, and that it was the 1948 shipment that came from Hiroshima because it had the advantage of being near the shipping point of Kure. Interestingly, all of the five strains of *gigas* oysters known in Japan are now found in Tasmania, the most obvious being the Kumamoto, easily recognised because of its very dark fluted shell.

Like much of Australia, Tasmania has had a long history of oyster production. Although the names Duck Bay, Moulting Bay, Bruny Island, Cloudy Bay, Freycinet, Great Oyster Bay, Spring Bay, and St Helens are now virtually synonymous with Pacific oysters, in the early days the state's industry, as elsewhere, consisted entirely of dredging the natural beds—with the usual results. Saville-Kent, who played such an important role in Australia's early fishing industries, attempted during the 1880s to revive the depleted stocks in various parts of Tasmania, by requesting the sum of £100 for the establishment of Government Oyster Reserves 'in which breeding stocks of oysters of the best quality should be carefully cultivated and permanently retained. Such Government Reserves ... would serve as models for the benefit of private individuals'. But the project was not without its difficulties. An 1883 Royal Commission report stated that, besides the obvious destruction caused by overfishing and dredging, there was some disease amongst the Native oysters so that 'on the pearl lining of the shell of a diseased oyster there is a yellow stain ... After seeing this appearance ... the beds in a short time (a season or two) became barren'. (Could this have been Bonamia again?) Floods and clearing the land for agriculture caused many rivers to be silted up, changing much of the original habitat. Epidemics of mussels, too, resulted in the disappearance of oysters, and in 1887 it was reported that the beds at Spring Bay had been invaded by an oyster-eating shark which left the shells empty, presenting 'the appearance of being smashed up with a hammer'. However, in spite of these setbacks, the initiative of the government reserves and Saville-Kent's experiments with spat-catching encouraged cultivation and by 1887 there were 33 established oyster farms. Oyster production in Tasmania recovered so quickly and well that a glut actually developed in the Hobart market. Saville-Kent, his reputation for saving the beds at Spring Bay preceding him, was subsequently welcomed as a saviour in Western Australia.

One might wonder, considering such success, what happened to Tasmania's Native-oyster industry? It seems, unfortunately, that with Saville-Kent's departure for the mainland to take up other work, there was a marked decline in the government's interest in marine fisheries. Although a Royal Commission report of 1883 had recognised a loss to the colony—

> astounding to contemplate ... that the quantity then brought to market in one year [1860s] would now, at current prices, realise a sum of £93,125 ... *more than the equivalent of the value of the last three years' export of grain, hay, flour and bran from Tasmania* [my emphasis]

—and bemoaned the fact that 288 000 oysters in the year current had been imported from Sydney to the value of £1200, the Tasmanian government was now unable or unwilling to put its money where its mouth was. The Native-oyster industry dwindled over the years toward its inevitable extinction. The Commissioner of Fisheries' report for the year 1907–8 contains only three references to oysters: that New Zealand oysters were being cheaply imported; no dredging of commercial importance had been carried out that year; and 'from some unexplained cause the oysters that years ago were numerous in the Derwent and Tamar have almost entirely disappeared'. (Some limited dredging for Natives was apparently carried on in the Tamar at Middle Island until the 1950s.)

Large middens of *angasi* shells are found all along the coast of Tasmania. They are particularly numerous around

Cloudy Bay, from Bruny Island to Risdon Cove, and on the Derwent River—some of the very places where the revived industry of the 1880s was situated and which later would be the sites of a new industry. The extraordinary size of these middens (in comparison to any others in Tasmania), especially those around Little Swanport estuary, caused archaeologists to call them a 'phenomenal deposit' and the 'most outstanding monument of the Tasmanian of the past'. On the southern bank of that estuary alone, 'they cover many acres, with dense extensions up to 2–3000 yards inland'. Some sections are up to 2.5 metres deep.

The midden on Col and Sue Dyke's leases at the mouth of Little Swanport estuary emptying into Great Oyster Bay is an astonishing and memorable image. Exposed as a bank at the edge of the sandflats and calm water, there is layer upon layer of large, round, Native oyster shells, making a kind of dry wall, each one lying flat, in most cases cupped side face down—a fluted, scallop design, white curves in the darker earth. Covering the beach are these same shells; Hayden, Col's son and the farm manager, handed us a black flake he had just picked up on the sand of what looked like obsidian, left over from the shaping of an Aboriginal tool. It was not surprising to find the ruins of a lime-burning company there, nor to read a facsimile of a letter, dated 1913, in which the original landowner discussed selling the once lucrative business in order to meet mortgage commitments. Out in the punt inspecting the racks and Pacific oysters in their different stages, I could see, beneath the clear shallow water, thousands of these same *angasi* shells scattered over the bottom, and I couldn't help feeling a little sad that the Native oysters were gone forever, in spite of the great beauty of the place and the superb Pacifics.

As are almost all of the oysters cultivated in Tasmania, those at Little Swanport and further up the coast at Freycinet, are grown from hatchery stock. The water temperatures are generally too cold to produce natural spawning, or, if this does occur, are not conducive to larvae survival and settlement. Seed had just been delivered to both farms and laid out in fine-mesh trays around the time we were there—that is, end of September. In both subtidal or intertidal cultivation, the oysters are graded and relaid between five and seven times before harvest—the subtidal the more often, the intertidal less.

Freycinet Marine Farm, owned by Andrea Cole, has around 6.5 hectares of intertidal leases in current use for hardening oysters that are later cultivated subtidally. According to the farm's fact sheet, 'Freycinet Oysters' (one of the few registered oyster names) are finished at sea for a plump well-developed meat only after the oyster has had at least twelve months of intertidal exposure'. In the subtidal stage, oysters are placed in baskets hanging suspended from a long line at a depth of 4 metres of water about 4 km offshore in Great Oyster Bay. This method of growing in the open sea gives the oysters a particularly complex and distinct flavour, known as *à pleine mer* by oyster growers at Cancale, Brittany. And anyone watching Andrea crouched down in the stern of her boat in the lashing rain, tasting the oysters which had just been pulled up from the water, would surely be reminded of a winemaker swilling the latest vintage around in their mouth, face registering each sensation on the palate.

Going 'to sea' in the large amphibious barge, the *Perseverance*, driven by Andrea's son Joe, was one of the adventures in this book's little odyssey, although certainly not the most comfortable. We headed out into a chop of grey and blue, guided by their exact knowledge of certain land features—that particular rock, the angle of that bit of land to the horizon—many of which most people couldn't even see. It was blowing pretty hard, cold and raining, although neither Andrea nor Joe seemed the least affected. Out on the lease, they winched up the long-line, pulling it along to attach the crates we had filled that morning with oysters and then the 'ladders' of mesh baskets. In the same way as on the Dykes' leases (where the distance between the racks is also an important factor), density—that is, the number of oysters placed in a tray or basket—is extremely important for maximum amount of growth. Though it may seem more efficient, too many leads to crowding and the oysters will not be able to get enough nutrients; they will

take longer to grow and never be in as good a condition — another of the fine balances an oyster farmer must constantly take into consideration and adjust accordingly.

A number of large black plastic containers (recycled hydrogen-peroxide bottles) are also attached to the longline. Everything, Andrea says, is in the buoying: too low and the starfish will get the oysters (even through the protective mesh); too high and the oysters won't get enough food. The level has to be checked every day or so, as there is so much change in the tides.

Although the Dykes have a very different set of variables in their quiet estuary at Little Swanport, they too take extreme care with the height of the racks on which their oysters grow. There is a relatively small tidal variation from day to day but certain atmospheric pressure systems can also affect the depth of the water and therefore the height at which the oysters sit. Only a 20 mm deviation is quite significant in terms of exposure and growth. The Dykes get around this by having permanent racks set at varying heights and moving the oysters as the need arises. Oyster Bay Oysters Pty Ltd produces and sells about 3000 dozen Pacifics (what I think would be deemed 'jumbo') per week from March until Christmas, when they close for a well-earned break. This is the period when Pacifics can normally be counted on to spawn.

～

There has been concern in Tasmania, as there has been in New South Wales, about the unwanted spread of escaped feral populations of Pacific oysters, and plans for more marine leases have at times caused some controversy.

It should be remembered, however, that oysters of any species have quite specific environmental requirements. For example, they cannot colonise an open sandy beach but tend to prefer rocky shorelines and brackish sheltered water of a kind generally not used for recreation. On the other hand, oysters are sexual broadcasters and we know that spawn can travel some distances depending on the currents, although their chances of surviving and settling are very low. Much of the protest has pointed to the extreme over-colonisation of the River Tamar, to where, it is said, spat from Port Sorell oysters migrated. Given that the larvae would have had to experience significant changes in temperature, salinity and turbulence, this would have been virtually impossible. But how then could it have happened? Marine biologist Colin Sumner has 'another explanation for the presence of oysters in the Tamar [which] is unfortunately founded on rumour'.

> At the time of the transfer of oysters from Pittwater to Port Sorell [1952] a number of oysters were lost. The transfer of the oysters was a laborious and unrewarding task, involving removal of trays from the muddy bay at Pigeon Hole Creek (Pittwater) to emptying the oysters into trucks and the long drive to Port Sorell where the reverse was carried out. On one occasion so the story has it, the oysters were being transported in a truck somewhere near Beaconsfield [a small town connected to the Tamar River by several roads, one of which runs to an area called Middle Arm]. It being a wet and miserable evening the persons involved stopped for some solace at a nearby public house. Later that night the oysters disappeared into the Tamar River and the truck then went on to complete its journey.

The introduction of Pacific oysters into Tasmania is fairly recent history and many of the persons involved are still very much alive to remember the sometimes embarrassing details. But in spite of the additional evidence Sumner found in 1973—of large living oysters in the Tamar which 'showed no signs of being or having recently been attached to rocks or any other such cultch' (meaning the oysters had not settled naturally)—the mystery remains unsolved. One can't help thinking of that old adage: where there's smoke there's fire ...

Since the beginning of Pacific-oyster cultivation in Tasmania, there have always been problems with low spatfalls and spat collection because of cold water temperatures. Then, in 1969, there was a marked spat decline, possibly due to a drop in water levels because of a prolonged drought and a year of bushfires. (There are some alarming stories here as well concerning a power station and the use of a chlorine trickle to keep the intake valves free of marine growth.) Oyster farmers in any case had to come up with something quickly to save their industry which was still in its infancy. Hence the first experiments with hatchery seed in the early 70s. The first hatchery was built in 1979, though it was not until 1985–86 that farmers could breathe a sigh of relief that hatchery production had reached sustainability and they would be ensured a stable supply of seed.

The area in Tasmania leased for intertidal oyster farming is approximately 1051 hectares, while another 300 more is suitable for subtidal culture techniques. Around 190 hectares (mostly intertidal) of the total are in northwest Tasmania—at the mouth of the Montagu River, in Big Bay, off Shipwreck Point, and in Duck Bay; the rest are spread around the state mainly on the east coast. Although Pacific-oyster culture has only recently become a viable industry, with intertidal culture becoming commercially practical as late as 1968, in 1998–99 the annual production of oysters had a farm-gate value estimated at over $12 million. And this does not take into account the potential for subtidal cultivation of flat Natives which Andrea Cole has demonstrated, nor the harvesting of wild Natives, or sales of large wild Pacifics to Asian restaurants. And Col and Sue Dyke have plans for land-based aquaculture, among other projects, to bring new life to the barren, over-cropped 140-year-old farm they have lately acquired at the head of the Little Swanport estuary. All, it can easily be argued, at no expense to the environment. As Colin Dyke says:

> We dig nothing up, chop nothing down, extract no non-renewable resources from the sites we occupy, and only harvest (hatchery) shellfish we put there in the first place.

chapter v

The Right Time

You want 'em to be *plump* as possible, you want them to be *big*, just ready to spawn ... that's what the processors want, he wants a *nice fat* oyster. Then there are some people who don't like eating them because they're too rich, they like an oyster where it's say ... 'half-conditioned' and they can sit down and eat a dozen but you get some that are *that fat* you eat about six oysters and say I could just not eat another. You just push them away because they're so fat.

Barry Allen (Shoalhaven Oyster Service)

One person's fat or conditioned oyster may be another person's nightmare. Confronted with a half dozen oysters naturel in Boston, British novelist William Makepeace Thackeray commented after eating one, that he felt as if he 'had swallowed a baby'. For some an oyster is never too big, too creamy or too many. For others it can be an embarrassment of riches, an overdose, too rich, too much. In Australia, Pacific oysters are generally large and of a creamy texture, and may, when full of spawn, be decidedly too much for most people. The Sydney Rock, however, is thought to be at its most delicious when just ready to spawn.

So the 'R rule' is important to consider when choosing the variety and 'condition' of oysters you most enjoy. Like many foods—lamb, sweet corn, asparagus, crab (you don't often consider buying strawberries in March do you?)—different oysters have a specific season when they are at their peak or most plump and flavoursome. Again turning the 'R' rule around, for the Sydney Rock this applies to our summer—the months of November, December, January and February. It will be quite different for a Pacific or Native, and unfortunately the confusion expressed by a writer for the *Good Weekend* is not uncommon: 'Oysters are at their best during autumn and winter, as they gain weight after spawning in summer, and become soft and plump'. If you like a fat, rich, creamy oyster which is full of spawn—and for many people, including most growers, this is the only kind of Rock oyster there is (you may find it convenient to think of the oyster as being 'ripe' or, in season, at this time)—then in most cases enjoy them during those months and choose them from localities where spawning is imminent but has not yet taken place.

The chancy bit in this, of course, is that if you are buying unopened oysters and are off by only a day the oyster, when opened, will be thin and unpleasant with a strong aftertaste. Theoretically, spawning is a continuous process throughout the summer months—provided the temperature stays above the essential minimum—though there are fluctuations in the actual presence of larvae in the water. A male oyster may take a few seconds to a few hours to discharge all its contents; the female, in a more complicated process, takes some hours, often with intervals between. The main spawning of a whole bed, or 'swarming' as it is called, can last up to two weeks or more, since not all the individuals spawn at the same moment. Oysters don't always spawn completely; they may only do so partially and therefore can be in 'partial condition' when you get them.

A reputable producer won't let oysters onto the market (s)he suspects or knows have recently spawned. If you're buying oysters already opened, it should be clear as to the condition they are in, although the way they look may be due to the drying out and shrinkage that can occur when an opened oyster is not properly cared for (covered and refrigerated) or if it is more than a day or two old.

If, like Thackeray, however, big, fat oysters full of spawn put you right off, then your best bet is to enjoy oysters when they are fit enough to reproduce but still have a while to go before spawning. Oysters are usually 'ripe', that is, ready to spawn, for some time before this actually happens. Otherwise, you might prefer to wait until a few weeks after they have spawned, when the oysters have regained some condition but are not 'fat'. Personally I rather like Rock oysters in the cold weather when they're generally smaller and have a kind of 'flinty' taste rather than a creamy one, and are not usually too salty. But many New South Wales farmers won't sell their oysters during the winter (June, July, August, September) as they consider them too poor due to lack of proper feeding in the colder water.

The Right Time

Most growers try to harvest their oysters when they are at their fattest, or, as they say in 'the condition'. Ideally for Sydney Rocks this is usually just hours before spawning. But it's not always that easy:

> ... we've brought the trays into the punt, then all of a sudden it sounds like a set of castanets all clapping away. They're just shooting spawn out—and the whole bottom of the punt, it was like standing in a big bowl of condensed milk! Then we put 'em all back on the rails or back in the trays, throw some water in the punt and bail it out. Dad used to say, 'Oh well, come back at low tide or when the tide's just coming in and pick 'em up when they're *dry*. Don't pick 'em up when they're *so fat* and there's water over them because as soon as you pick 'em up and they got a belly full of water, they're ready to go.'
>
> Brian Allen (Shoalhaven Oyster Service)

> Now with purification they'll get to about 34 hours out of the required 36 and then *bang*, they're gone! A lot of farmers are having that problem. Before we built our shed down on the waterfront, we used to have a 'plant' in this [upper] shed and we had to be very careful to have that window closed because if we had a southerly wind come up and it put a ripple onto the water [in the purification tank] bang, away they'd go, they'd spawn, that's how temperamental they are ...
>
> Barry Allen (Shoalhaven Oyster Service)

When the grower deems the time right, having sampled the crop and taken into consideration the condition the supplier wants, it is time for the harvest. This is entirely dependent on when the oysters spawn. Generally the Sydney Rock has two main spawnings: one frequently occurs during the abnormally high tides around Christmas; the other possibly in late summer. If, however, the spring has been unusually cool, sexual development is relatively slow and spawning may occur as late as January or April or even May. At other times it can be a partial process during the summer months, with even some light intermittent spawning in winter. And of course, there is always that element of chance and mysterious forces at work. Describing the process of harvesting Barry Allen says:

> You go out on the water but before you pick any oysters up at all we open two or three and have a good look at 'em—yeah, they're fat, they're good; pick some up there. You might go for a row of oysters on sticks which a few weeks ago was *poor*, spawned; go over there another fifty metres and that row is *fat*. We just don't know what it is— just the luck of the draw.

Because of our different species and the seasonal variations, different oyster-growing areas come into condition at different times, so that in Australia we can have a good, fresh, fat oyster every month of the year. This is not necessarily the case in the rest of the world where the R rule applies. About America (and our oyster suppliers would agree, at least with the first part), MFK Fisher, in

1941, writes: 'They say all oysters are all right any time as long as they are healthy ... all except the oyster farmers ... Their main interest is in growing as many good crops as they can, and it stands to reason that if a healthy female, round with some twenty million eggs, is taken from the water before she has a chance to birth them, farmers lose'. In many American states and some European countries there are strict laws regarding seasons in which oyster harvesting is allowed. The season usually begins in September—the first R month.

So besides the unpleasantness of the larvae shells in the *Ostrea* during the breeding season, the stipulation not to eat oysters in the months without an R was also an attempt in the Northern Hemisphere, to ensure 'the protection of the sexually active adults and the reproduction and preservation of the species' (remember the Reverend Sprat's account of the severe penalties for anyone removing a cultch during that period). This is not the case in Australia where spat is produced in hatcheries or the warm climate and water temperatures normally create ideal conditions for spawning and larvae survival.

In New South Wales, as the weather warms (and therefore the water temperatures rise) the Rock oyster becomes fully mature in most places by December. However, up north, where the water warms sooner, oysters can begin spawning as early as August. Further south temperatures begin to hit 20°C around September and become the average in October. Around the Shoalhaven and Clyde rivers and further south, temperatures do not begin to steadily reach 20°C until December.

There is a pattern then, clearly not always foolproof, but reasonably reliable—running down the eastern coast from north to south based on temperatures, rainfall, etc.—that will give a fair idea of which Sydney Rock oysters to buy at what times. (This pattern does not apply in the same way to Pacifics or Native *angasi*.) There's not always as much choice in restaurants, where the quality and variety of oysters are as dependent on the individual supplier's knowledge and care, as what's available. Often when the local oysters run out, other kinds will be brought in by the supplier to fill the demand. If you want an authentic, locally grown oyster you'll have to check, and even then the restaurant may tell you only the location of the suppliers from which they got the oysters. It is perfectly possible to be served Pacific oysters from Port Stephens when you think you're ordering the local Greenwell Point Sydney Rocks. On the other hand, restaurants like the Rockpool and Boathouse (Sydney) or Marchetti's Tuscan Grill (Melbourne)—which takes its oysters so seriously it holds a special tasting annually—pride themselves on the number of different oysters from different localities and may have up to sixteen kinds at any one time. The only problem here is that in order to provide such variety, even the most scrupulous purveyor will be forced at certain times of the year to offer some oysters that will not be as 'good' as others. And this again will depend on *your* preferences.

FATTENING THE GOOD OYSTER

Most farmers make special arrangements for the maturing crop they intend to harvest. *Affinage* is the French term for 'finishing' or what we would call 'fattening'—that is, improving the flavour of the oyster and getting the size to marketable quality. This is different from the *élevage* which is the term for the growing or raising phase described in the previous chapters. Because oyster larvae normally settle in sites with weaker currents, they eventually run short of nutrients as they grow larger, since, as Korringa remarks, 'it is the tidal currents that transport the planktonic food to these sedentary creatures'.

Simply put, to fatten an oyster means, for farmers with the resources (and the appropriate 'portfolio' of leases, as one grower put it), moving the maturing oysters to a specially reserved, sheltered and highly productive area. The oysters are also further spread out so there is more room for the food-bearing currents to flow easily between them. Sometimes, as is the case at Andrea Cole's, rafts or long lines, with stacks of trays or baskets hanging beneath them, are also used for short-term fattening, since totally submerged oysters are able to spend the entire time feeding with no interruption at low tide. In Europe, oysters are usually moved to *claires* or basins for fattening.

This phase, for the oyster, is the equivalent of a stay in a luxury hotel and in it the oyster leads a country-club life complete with a five-star menu, pampered and protected from any predators or pests, its waistline expanding accordingly. In such warm sensuous surroundings, its thoughts naturally turn to love and all of its bodily functions and fibres begin to prepare for the big moment. The oyster for once has nothing to worry about and can relax, bask in the sun and stuff itself on its own equivalent of truffles and *foie gras* while sipping sea-champagne, happily ignorant of its imminent fate. With luck this blissful stage of an oyster's life can last up to six months or nearly a year, although frequently it may be only for a few weeks.

> A fine purple thread should run around the beard, this being looked upon as a sign of superior quality.
>
> Pliny

Not all the 'breedy creatures' are fortunate enough to go through the *affinage* which will produce the prime, grade-A restaurant plate oysters; many will achieve good condition right where they spent most of their lives, although it may take a little longer and they will never be quite as sleek and plump as their luckier cousins. How 'good' or conditioned an oyster is is usually indicated by the proportion of meat to shell. Although it is difficult to tell this when the oyster is closed—except by weight and even that may be only water (which is interesting in terms of buying oysters, especially if you are buying them by the kilo which is as it is often done in France), it stands to reason then that when open, a fat prime oyster has more meat than space in the shell. A poor oyster barely fills its shell and looks pretty forlorn. (In Japan, oysters from certain areas which remain in this deprived state all year long due to lack of food and are mostly water, are actually called 'water oysters'.) When buying oysters, if possible, always check for weight. Jerry Fraser, of Mead's Restaurant in Perth, advises tapping the oyster with the back of a knife: 'If it sounds hollow then the meat is weak—do not purchase. If it sounds with a thud, then it should be fine.'

The Right Time

Besides filling the shell, a good oyster in prime condition is plump, opaque and fairly light coloured or even white, often, if a Rock, with lines or 'silk threads' across its surface (actually ducts full of spawn) which Laurie Larner, founder of Larner's Oyster Supply (Fremantle), calls the 'strawberry texture'. At the 1999 and 2000 New South Wales Oyster Farmers' Association annual lunches in Sydney, the dozen judged to be the best (these two years they happened to be from Tathra, near Bega) and all of the other oysters in the competition had these features. (A very impressive dozen was disqualified because one of its stars had disgraced itself and secretly spawned *en route*, which goes to show that even experts find it difficult to judge a good oyster until it's been opened.)

Generally an oyster increases in body size first and then enlarges its shell to accommodate it, rather than the other way around, since it is a particular part of the body which secretes the shell. A Pacific oyster can grow to a massive size of 450 mm in length but is usually marketed at about 70–80 mm, while a Sydney Rock oyster rarely reaches 100 mm in the wild (some cultivated individuals have exceeded 250 mm). Nowadays, a flat Native averages around 100 mm in diameter, although Saville-Kent described the *angasi* from Spencer's Gulf, exported to the Victorian markets, especially Ballarat around 1890, as being of such 'Brobdingnagian dimensions' that it was normal practice to cut them into four pieces for sale in the oyster saloons, the quarters being put into empty shells of ordinary size and sold as single oysters.

Sadly for those of us buying unopened oysters, a large shell does not necessarily guarantee a large oyster. Size isn't everything. It can even be, on occasion, quite happily misleading. I am thinking particularly of the Kumamoto oysters we had in Spokane, Washington, donated for research by the kind owner of Milford's Seafood Restaurant, Wally Tamamura. These Pacific oysters were grown in Puget Sound and, to look at, were not promising; they weren't as tiny as the native (*Ostrea*) Olympia, but still very small, less than half the size of the average Sydney Rock. But when we opened them, they were absolutely full of delicious oyster—so much so that there was hardly any room for juice at all.

THE OYSTER OPENS

Thomas Welsby, writing in 1919 about Queensland Aboriginals' knowledge of and choice of food recorded:

> The oyster has its sign as to time of opening or being in fit condition to eat. Of course, all through winter, as a rule here [Stradbroke Island] oysters are poor and unfit for food but in spring they begin to fatten up and become succulent. This time for commencing to eat them is known to the Blacks, not by the warmth of the season, nor by any record of the month ... but by the flowering of the wild hop plant. When this shrub begins to bloom they know it is time to summon their friends from the bush along the sea coast ... the native name for this plant is *kinyingga gilyural* or 'the oyster opens'.

Those of us who wouldn't recognise a wild hop plant if we fell over it have to rely on other methods. A general rule of thumb offered by John Susman (lately with the Flying Squid Brothers, who sold oysters from twenty-one regional locations with different optimum seasons) as quoted in *Gourmet Traveller:* 'you should eat north coast [of New South Wales] oysters in summer and south coast in winter'.

My own experience bears out the comments about south-coast oysters in winter (by this I mean Rocks from the Clyde River which are the oysters I'm most familiar with at this time of year); they're not big (but then they rarely are since the water is cooler and there is not so much food available) but they are fresh-tasting and delicious. In the summer—the time when one would usually expect optimum growth—cool spring melts have lowered water temperatures which limits food and slows down the oyster's metabolism, while conversely, there's actually some growth in winter when the water tends to be clear and the water temperatures warmer. It makes sense if you think about going to the beach on the south coast of New South Wales where the water is really cold in early summer. By autumn it's warmed up enough so you can still have a pleasant dip long after Easter and also get good Rock oysters. (Only a few kilometres further north at Greenwell Point, the Allen Brothers don't even sell their oysters from June to October.)

I'm a little less convinced about a blanket dictum for eating north-coast oysters in summer. I've found some north-coast Rocks disappointing at that time of year, because of weather conditions or suppliers' carelessness and seasonal market complications. There are numerous exceptions and variables, depending upon whether it is a dry or wet season and what the temperatures are like for that time of the year. For example, in the north, rivers flowing eastward from the Great Divide come off the Dorrigo Plateau, bringing with them an influx of fresh water. The lowering of saline levels can be detrimental to the oysters' growth and may kill them, not to mention the problems caused by the resulting run-off. This influx usually occurs in early autumn but can be earlier.

So, to go back to general rules, the advice I've been given by New South Wales oyster farmers is that their oysters are best in the summer months when all the rivers are in season (some more than others). During winter and into early spring if you can't live without your Sydney Rocks, try and get them from south of and including Port Stephens. Christmas and the New Year tend to be the height of the season for growers in the north; Easter for those in the south.

SEASONS*: When to eat Sydney Rock (R/r) Native *angasi* (N/n) Pacific (P/p)

JAN	FEB	MAR	APR	MAY	JUN	JUL	AUG	SEP	OCT	NOV	DEC
R	R	R	r	r	r	r	r	R	R	R	R
			n	N	N	N	N	n	n		
	p	P	P	P	P	P	P	p	p	p	

* capitals indicate prime season, lower case indicates coming into and going out of season depending on environmental conditions

The flat Native oyster (*Ostrea angasi*) generally spawns in late spring and early summer with a possible second spawning at the end of summer and, unlike the Rock, is usually thin and poor during December, January and February. In South Australia its breeding season extends longer—from October to March—while in Tasmania it is thought to occur a little earlier. In southern New South Wales the breeding season appears to be considerably longer—from June to December—but with the manipulation of hatchery brood stocks, there is potential to extend what is now, because of the incubation of larvae in the female, a fairly short harvesting time.

In Victoria the main season for our Native *angasi* exactly corresponds to that of the *Ostrea* in the Northern Hemisphere and is almost the opposite of the Sydney Rock's (another reason for hoping the flat oyster industry will eventually get off the ground), lasting from around April through to October with the peak months being May, June, July and August.

The fact that both Tasmania and South Australia rely on hatchery-produced spat might suggest that there is no natural spawning period and that Pacific oysters from these areas are in good condition all year round. Actually Pacifics do spawn in these areas even if only sporadically, generally in summer's warmer weather, but there is little or no settlement due mainly to water temperature which is usually not high enough for long enough to support larval growth and survival. Because Pacifics are temperate-zone oysters, they normally spawn only once in Tasmania, mainly between November and February. South Australian Pacifics may spawn slightly earlier because of warmer water temperatures there. Pacific oysters in less temperate areas like New South Wales may spawn twice (this is one of the reasons for the problem of overcatch in that state). In Port Stephens the spawning period for these oysters can last from October to May.

Pacific oysters tend to have poor growth after spawning—the period from December to around April—and may take a long time to return to condition. They are considered at their peak from around April to early October. South Australian Pacifics are best from March through November, and those from Port Stephens from August to December. Unlike the Sydney Rock, a Pacific oyster is not considered in good condition when full of spawn since its texture, which is ordinarily creamy and rich, becomes 'oozy'. It is fairly easy to tell, if buying them open, when one has gone past its prime: the tip of the oyster—that is, the little part up near the beak or pointy end—will be clear and there will be evidence of fat on the 'frill' (margin or edges). The advice from the experts is: don't even think about eating Pacifics in January and February.

The Right Time

By now it should seem logical that areas with higher water salinity produce a saltier-tasting oyster (this seems to be the case especially in summer when freshwater levels are low and rainfall scarce). It would follow that a lower salinity of the water in which the oyster lives results in a less 'briny' taste. But it seems futile to try to describe what particular oysters from specific areas taste like. After all, one person's salty is another's bland. A good illustration of this is of a friend who ordered Ceduna oysters in a Melbourne restaurant and thought they were so salty they were 'inedible'. In Perth, another friend and I shared a dozen oysters from Ceduna and Albany. I thought the Ceduna very salty and preferred the Albany Rocks but my friend enjoyed the Ceduna Pacifics. (South Australian oysters are generally more salty because the areas in which they are grown get little 'fresh' in terms of rain, rivers or run-off.) Generally, *unrinsed* South Australian and Tasmanian Pacifics are fairly 'briny' but pleasantly so and some people think they have a much stronger flavour than Rocks. This seems surprising, and may actually be the reaction to the natural saltiness of the liquor when a Pacific is freshly opened and not rinsed—if they are used to having their oysters washed.

Average salinity (measured in parts per thousand/ weights of salt per litre of water) can range from lows found in the Hawkesbury and the Richmond River in February, of 19.11 and 12.01 respectively, to extreme highs in January of 36.24 for Wagonga Inlet and 37.8 for the Tweed River. Low salinity rates—such as for the

Hawkesbury, which generally has low salinity all year round (and as a result produces a creamy oyster with very little saltiness), or the sudden very low rate for the Richmond—indicate an influx of fresh water due to end-of-summer rains. Much of Port Stephens, for example, has a salinity similar to that of the ocean for most of the year, but it may drop as much as 25 per cent during February and March—a time of heavy rains—and even lower in the areas near where rivers are discharging into the bay. The high rates for estuaries at other times of the year usually signify high temperatures and little rain. As a general rule, the nearer the mouth of the river and the smaller the body of water, the fewer rivers or creeks emptying into it (usually because they are in an area of scarce rainfall), the saltier tasting the oyster. So again, it's a good idea to consider geography when ordering your oysters.

Bringing in the Catch

Harvesting is carried out in many ways all over the world: raking into baskets, loading *pochettes* onto trucks or 'sleds' (which are designed to glide over the *vase*) when the tide's out and/or the *claire* is empty, diving, dredging or tonging from a boat. In Australia, the most common method is to load up an aluminium punt with the trays, baskets or sticks (using iron hooks or mechanised lifts), then take them back to the 'plant' (or shed) to cull and sort. The oysters on sticks are dislodged by jarring the stick with an (often handmade) axe-like tool so they fall off. Immature oysters are usually returned to the leases unless bagged and sold to other farmers for growing on. In New South Wales the oysters that are ready for market undergo 'depuration' before being sorted again and packed into waxed cartons or plastic crates for shipment. Until recently all growers used hessian bags (some still do) holding approximately three bushels or about one hundred dozen plate-grade oysters. Oysters that are too small to sell as plates or bistro are also returned to the leases to get over the shock before being purified and bottled.

In New South Wales the 36-hour purification period for oysters prior to sale has been mandatory since 1985 in accordance with the Shellfish Quality Assurance Program run throughout the state. Most farmers 'depurate' their oysters by placing them in a tank of high quality water that has been purified by being exposed to high-intensity, ultraviolet light. Where possible, salinity, temperature and oxygen levels are also controlled. Because the oyster is a filter feeder, in this situation it will naturally flush itself of food and impurities. (One wonders how this affects the natural 'sea' taste, although usually, the water has been pumped in from the same estuary in which the oysters were grown.) The growers at Ocean Foods in Western Australia don't, as yet, have to be worried about such a thing because the water quality in Oyster Harbour is still very good. In Tasmania, as already explained, a statewide quality assurance program eliminates the need for purification. This is the same for South Australia.

Purification is all well and good for most bacteria, but it does not kill viruses. And even after purification, like any food, incorrect or unhygienic handling can encourage harmless amounts of remaining bacteria to multiply. A simple warning to the wise: get your oysters from known, reputable growers or suppliers. Bags or nets, if sold at an indirect outlet, should bear a tag with dates and licence numbers. Elderly persons who are not in good health or persons with diabetes, chronic liver problems and/or lowered immune systems (similar to the risks they face associated with 'flu') should avoid uncooked shellfish, especially after heavy rain.

A 'bad' oyster or one that is 'off' is quite a different thing. This is usually due to careless handling and storage and can be easily smelled. A discreet sniff before eating is always accepted in polite company (although your host or hostess should have done this for you already). If by chance you have a cold or are 'hard of smelling' and somehow slip up and swallow what M F K Fisher describes as 'that gastronomical rarity' (the taste will tell you!!), she suggests you 'should leave the board at once and do what men have always known how to do, even the dainty ones, and get rid of it'.

The Market

When we first started buying and eating oysters at Batemans Bay on the south coast of New South Wales, they were known as 'Sydney Rock' and that was it. We'd buy them by the dozen already opened on styrofoam trays from Pearly's, but that meant trying to keep what was left of the precious liquid from spilling during a bumpy 35 km drive home. So we decided to take the plunge, invest in an oyster knife and open them ourselves. We used to get them (and often still do) in small net bags with a date tag at the fish and chips or the bait shop. We'd take them home and wrestle them open, eating them and slurping the juice during the clear evenings on the deck of our friends' house, listening to the ocean pound below on Depot Beach.

When we moved to Sydney in 1991, things were much the same at the city Fish Markets. 'Sydney Rock'—that was it, and you couldn't for the longest time find oysters that weren't already open and lying on the styrofoam trays in stacks. Then we discovered the New South Wales Oyster Distributors outlet at the Fish Markets where we could buy unopened oysters, but there was usually only the one kind and we were never sure where they came from.

A few years later (only as recently as 1995), things had certainly changed. I was astonished at the number and kinds of oysters available. Sydney Rock of course, but of different sizes and grades; Georges Basin, Tasmanian Pacific, Clyde River, Coffin Bay. And this day, besides the amazing variety, more than one of the fishmongers had oysters that could be bought unopened! One even had large, flat, horny Tasmanian Natives (*Ostrea angasi*).

On the next visit to the markets only a few weeks later things had changed again. Suddenly, for some reason (now I know it was probably to do with seasonal supply) all the oysters were reduced to 'Pacific' or 'Rock' and that was it, though when I asked a girl at one shop where they were from she said without hesitation 'Nambucca'. Today, it varies with the season at the Fish Markets as it always does, but also from retailer to retailer. In some places, we are told whatever name they happen to think of when we ask—for a time it was almost always 'Brisbane Waters'—and so have taken to checking the box. The last few visits (in June) we had very nice oysters which we were told were from Port Stephens but in reality were from Tuross Lake.

I have to wonder if 'Brisbane Waters' has become a *nom de plume* for Wallis Lake? You will also find some Clyde River oysters disguised as 'Batemans Bays' and Georges River as 'Quibray'; while quite delicious *à plein mer* oysters grown in what could officially be called Port Stephens, have distinguished themselves as 'Corrie Island Rocks'. The confusion is compounded by the fact that nomenclature used for oyster-growing areas and their produce varies. In New South Wales oysters and their place of origin are usually identified by the name of the river, lake or estuary but not always. In South Australia and Tasmania, they may be identified by the body of water they're farmed in or by the town nearest. Sometimes oysters are referred to by the names or companies of the individual growers and sometimes by another descriptive made up by the locals. As is the case with Australian wines, there is as yet no set system or rules for naming practices.

(If anyone or any oyster finds that they are misplaced or misnamed, I hope they will excuse me.)

One has to ask why oyster-growing areas do not have registered names, as is done with so much produce in France—a kind of *appellation contrôllée*, which would help the consumer determine quality and would reward the careful, skilled producer? Apparently one of the biggest problems with issues of food safety *and* quality control is the mixing by distributors—the middlemen—of oysters from various places into singly marked boxes, a practice known (and not appreciated by most) farmers as 'comingling'.

～

Originally fresh oysters were transported to Sydney by boat or by rail and then distributed by 'commission agents' throughout the city and out into the suburbs and country districts. Of course this was not without its casualties. According to G S Smith, some freighters in Queensland, notably the SS *Peregrine*, were 'avoided by oystermen as they had a reputation for killing their cargo as a result of engine vibrations'. There were other mishaps:

> I have been informed on very good authority that, on the 2nd of January of this year [1887], the coal-lumpers employed filling the bunkers for the 'Rockton' steamer in Sydney, dumped the coal from the lighter on to a bag of oysters from Moreton Bay. To the tender shells of fat and well-matured oysters one night of this work would be destruction, and the necessity of more care in their carriage between ports is very apparent.
>
> C S Fison, 1887 Report

A portion of the New South Wales harvest has always been shipped to the southern states (mainly Melbourne) and other areas where the Sydney Rock does not grow, but even today the Sydney market accounts for most oyster sales, with local and interstate markets about equal to each other, at a third of the total. Very few New South Wales oysters are as yet exported overseas (about 3500 dozen). Tasmania has some export market for its Pacifics and South Australia sends a weekly shipment to Japan.

In the early eighties when concerns were remounted about export markets for New South Wales oysters, farmers bemoaned the cost of freight. It was felt that for every 70 kilograms of oysters, only 6 kilograms of flesh was actually being transported. At least one farmer believed that the oysters should be shelled before shipping—which would cut the cost—and then served in a 'realistic plastic shell manufactured so that it could be hygienically used more than once'. We can probably be grateful this was one idea that never got off the ground.

At the turn of the century Native *angasi* oysters, though prolific in southern areas, were not marketed in New South Wales but a considerable quantity was available in the Melbourne and Adelaide markets, where they brought only from one third to one half the price of the 'imported' Rocks from New South Wales and Queensland. Until recently, when it was made into a marine park, wild natives were dredged from a small part of east Jervis Bay in New South Wales and they are still harvested under licence at St Helens in Tasmania. Modest quantities have been farmed on leases at Freycinet in Tasmania and Albany in Western Australia.

In the last few years however, successful production of Native *angasi* seed at the hatchery at Port Stephens Fisheries Centre has meant that trial cultivation by a handful of farmers in southern and central New South Wales has been possible, and Native *angasi* oysters have occasionally become available, particularly from Bermagui, Merimbula, Pambula Lake and Narooma. In spite of the good prices for and interest in Native oysters, few growers have as yet attempted commercial production. This is because generally the *Ostrea* is less hardy in our modern waters, more susceptible to disease and sensitive to changes in environment—even unusual rains. They require more finicky handling and, although recent experiments at Port Phillip Bay in Victoria have shown this can be almost halved, a far longer time (up to four years) to attain the size necessary for flavour and quality.

In 1924 the price for a bag of Sydney Rocks (about 100 dozen oysters) was between £3 and £4/10s depending on the quality, and in that year 28 380 bags of oysters were produced in New South Wales. Apparently the prized Queensland oysters sold in Sydney went for as much as £3/10 per sack in 1908. Early in the days of the colonies, Native-oyster fishermen in Hobart sold their harvest to town vendors. Hobart Town at that time consumed most of what was produced and 'export' trade was very small and usually went out of Melbourne.

Interestingly, one of the largest and best-known oyster supply companies in the first half of the twentieth century was called the Melbourne Oyster Supply Ltd. It began humbly in 1913 as the Pindimar Oyster Company operated by F Phillips and other members of the family, who grew oysters on their leases in Port Stephens. Phillips, who researched various methods then in practice, began to experiment with the idea of producing oysters 'that could not be surpassed in quality'. By 1916 he was ready to market his crop but found that almost all the growers concentrated on sending their harvest to Sydney. Melbourne, on the other hand, had an inadequate and irregular supply. As a result, the oysters from these Port Stephens leases, until at least as late as 1957, were regularly consigned to Melbourne.

Eventually a partnership made up of the next Phillips generation extended their operations until they owned many of the best leases in the Port. Concerned to provide oysters of prime quality all year round, they perfected in the 1930s the stick and tray method which became the standard for oyster cultivation in the rest of New South Wales. ('Port Stephens oysters', commented Korringa in 1976, 'are of usually a good quality during the winter season when other areas are poor'.) At one time the company owned up to 1000 acres of leases, including many on the Georges River. It also owned a sawmill, a 5500-acre forest and a fleet of ships—the flagship *Stella Maris* was in fact released to the navy and saw service for three years in the seas around New Guinea.

In 1948 the Port Stephens interests (C W Phillips & F S Phillips) merged with what was then the largest oyster distributor in Australia—the Melbourne Oyster Supply Pty Ltd—and took on that name. Additional company offices were set up in a property purchased on Flinders Street in Melbourne from which, along with the oyster bar at the Port Phillip Hotel, the oysters were sold—over 10 000 bags yearly. By 1966 the Melbourne Oyster Supply Ltd was located at Taren Point, New South Wales. In Melbourne in 1973 it had resumed trading as Phillips Oysters (Vic) Pty Ltd. The Sydney telephone directory last listed Phillips Oysters in 1990.

Another important company typical of its kind was the Moreton Bay Oyster Company operating out of Queensland. Registered in 1876, this held extensive leases in Moreton Bay, Great Sandy Strait and as far north as Rodd's Bay. It began with a capital of £2500 and its investors were some of the most prominent men in the colonies, including past and future premiers, bank managers and board members, and a chemist. (Perhaps not surprisingly, a number of those on the board of the Queensland National Bank were in many other business ventures together and later this same bank was implicated in some questionable loans to its own directors.)

Shareholders took little part in the running of the company although occasionally one of them would become manager. European regional managers or foremen were employed to manage the beds and to oversee labour, which was usually Aboriginal. As with most other companies of this kind, cottages were provided for the workers and their families and better houses for the managers near the areas in which the beds were located. Some large companies provided schools and shops as well.

Because companies generally had more money behind them, they could better withstand the slumps in the industry than individual oyster farmers could. (Though they could also do more damage: it is said, for example, that wholesale dredging by these companies was one of the main reasons for the devastation of beds in Queensland.) And they were large holdings—in 1884 for example, 39 dredge sections were available for lease in Queensland. Of these only 16 were actually leased, 11 of them by the Moreton Bay Oyster Company. In 1887, it held 78 of the 199 existing leases in the colony.

The objects for which the company was originally established, as stated in the Memorandum of Association, covered every possibility and eventuality, and give a sense of the emerging industry at the time. These included licensing, holding, purchasing, leasing or 'by any other means acquiring land for the purposes of farming and improving of Oyster fisheries; collecting, preserving, breeding, fattening, selling, or otherwise disposing of oysters of every or any prescription'. And as the company began to acquire more leases in other areas, they began to ship immature oysters by coastal freighter or their own boats, from Sandy Strait down to Moreton Bay which was more suitable for fattening. From there after eighteen months or so, the oysters, now in prime condition, continued their journey south to the markets of Sydney and Melbourne.

Though for most of its history the company relied on dredging and re-laying, in the 1920s it experimented with wood and wire trays. But to no avail, as it was probably too late—mudworm infection, the cost of labour and interstate shipping, and the competition of the growing New South Wales industry substantially bit into the company's profits. The last beds leased by Moreton Bay Oyster Company were in 1945.

Up until recently there were only two grades of oyster: a 'plate' or first-grade oyster was considered between 15–25 oysters per kilo. (To give you some idea of difference in sizes between the species, large *Crassostrea* oysters from the Bassin de Thau in southern France generally weigh in at about 10–12 oysters per kilo.) The other grade was 'bottle' (what used to be called 'seconds') which make about 25–35 per kilo. At one time in Australia, in the cities, oysters were often sold in jars—salt-glazed pottery ware manufactured specifically for the distributor, and later, the traditional and distinctive 'lady's waist' curved bottles.

The weight figures given above are courtesy of an Oyster Farmers' Association of New South Wales fact sheet, and I will say, as a fairly average oyster lover, that these are pretty wide categories; the variation of *ten* oysters per kilo seems quite a lot. Grading was, and is, generally done by hand and eye, and is therefore quite subjective. This has been a problem for the industry and consumers alike.

Within the last ten years a new grade, 'bistro' was introduced for an oyster of medium size—that is, not as big as a plate grade but bigger than bottle. This gave the grower a chance to do something else with those in-between oysters besides slip them into a grade A bag or give them away as bottle-o's. Suppliers and restaurants loved it: it meant they could offer smaller, cheaper oysters in buffet-type situations or serve them at table for the same price they had charged for plate-grade before. Anyone who remembers eating oysters a decade ago, and bemoans the fall in size and quality, will know what I'm talking about.

In recent years the situation has become even more confusing with 'jumbo', 'large', 'standard', 'large bistro', 'bistro', 'mini bistro', etc.

While we will always be at the pride or mercy of the individual, efforts are being made to rectify the situation — some cooperatives and companies, for example, are employing mechanised grading and weighing systems and there are attempts at regulating minimum meat content. Ocean Foods International produces drop-shaped oysters of almost exactly the same size for its market at the moment. This is possible because of precise grading at the larva stage and during the oyster's growth. These oysters are also single seed (which guarantees a certain size and shape), and they are harvested by size, rather than by age as has traditionally been the case. This method is also the usual practice in Tasmania and South Australian with Pacific production. For example, South Australian Pacific oysters marketed through OYSA are measured by the length of their top shell and standardised as:

Bistro	50–60 mm	45 doz/bag
Plate	60–70 mm	30 doz/bag
Standard	70–85 mm	20 doz/bag
Large	85–100 mm	20 doz/bag
Jumbo	100 mm+	15 doz/bag

Up-market or seafood-specialty restaurants buy some of their oysters directly from the producer rather than a supplier/distributor if they can, and this allows them to stipulate more precisely the size and quality they want. But as always, the best rule of thumb is to know the season,

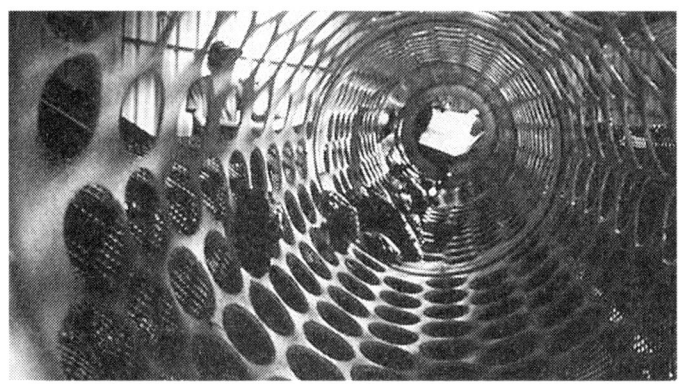

growing area, your supplier or the restaurant, and to *ask*. If they don't seem to know what you're talking about, the chances are they don't know much, and it may be better to order something else.

By 1970 the price of a 70 kg bag containing 80–110 dozen Rock oysters was $41. In 1992 the price of a bag of plate oysters jumped to around $340; on the half shell, a dozen plate-grade oysters sold for $5.60. In 1998–99 the farm-gate price of a bag of plate grade Sydney Rock oysters was $445. (There are around a 100 dozen to a bag normally, although a *good* oyster, according to Laurie Larner, is only 90–92 dozen. Approximately fourteen bags of Sydney Rock oysters make a tonne. Imagine, a tonne of oysters!) A bag containing 76 dozen Select and Prime Pacific oysters from Port Stephens, which are generally larger than Rocks, currently costs around $364. The farm-gate price of a 50-dozen bag of Tasmania Pacifics is around $220.

At the time of this writing in 2000, the price of a dozen Rock oysters sold unopened varies from between $5–9 depending on the place, producer and season. Oysters on the half shell (opened either by the farmer or by the supplier) are usually sold in waxed boxes of ten dozen, layered between dampened butcher's paper. The best prices are almost always to be had directly from the grower. Most areas where oysters are cultivated will have one or two outlets where you can buy them fairly direct and some farmers are happy to sell their oysters from their own outlets or sheds, like Jim Wild at Nowra or M&E Ralston, at Batemans Bay. In Freycinet you can get fresh oysters at Freycinet Marine Farm, Coles Bay and in South Australia at Stansbury through Dee's on the main road. (Farm-gate Pacifics are around $4.50 per dozen in Tasmania and $5 in South Australia.) The best thing to do if you don't see a sign is to ask around—someone will know where to find them. It may be a bit of a drive but it will be worth it, if only to see off-the-beaten-track country and the farm operations. Keep in mind however, the story told by an old-time oyster farmer from Port Stephens.

During the 1930s, when plate oysters were selling for six pence a dozen, he decided to make a fortune by selling his oysters straight from the shed to the public and proceeded to put up a sign advertising his wares. The very first day a lady called him in off his leases. He was at least 275 metres out but certain of a large order, he pushed his punt back up the drain and almost 'blew a fuse' when the lady ordered a half dozen. Speechless but polite he gave her the oysters and followed her back up the road. As the story goes, when she pulled away so did the sign.

For some reason, there is usually only a 50-cent difference between opened and unopened oysters per dozen at the Sydney Fish Markets. If they are on styrofoam trays already opened, they may cost between about $5.90 and $10.90 depending on the size and quality. Because of their larger size, Pacific oysters, especially Tasmanian, are usually slightly more expensive—ranging from between $7.50–11 per dozen. In a restaurant, expect to pay anywhere from $7 per half dozen up to $35 for a dozen oysters natural. (One should also expect, at the higher end of the scale, that they are opened on the spot—again ask.) Places specialising in freshly opened oysters often sell them at between $2.50 and $3 per oyster, which means you can try a few different varieties at the same time.

One wonders what our predecessors would have thought of ordering per oyster! In the past where oysters were eaten, a half dozen or dozen, according to Eleanor Clarke, 'would have been considered ridiculous'. Since the beginning of last century, however, when oysters were becoming scarcer and more expensive, they have been sold and consumed increasingly according to what is really a fairly arbitrary measurement—the dozen count. Though some dozens are more arbitrary than others, as the following story from Australian writer, Frank Moorhouse illustrates. Having ordered a dozen oysters in a restaurant in Cambridge, Mr Moorhouse was brought six. He consumed these with pleasure, thinking that perhaps this was an idiosyncrasy of the house (meant to keep the oysters as fresh as possible? or because they were so large no one could eat twelve?) and that his next six would shortly arrive. Nothing happened. Moorhouse ordered a second half dozen and was brought three oysters. By this time, determined to get his dozen, and suspecting that the waiter (or kitchen) had absolutely no idea what a dozen was, he had a careful chat to the young man and ordered three more oysters. Surprisingly, at this attempt, he was brought the three (not one and a half). The best part of the story, which the author suggests could be titled 'The Man Who Worked in the Oyster Bar Who Did Not Know How Many Made a Dozen', was that Mr Moorhouse was only charged for nine!

At its peak in 1976–77, the combined New South Wales and southern Queensland industry produced 9267 tonnes (net weight including shell) or 154454 bags (1200 oysters per bag) but it declined through the eighties to a production of 5306 tonnes or 88429 bags during 1990–91, worth about $30 million. In 1998–99, New South Wales marketed 70337 bags (that's 7880234 dozen) for a total value of $25897853. This decline in production is due partly to state restrictions on leases in an attempt to return waters to the wild or to recreational areas, and due partly to problems with pollution and disease. However, it is also because the oyster growers themselves have found it more economic to produce fewer oysters of a better quality using only their best leases. (Interestingly, general production in New South Wales has inclined toward growing 'bistro'.) But clearly, the difference between what the growers get for a box of oysters and what they cost on a menu in a big city restaurant indicates the amount of middlemen and, questionably, the cost of handling. If the restaurant gets

$2.50–3 per oyster, the oyster farmer is probably getting less than 40 cents. According to New South Wales Fisheries, the retail price of oysters is around 300 per cent greater than farm gate price. In 1974 Sumner reported that the retail price of Pacifics in Tasmania was approximately four times greater than that paid the farmer. Colin Dyke tells me its more like five times greater today.

THE BUREAUCRATIC OYSTER

Oyster farming in Australia is carried out under a system of leasing Crown land, or other land under the jurisdiction of the Minister for Fisheries or other public authorities. This land is leased to the grower for a renewable set term (15 years in New South Wales). The yearly rental in New South Wales is $37.10 per hectare while in South Australia it is $160 per hectare. In most states an aquaculture permit issued by the regulatory authority is also required, with heavy fines for anyone operating

without a permit. There are 542 permit holders in New South Wales, who between them hold around 2400 leases covering an area of 3200 hectares. In Tasmania 1351 hectares are leased for oyster growing, with 89 leases distributed among 67 leaseholders, producing over four million dozen oysters. In South Australia there are 1600 hectares of leases held by 134 farmers.

The lease system in Australia is similar to the system in France and other countries of Europe. In the United States, most oyster culture until recent times was based on the harvesting of naturally occurring public beds, although leasing is becoming more common in many states, especially on the west coast; leaseholds there are still usually incredibly cheap. It's been found (as in Holland), however, that making leases more expensive tends to lead to more and better oyster production as well as a lessening of the number of derelict leases—that is, areas leased where cultivation is no longer carried out. Such leases have been found to be a problem in Australia. They may become havens for predators and even breeding grounds for pests and unwanted species such as feral Pacifics, as well as presenting a danger to swimmers and recreational boaters. For example, statistics from 1998–99 showed that in New South Wales, more than 28 per cent of permit holders had no production, while 13 per cent produced under 50 bags. Thirty per cent of leaseholders produce 90 per cent of the state's oysters. At the time of this writing the state government is instituting a bond system based on the number of hectares held by the leaseholder, which it hopes will lessen this problem. Unfortunately it may prove so financially difficult that many small farmers may be forced to go out of business.

Generally oyster production all over the world has been a family-owned and run business, the family members doing most if not all of the work, often two or three, even four generations together. In his study of Australian oyster growing at Port Stephens in 1970–71, Korringa remarked that 'it is very difficult to attract and keep labour'. Clearly the work is hard and long and the pay is not great. The situation is changing somewhat and today you'll find almost anyone and his mother—accountants, schoolteachers, diplomats—trying their hand at oyster farming, though these smaller 'hobby farms' are rarely successful in such a demanding business. Predictably, the trend at the moment is toward modernisation of the industry, which means bigger farms and fewer leasees, although these remain, as far as I have seen, usually still family owned and run.

chapter vi

Breaching Those Stony Doors

SHELL NEARLY ROUND, THOUGH VARIOUSLY SHAPED, INEQUIVALVE; THE UPPER VALVE FLAT, OR NEARLY SO, WITH SCALES OR LAMINAE OF A YELLOWISH-BROWN; THE LOWER VALVE CONVEX, AND FOLIACCOUS, OF A PALE PINKISH-WHITE, WITH STREAKS OF PURPLISH-PINK; TRAVERSELY STRIATED.

OBVIOUSLY EVEN THE eminent biologist Linnaeus had a great deal of trouble managing a precise description of an oyster. The poet Lucilius put his pen exactly on the reason:

> When I but see the oyster's shell
> I look and recognize the river, marsh or mud,
> Where it was raised

The appearance of oysters varies to such an extent because of myriad ways it has ingeniously adapted itself to local conditions. For example, muddy conditions usually produce an elongated or 'shoehorn'-shaped oyster, as it attempts to enlarge its shell upward and limit its intake of water to the highest point where the water is clearer. In deeper water with a firmer bottom surface, the shell grows more uniformly around and tends to be broader.

So many are these variations that in Britain and elsewhere, studies are continuing to divide the 'British Native' and the 'Pacific' oyster (among others) into further differentiated species and varieties. As illustrated by the reclassification of the Sydney Rock, exact groupings, especially since many were once based on shell characteristics, are currently being disputed by experts. For example, the study of ligament or hinge shape in the Stewart Island mud oyster of southern New Zealand, has determined its close relation to a Chilean oyster and a change of its name (now *Tiostrea chilensi*) — in spite of its apparent geographic distance.

And yet, for all its variation, the shell of the oyster is so well known that we can recognise the empty ones even on shores where they no longer exist, or dug up in gardens where they may have been left in the past from sumptuous banquets or paupers' meals. But for most of us, as in the frequently quoted lines from Shakespeare's *King Lear*, how the oyster actually produces it remains a mystery.

> Fool: Canst tell how an oyster makes his shell?
> Lear: No.
> Fool: Nor I either.

Nor did I until I read Professor Yonge's invaluable book. As Reverend Williams remarked, the oyster does make for a very worthwhile study. Sir Anthony Carlisle, Surgeon Extraordinary to His Majesty, must have agreed when in 1826 he devoted the Hunterian Oration to the Royal College of Surgeons entirely to the oyster, because 'the various facts of its structure and many of its detached offices are analogous to several occurrences in the Human body'. In a more modern context, a friend who is a physicist, is doing a great deal of work on surface chemistry and has become fascinated by the atomic and molecular structure of shells (apparently enigmatic on many accounts) which he has been able to apply to such problems as the design of molecular sieves and other so-called 'smart materials'.

THE ENCLOSING SHELL

> The most prominent fact in the organization of the oyster is its shell. Its body is shut in between two long concave stony doors, which are made of limestone, and are fastened together at the end, somewhat in the same way that the covers of a long narrow check-book are bound together at the back.
>
> W K Brooks, *The Oyster*

The oyster's 'solid box of stone' provides protection for the animal inside, which, because it can't move, would be otherwise completely helpless. The sooner a young oyster can produce its shell the better chance it has of resisting predators and completing its growth. During the entire span of its life, its survival is most certain when there is a good supply of minerals in the water so that it is able to construct a thick, relatively massive shell as quickly as possible.

This shell has three main parts: the two valves and the connecting horny ligament near the more pointed end, known as the 'beak'. The basis of the shell is organic—like our own fingernails—made up of a material called *conchyolin* with much calcareous matter in the valves but not in the ligament. The ligament forces the valves apart to let in the water which contains the oyster's oxygen and food. A thin sac or 'mantle' covers the animal completely and actually makes or secretes all parts of the shell, as well as controlling the contact between the oyster and the surrounding marine environment.

The mantle in turn is made up of three folds, each with its own particular function: the first or outer layer (nearest the shell margin or edge) is concerned with the formation of the shell; the middle one is sensory, having basically taken over the functions of the head; the inner, and the largest, is a moving muscle which adjusts the inflow and outflow of water. In a Sydney Rock and flat Native oyster the mantle edges are pale, as distinguished from those of the Pacific which are black.

The shell of an oyster also consists of three main layers, each formed by different parts of the outer mantle. The first or outer layer (known as the periostracum) is thin, horny and organic, made, surprisingly, by the *inner* surface of the outer mantle fold. This outer layer of the shell is so fine that it is transparent and, at the edges in particular, also somewhat soft and elastic in a way similar to cartilage. Because of this, when the two valves are closed they 'form a perfect marginal contact, so much so that not a drop of water can escape when the oyster is removed from the sea'. (Yonge, 1960.)

The next two layers are thicker and mostly made up of calcified conchyolin. (Quite magically, the calcium is actually absorbed from sea water.) The middle layer of the shell consists of calcite prisms arranged vertically, while the innermost layer, the iridescent 'mother-of-pearl', is composed of crystals of aragonite. The mother-of-pearl, because it always remains in contact with the part of the oyster that forms it, increases in thickness throughout the life of the animal and, except for the margins, is the only one of the three layers of the shell that can be repaired if they are damaged.

Generally the shell of the Rock oyster (*Saccostrea glomerata*) is described as 'triangular', although it can often be distorted by growing conditions into all kinds of weird and wonderful shapes. Its shell tends to be crenellated at the edges and more smooth than those of Pacific oysters (*Crassostrea gigas*) which are fairly uniform in shape—usually oval (or slightly more elongated)—due to carefully regulated growing methods. The shell surface of a Pacific oyster is chalky and much more spiky than a Rock, with lobes and protrusions, or prominent radial grooves. Native or mud oysters (*Ostrea angasi*) are almost always round and relatively flat. The surface of the wild Native shell from

St Helens (Tasmania) can be fairly smooth with subtle (but definite) regular frill or growth 'rings', while other Natives, including cultivated ones, tend to look more like their European cousins with many thin, horny, quite brittle layers.

Oysters actually 'fix' carbon in growing their shells, removing it from circulation, so that in their own small way they help to mitigate the greenhouse effect. Some are also able to produce large quantities of what are called 'chalky' deposits. These deposits alter the shells' inner contours like a kind of padding, and are the oyster's reaction to different seasons and altered conditions. (You might notice the subtle modelling of the inside of a shell next time you eat an oyster.) These alterations of its inner world help the animal to function more efficiently, by more or less adjusting its body shape. Older oysters, especially, are also subject to a condition known as 'chambering' in which the oyster produces spaces in its shell that inevitably fill with water, and then seals them over. If the chambers are broken when trying to open the oyster, the water smells as if something has died in it and it can be confused with a bad oyster, which it is and is not. This condition is thought to be caused when the shell-forming part of the mantle shrinks, either when the water the oyster lives in becomes more saline or because of the body's weight loss immediately after spawning. (Some chambering in oysters was also believed to be caused by the effects of 'tributyl-tin', anti-fouling paint used on boats and now banned.)

Except for the delicate, almost invisible attachment at the margins (it is possible to see this when opening an oyster by gently lifting the flat valve or lid and looking inside before removing it), the body and mantle are attached to the shell entirely by muscles. The main one, and the most noticeable, is the 'adductor', once called the 'heart' by some oyster openers because it was thought that the oyster died when the 'vital point, the seat of the oyster's life' was severed. (This is not true.) When the oyster is opened and removed from the shell, a scar will be left where the adductor was. In the Crassostreinae, this is a fairly dark purple circular mark, slightly off-centre in the shell; in the *Ostrea*, it will generally have no colour and will be at the centre. The position of the adductor, somewhat away from the hinge, affords it maximum leverage.

The adductor is made up of two different kinds of muscle fibre: one semi-translucent and nearer the hinge, known as the 'quick' muscle; and the larger opaque area known as the 'catch' muscle. Both play a significant part in the life of an oyster. The quick (appropriately named) contracts very suddenly—as when expelling water with accumulated waste or sediment that has become too much for the oyster's regular filtering system—but soon tires and must relax. This ability to contract quickly is most important for the survival of the oyster that might find itself lying on a soft bottom in danger of being suffocated by mud. It is the means by which the female expels larvae. And it is also the quick muscle which responds to the impulse sent by the sensory portion of the mantle and snaps the valves of an oyster shut at the approach of predators. Whole beds of oysters have been observed to stop feeding and suddenly close at the passing of a shadow. (Apparently the valves of Crassostreinae oysters snap with greater efficiency than those of the *Ostrea*.)

The catch muscle contracts more slowly, but can remain contracted for a long time with apparently little expenditure of energy. This accounts for the oyster's well-known ability to stay tightly shut for long periods, using the oxygen in the small amount of water trapped within the shell. The catch muscle allows the oyster to survive extremes of temperature or salinity, attacks by predators, or lengthy exposure at low tide. Anyone who has ever tried opening an oyster knows the power of this muscle. One of the stories told as proof of its strength is of a mouse, investigating a plate of shellfish, being found half in and half out of an oyster that had closed on it; another is of fishermen being caught by the hands or feet in the valves of a giant Pacific clam and 'held, as if in a vise, until the tide rises and drowns them'. (Brooks, 1891.)

BREAKING AND ENTERING

Far in advance of human beings, natural predators have various ingenious and efficient methods for 'breaking and entering' which, as Toussaint-Samat remarks, would be 'almost comic if they did not portend disaster for the oyster'.

Clarke describes women workers in France spending whole days in the *parcs* beating crabs off with sticks. In Australia, in the north, and especially on the Macleay River, the mangrove crab—which can grow to quite a large size—is able to crush even mature oysters (mainly the ones with slightly softer shells due to fast growth), with their powerful nippers, much like we would crack a nut. Careful and delicate feeders, crabs don't seem to mind the shell bits. On the Oregon coast of the United States, the endangered tiny native Olympia oysters (two of them, shucked, will fit into a thimble, and it takes 350 to fill a litre), are being devoured by a European import, the green crab, which 'eats them like popcorn'.

Fish of various species, as already mentioned, are able to feast on oysters by means of powerful flattened teeth: the toad and porcupine fish in Australia have teeth modified into a kind of beak like a parrot; and the bream, which has canine teeth that it can use to pull an oyster from where it is attached, and molars adapted to crushing the shell. Eagle rays can grow to over 1.5 metres, and are equipped with hard jaw plates which can crack the shells of even relatively large oysters.

One of the neatest ways of eating an oyster is accomplished by whelks—drills and borers—which have their own special tool for doing so (hence their names). They are a large genus, with many different species that cause havoc to oyster beds all over the world, particularly where the salinity of the water is fairly high. In Australia they are found in large numbers at the mouths of rivers and estuaries—for example, the New Brunswick River and the entrance of Port Macquarie—where there is little fresh water; heavy rains will kill them or drive them back out to sea. In this country, there are three species of these 'boring' whelks, known as the common borer, the black borer, and the hairy borer. These are those often pretty, pointed, cone- or spiral-shaped shells found on the beach or in tide pools, sometimes still complete with borer. Each borer possesses the ultimate oyster opener—a tongue-like rasp or radula, sometimes called a proboscis, rather like a two-edged saw, with which they simply drill into the oyster (or any shellfish, for that matter) and then extract the flesh as it pleases them. A secretion of acid helps to reduce the hardness of the shell and makes the job even easier. If you've ever wondered, when collecting shells to string on a necklace or wind chime, why there is often a convenient, small, perfectly round little hole in the shells—the borer has been at work getting its lunch.

But, by far, the oyster-opening method of the 'five-finger' (picked off by hand in most places or, as on the eastern seaboard of the US, cleaned up en masse with a starfish 'mop') must be the most subtle and dramatic. '[F]ar from being the placid, decorative forms of marine life they may appear' (Toussaint-Samat), the sadist starfish creeps up with its tiny feet and wraps its arms around the unsuspecting mollusc. It has no means to kill the oyster quickly but in this 'horrible embrace', which can last for hours, it pulls and pries with those sucker-like feet ever so gently until the oyster becomes exhausted. The catch muscle weakens, and the oyster, suffering from lack of oxygen and despair, is already dying. The starfish is ready. When the shell begins to gape—only a millimetre is enough—it extrudes its stomach through its mouth and literally sucks the poor oyster out, more or less digesting it with gastric juices in the shell first. Apparently this death dance is so intense and covert, taking place hidden within the starfish's arms, that no one has really ever been able to see it, only the final evidence—an empty shell and a satisfied starfish slinking away. At worst, whole armies of them can pass through at 140 starfish to the square metre, extending over several kilometres.

Shucking/splitting/opening

Among us less adapted, there is a fair amount of disagreement as to the proper way of opening an oyster and certainly no hard and fast rules. Most, however, seem to agree on the fact that the hand holding the intended victim should be wearing a glove or at least be safely protected in a tea towel. My partner, who has opened many oysters for my pleasure (even long before he ate them himself), holding the oyster with the cupped side down, flat side up, goes in from the hinge end—in the case of the Pacific or Rock this is the more pointed end—and severs the ligament. He then runs the blade of the oyster knife (don't try to do this with an ordinary knife) around the upper valve separating the flesh from the shell and leaving it in the lower or more deeply cupped left valve, where the most amount of liquor can be retained without spilling. We, the receivers, then finish the job of cutting the flesh away from the shell with a fork on our own plates with more or less struggle and tenacity. (In France an oyster is served to you in much the same way, as it is believed that severing the adductor in the bottom shell causes unnecessary premature damage and hastens the demise of the oyster so that it's better left later rather than sooner.)

Experienced oyster farmers, who have opened thousands in their day, out in the punt or at the culling bench, hold an oyster in their torn rubber gloves or bare hand with the flat side down; a quick shove, jerk at the margin (the more rounded, fragile end) and it's presented dripping on the flat or smaller half shell. I'd say the disadvantage of this method is that much of the liquor is lost, but on the other hand it does seem very fast and efficient.

I myself, who cannot claim any expertise, have sometimes managed to pry open the shell by bashing a blade in at the same place (the margin) and turning it sideways, but with hardly the same result. The problem was that while I may have finally gotten at the delicious creature, I had usually broken and chipped a good deal of the edge of the shell, which adds to the offending grit and looks pretty unsightly on the plate. And if nothing else, one wants to enjoy, arranged on ice, the beauty of the lemon and shellfish that has taken so much effort to get to.

After a half hour's lesson with an expert, however, I was actually able to open an oyster fairly easily with a minimum mangling of the meat and no glove or tea towel at all. Here's the method: On an old chopping board (or your regular one covered with something) place the oyster cupped side down (flat side up), beak end away from you. Push the oyster knife (or chop with the pointed end) into the indented space on the shell near to the lip edge. It's actually surprisingly soft if you get the right place. (You can also get a kind of pincer/plier-like device or a 'gun' which will puncture a neat little hole in it with a minimum of effort and destruction.) When you have a small hole, push the knife half or all the way in, depending on the length of the blade (I find a knife with guard handy for this), but keeping the point angled well down toward the bottom shell. Wiggle (yes, I said wiggle) both the knife and the oyster, at the same time moving the blade, pointing downward, gently around toward yourself (the adductor is located in this area). The oyster will open slightly as you add pressure, levering off the top shell and cutting the adductor. I then remove the lid and slurp down the oyster (to Brian Allen's professional horror).

Brian, on the other hand, like most suppliers and distributors, would then carefully rinse it, cut it away from the lid, flip it over into the cupped shell and present you with a perfectly clean, plump (no gills showing) oyster. The reason for rinsing is because of the grit which restaurants and suppliers don't like customers complaining of. And unfortunately the way I bashed the shell to get the little hole started produced a fair amount of broken bits. Still, I could open my own oysters! When I told Ted (Brian's father) of my triumph he asked whether I had stabbed myself yet? When I proudly told him no I hadn't, he dryly commented, 'you will'.

Since then I have gone from being totally helpless in the face of an unopened oyster and in danger of amputating a finger, to being able to open one from the hinge end with relative ease and almost no chipping. Depending on how fresh the oyster is—it seems that the fresher the oyster the healthier and therefore stronger the adductor muscle is—and where and how they were grown (see pp 95–96), I find most Pacifics generally easier to open, or 'split', than Rocks, and for the first-time opener they may be the best choice. A little confidence goes a long way and so does a good oyster knife. These come in various sizes and shapes, with different kinds of handles and blades. Most openers have their favourite, whether

Breaching Those Stony Doors

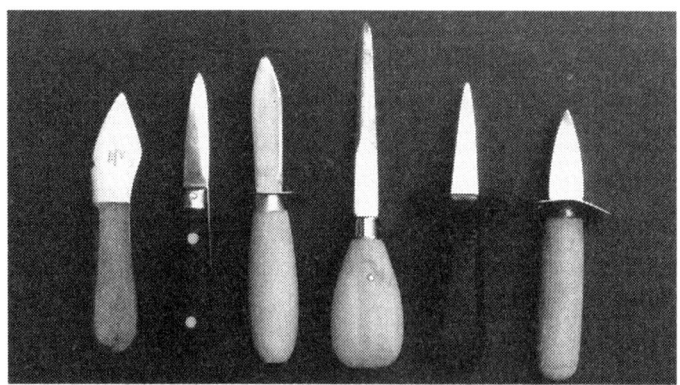

one with a bulbous wooden handle and a short blade, or very pointed slim blade with a slim plastic grip. Some actually make or customise their own knives, and if you go to where oyster farmers or processors are working, you will find they always use the same knife that is known to be their own—no one else uses it. Some openers wear them out at a prodigious rate and replace only the blades. Other knives I have seen have been so beloved that the grips are bandaged and held together by tape, so loath is the person to give them up. What they all have in common, though, is a very strong, sturdy blade which will not bend or snap under the pressure of prying the oyster valves apart, and a handle designed to cushion and protect the hand—some have a guard which can help keep the inexperienced from going in too deep or cutting their fingers on the sharp shell. The main thing is to find one that is comfortable for you and suits your particular opening style. (I find a slim blade with a very pointed end to work best.) This makes an enormous difference to the ease and confidence with which you shuck.

An American magazine article on 'Shucking Oysters Made Easy' shows the knife going in at the hinge end and running through the muscle in the top valve and then the lower, removing the oyster, then rinsing the shell under the tap before replacing it. Many regard rinsing the oyster as sacrilege—the purist will happily put up with a little grit in order not to lose the precious liquor. It may be a good idea however, to scrub the unopened oysters first with a stiff brush, particularly if they are muddy. South Australian oyster farmers suggest putting them in a bucket with a small amount of clean water and shaking or stirring it to rumble the oysters against each other. If you have a large number, Laurie Larner recommends using a cement mixer—a clean one of course.

A 'trick for opening oysters' is given by Toussaint-Samat in his *History of Food*:

> ... there is a clever method of opening oysters, a job which alarms many people. If you are afraid of cutting yourself with an oyster knife, you can put oysters in the freezer for three hours, the right way up [that is, with the cupped side down] ... (however, this is not something you mention to the purist who simply waits in front of his plate). Three hours before you want to eat the oysters, you take them out of the freezer again. The low temperature will have made the flat shell gape; you only have to slip a short, strong knife into the gap, and your oyster opens as if by magic. You give the oysters just over two hours to return to normal temperature ...

He claims that 'they will be as delicious as when they came out of the water' (and yet earlier on he also states that freezing will kill an oyster ...). I am still in the process of experimenting with this, and have as yet little to report on the efficacy of the method, although I have frozen oysters before and they didn't seem much easier to open. The problem is waiting that long, eight hours total, which seems aeons more than just wielding a knife. Toussaint-Samat's method does have an advantage though; as he says, 'they will be perfectly free from bits of shell'.

This is much the same method in theory as steaming or roasting oysters to open them. And if you're desperate, an American *Connoisseur's Guide and Cookbook* recommends cracking the shell with a small hammer. Apparently you can also microwave oysters in a glass casserole dish for 5 minutes on warm (Andrea Cole suggests 30 seconds on high) which is enough to make the shell gape so a knife can easily be inserted. Given a couple of dozen Freycinet oysters, restaurateur Gay Bilson quickly began to experiment, placing some in a dry pan that could withstand a fair amount of heat. It was about 15 minutes when the oysters began to froth at the lip and could then be opened easily. They were not cooked, only gently warmed — and, she said, you could now smell the true scent of the oyster.

On the quay at Cancale, bought oysters are handed to you in a plastic bag with a particularly well-illustrated *'Les huîtres ... une ouverture facile: 1) Bien tenir le couteau, en plaçant le pouce à 1 cm du bout de la lame. 2) Placer la pointe du couteau au niveau du muscle. Introduire le bout de la lame en la faisant vriller légèrement. 3) Enfoncer la lame plus profondément et couper le muscle en ramenant le couteau vers soi.* [sounds pretty dangerous!] *4) Racler la partie supérieure. Soulever et détacher la coquille'. Voila!* What is particularly interesting about this method is that it suggests going in at neither end but at the *side*—that is holding the cup side down in the palm of your hand, hinge end toward you—about two thirds of the length of the oyster from the hinge (approximately where the adductor muscle is located), twisting the blade slightly and then running it toward you to detach the lid. Notice NO RINSING. (By the way, it also says that the oysters may be kept for five days at +5°–15°C compared to almost two weeks for a Sydney Rock.)

Here is the official method given by the New South Wales Oyster Farmers' Association:

How to Open an Oyster

1. A knife, oysters and gloves if you are inexperienced, is all you need. Note where the hinge is.
2. Rest oyster on a sturdy surface, flat side up, hold firmly, push knife through top shell opposite hinge end.
3. Press downward on the knife, levering top shell up. Separate top and bottom shells completely, then rinse them.
4. Insert knife under oyster, cut adductor muscle.
5. Lift oyster out of flat shell, place on the other half, turning it as you go.
6. The smooth side of the oyster presents a more attractive appearance than the bearded side. (All opened oysters are turned over by hand before being sold.)

Jerry Fraser says turning the oyster over is actually to check whether there are any mudworm blisters. Laurie Larner goes even further and also turns the oyster around so that its front end (margin, gills, etc.) faces the hinge end of the shell. He does this because if that's the end the oyster takes in water, then after being opened, logically, he says, it will stay fresher and keep longer if it's 'breathing' liquid rather than air.

According to the French *Comite National de La Conchyliculture*, the world record for opening oysters is more than one hundred in 5 minutes. Oyster farmer Jim Wild of Greenwell Point, four times Australian champion, has been able to dine off the fact that in 1988 he opened 30 oysters in 2 minutes 56 seconds bare-handedly to win the World Championship at Galway, Ireland. Jerry Fraser opens an average of 210 dozen a week and on a particularly busy night may open between 900–1000 oysters. The 1999 Australian champion, Jim Angelakos (Claudio's Seafood, Sydney Fish Markets) had the winner's time of 2 minutes and 54 seconds for opening 30 Sydney Rock oysters.

Brooks tells a charming story about a young oyster shucker he observed 'watch in hand' at a Crisfield canning factory in Maryland while on the State Oyster Commission (around 1900):

> With nothing but a small thin knife, [he] opened thirty oysters in a minute. He worked with the precision of a machine, and made six motions for each oyster ... He was very proud of his skill and of the prizes he had taken, and although he seemed to have abundant assurance, he explained that his movements were retarded by his diffidence in the presence of state commissioners and he said that, when free from embarrassment, he could 'shuck' thirty-six oysters a minute.

However, it's unlikely he would have gained any points for presentation!

※

The Dutch researcher, Korringa, concluded his year-long study of Australian oyster farming with an observation about the shortage of skilled oyster openers: 'the Australian market can absorb large quantities of high quality oysters *at least as long as labour can be found to open the oysters to be served in the restaurants*'. This was in 1971, when production and consumption of oysters in this country were at their height. One wonders whether the decline in the availability of such skilled labour inevitably led to the high cost and poor quality of oysters in restaurants and/or the eventual decline in demand for oysters (oyster bars, parlours, oyster-eating contests, roasts were all once very popular) and thus the downward curve in production. Or whether the opposite has occurred—that decline in the popularity of fresh oysters meant few people would consider pursuing oyster shucking as a proud and serious profession. Ex-oyster farmer Andy Derwent, now with New South Wales Fisheries, lamented in 1996: 'Young people in particular just don't seem to be eating oysters anymore. When I was young, oysters and prawn cocktails were the only entrées we knew. Now the entree list is two pages long'.

A large part of the problem may be that most of our restaurants which serve oysters get them already opened from a supplier and they may sit around for a day or so if no one orders the dozen. Some oyster distributors open 1000 a day at least, in an assembly-line system of sometimes up to fifteen workers, who open, rinse, turn and pack the oysters for distribution by truck. Often these oysters may have little in common with a freshly opened one. They will not necessarily be 'off' or 'bad', just ordinary and not terribly enjoyable. We do not have or expect, unless the restaurant is an exceptional one, an *écailler* in the kitchen or outside the door (as in France where no one would dream of serving a pre-opened oyster, or at least admitting to it). The restaurant people and the sales staff I've asked about this in Australia tell me that most of the time it is 'just too busy', and 'what would we do if someone comes in and wants a large order?' I say tell them to wait; it will be worth it. But unfortunately, the kind of master Ted Allen remembers are few and far between: 'One I used to know (he's probably dead now) opened eleven bags a week—that's eleven hundred dozen. All the hotels used to have their own opener'.

At a fashionable Sydney brasserie in November 1997, there were at least six different kinds of oyster on the menu: the usual Tasmanian, various assorted Rock and one name I had never heard of before. I asked a young waiter passing if the oysters were $2.50 *each* (remembering ten cents in South Carolina). 'Yes.' Are they all freshly opened on the premises? 'Yes' he replied, 'we "chuck" them ourselves, otherwise they would be $1.50 each.'

What he probably didn't realise was that even some of the best restaurants still haven't got their act together as far as opening fresh oysters. And those restaurants that do 'chuck' their own (instead of buying them pre-opened from a supplier) often do so as part of the ordinary preparation usually done by apprentices or kitchen hands, and let them sit around until someone orders. (I'm told that now, in many of the best restaurants, it's not uncommon for apprentices to spend much of their first year in the kitchen opening oysters.) Those restaurants that advertise an oyster bar and 'opened on the spot' don't always have a full-time professional opener. At a well-known restaurant in Fremantle, we sat at the oyster bar until someone could be found (granted, it was late afternoon) to come out and open the oysters—a young chef, who didn't have a particularly easy time of it, finally did the honours. And recently, an establishment known for its freshly opened oysters had to enlist the services of the pastry cook, among others, to meet the demand on a Saturday night.

It was gratifying, pastry cook or not, to see that no one there rinsed the oysters. Unfortunately many restaurants are still washing away the all-important liquor so 'no one will complain of grit'. This is what we were told by the manager of the Indiana Tea Rooms in Perth, a restaurant that actually opens the oysters at a counter but still rinses them. Besides the continuing controversy that rages over the introduction and/or superiority of the Pacific versus the Sydney Rock oyster, probably nothing else brings out such strong opinions as whether to rinse or not. In 'The Grave Case of Australian Oyster Abuse', Frank Moorhouse rates rinsing ('a brutal act of essence-cleansing') as a very serious offence, second only to the 'marketing and serving of dead oysters'.

Michael Klausen, executive chef for Sydney's Boathouse and Bayswater Brasserie, is clearly against rinsing, as he said unequivocally at a recent seafood school: it loses the juice—the 'gold' that makes the oyster different from any other grown elsewhere. Consultant Nick Ruello suggests the oyster is much cleaner and safer if it has been rinsed; I'm not sure exactly how this works, nor do I think anyone should fool themselves into thinking a contaminated oyster from polluted waters would be improved if washed. Certainly the opposite would be true: you could contaminate a good oyster by washing it in dirty water. In New South Wales at least, there are no health regulations requiring the rinsing of oysters (there are in Tasmania), although recently, legislation has been passed regarding the quality of water they are washed in. (A new sign at the Sydney Fish Markets: 'Customers, our oysters are opened using water filtered to Australian Health Standards'.)

If your unrinsed oyster has been opened with less finesse than you'd like and there is some grit in it, this can easily be removed with the point of a knife, the edge of a napkin, your finger or your fork before eating. One restaurant specialising in freshly opened oysters, cleverly uses a small pastry brush dipped in salt water.

'The oyster-eater', wrote Philpots in 1890, 'eagerly seizes that double-shell, thrusts his knife forcibly between its valves, gives it a wrench, and extracting daintily the little creature within, instantly swallows it.' Clearly, opening oysters used to be a fairly personal business performed on a plate (or pile) of succulent molluscs by the diners themselves. But it seems that somewhere or other, we, as a nation and a generation, have lost the habit of knowing how to open an oyster (so much so that Toussaint-

Samat could comment that oyster opening was something people could be expected to be *afraid* of) and, perhaps with that, the taste of what a really good fresh oyster is like. One hopes that both are on the way back.

THE SECRET LEVER

Whichever way you choose to open an oyster, it is the adductor muscle and the tough ligament or hinge that make it so difficult. In the oyster, this ligament is not smooth and pearly-looking, as you find it on other bivalves. Instead it is uneven and at the top or outer layer, having been worn away by the opening and closing of the different-sized valves (a wider separation as the oyster gets bigger). Before DNA matching, it was often the shape, size and texture of the ligament that some scientists studied when trying to determine the species of an oyster.

The ligament acts in opposition to the adductor—a good thing to keep in mind when shucking, as it has been estimated that the elastic power of this hinge in an average sized oyster is equal to the pressure of 32 pounds per square inch. Closure of the oyster shell is actually distortion of the ligament being subjected to a tensile strain through the energy of the adductor muscle. Another way of looking at it is that when the adductor relaxes, the valves more or less 'spring' open, in much the same way a stiff piece of rubber, bent in half, will snap back into shape when it is let go. An intact shell, when the oyster is either removed, dead, or very close to death, is said to 'gape', as it will when the oyster is suffering from winter-mortality disease. The 'catch' part of the adductor can hold the oyster closed for a long time, but when the small amount of oxygen is used up from the water trapped in the shell and the muscle begins to tire, it will eventually relax—a good indication that the oyster has been out of the water for longer than it can stand and is not fresh. This is why one should never buy or eat oysters that are not tightly shut or, if open, do not close when tapped. (Another rule of thumb—if an oyster opens *too* easily, check it carefully, since this may mean that it should be thrown away.)

If one is dealing with Native *angasi* however, this is not always the case. For some reason (probably because it is a subtidal oyster) the Native tends to gape soon after being taken from the water and this is not necessarily an indication that the oyster is dead or dying. Smelling it will tell you that. Even more mysterious, this delicious indigenous oyster when closed, can be so difficult to open that I'm told very few processors want to deal with it.

Sydney Rock oysters are actually capable of living out of water for up to three weeks (that is, from their 'pull' date, or the date they were actually taken from the water, rather than when they were purchased) and can be stored for as many as ten days if kept in cool moist conditions, ideally between 12 and 14°C. Find the darkest, dampest corner in your house (the hall closet? the garage? the bathroom?) and remove them from the plastic bag if that's how they've come to you. Keeping unopened fresh oysters in plastic is a sure way to lose the lot.

Larner's Oyster Supply, until recently, the only source of live oysters in Western Australia, brought them in by truck or rail from the eastern states (now it's South Australia). Laurie Larner, who in his time has arguably transported oysters farther distances and through greater temperatures than anyone else on earth, says the *only* way to keep oysters (by which he means Sydney Rocks) is in hessian bags—a practice he is sad to see being left behind. He tells the story of a time when it was so hot over the Nullabor that rail tracks buckled and birds fell out of the sky. The train was derailed and a large and valuable shipment of oysters was left sitting in the desert for almost a week. It was at least a fortnight before the oysters finally got to Perth. They were in hessian—dry—and, he says, he didn't lose a one! (South Australian Pacific oysters are also shipped in 'jute bags' by refrigerated trucks, having to contend with similar high temperatures, over 40°C in summer.) Laurie's theory, and here would be a man who knows, is that when a dry, tightly closed oyster is wetted it thinks it is back in water and begins to open, or loosen that hermetic seal it's capable of—and that's the beginning of the end.

Jerry Fraser, on the other hand (and this seems to depend on whether you're dealing with oysters from warm or temperate waters), suggests that the way to keep oysters for more than a day is to run cold water over them and place them in the back of the refrigerator on a dry tray. But then he also recommends making sure they are stored cupped side down, which would have been impossible to ensure with huge quantities such as Larner's used to handle. Toussaint-Samat's advice is to store them the other way—that is with the upper/flat shell downwards so that they can't open. But everyone else suggests placing the cup side down so the juice won't be lost if they do open.

Again with Native *angasi* the situation is slightly different because of their natural tendency to gape. I suspect it was their European cousin, *Ostrea edulis*, Toussaint-Samat was referring to when he suggested the weight of the heavier bottom shell would help keep an oyster closed. Experiments with storage of Native oysters indicate that beside keeping them cool and moist like all oysters, the next most important factor is to put a weight on them or pack them tightly into a container with a lid pressed down so they can't open. Losing liquor dries out any oyster and hastens spoilage.

In the absence of a hessian bag, a basket, wooden box, bucket or similar container covered with a moist tea towel, especially one soaked in salt water, or with a little damp seaweed, is ideal. It is best to cram the oysters together as much as possible so they will stay closed. *Do not put them in water*, even though this was the preferred method most oyster mongers used at the turn of the century (with the addition of a little oatmeal). Fresh water will drown an oyster. Also, if you have purchased unopened Rock oysters in New South Wales, don't take them home and store them in the lake behind your caravan or the river in front of the house. Remember they have been cultivated in clean water and/or purified, and you have no idea of the quality of the water outside your door.

After the development of the canning process in 1810, another way of preserving oysters became available. In the United States the canning of oysters was a major

industry, so much so that collecting the incredible number of different cans and labels has actually become a legitimate and lucrative hobby there. In Australia, where food storage was so difficult and variety scarce, tinned oysters were an important item in relieving a monotonous diet. As early as 1876, a canning industry was set up by the Campbell family in a blacksmith's shop at Streaky Bay, using the abundant oysters found on Oyster Spit. Apparently a tin of these oysters, discovered and opened in 1930, was still in perfect condition. (Who would have been brave enough to test them?) But the canning industry, though valuable, also helped to decimate the natural oyster beds in Australia. Now, of course, the only tinned oysters available here are smoked (and usually from Korea).

If you have too many oysters to tackle and are desperate, they can be kept frozen for up to three months if stored in a strong plastic bag, but freezing does kill them, so they must be eaten as soon as they defrost. I would not personally recommend freezing—although oysters are often sold snap frozen and some restaurants do serve these as natural—because I've found that home freezing alters the texture of the meat, making it flaccid and the oyster develops a strong, cloying, fishlike taste which is unappealing and quite unoysterlike.

Although oysters should be kept cool, I would never ordinarily recommend putting *unopened* oysters in the refrigerator. Too cold and the fridge will kill a Sydney Rock. If the weather is very hot, an Esky or styrofoam box without ice or just a little ice not directly in contact with the oysters will do, but don't close it up tightly— they need to 'breathe'. Unopened oysters from colder waters, such as Pacifics from Tasmania and South Australia, should be stored in the refrigerator and can last up to five days depending on how they were grown. If you have purchased Pacific oysters unopened, keep them properly chilled at between 5°C and 10°C until you are ready to eat them.

Opened oysters that cannot be eaten immediately should be treated like any other seafood. The worst thing for an open oyster is fluctuation in temperature. They will keep at below 5°C for two to three days, although you'll lose the best flavour after a day; so yes, by all means put them in the coldest part of the refrigerator, but prevent them from drying out by covering with plastic wrap. The rate of deterioration for *opened* oysters doubles for each 5°C increase in temperature. A good analogy is to treat open oysters as you would fresh milk—they are just as perishable. But the best way to store oysters is *not to*. Eat them as soon as you get them.

Those empty shells

> Oysters are an uncharitable meal, for we leave nothing but empty shells to the poor ...
>
> old English saying

Oyster shells were used by the Romans as medicine to cure wounds, ulcers, skin complaints, and chilblains. A mixture of figs, pitch and powdered oyster shells was recommended for repairing baths. They also used them, ground, as toothpaste. At one time the oyster shells which accumulated in the shops of Sydney and its suburbs were regularly collected and either burnt for lime or ground into grit for bird feed. Licences were granted (and leases carefully protected from poachers) by the Fisheries Department in Western Australia after World War I, for gathering shell grit, probably to be used in roads and footpaths. It's a pity that paving is no longer made with oyster shell, which is still used in many countries, and provides a natural and pleasingly irregular, crazy-quilt pattern.

Nowadays shells are a problem—growers and suppliers can hardly give them away. Those from restaurants go into the rubbish. At home, an alternative is to dig empty shells into the garden or throw them in the compost. They take longer to break up than mussel shells but are still an excellent means of aerating and providing organic lime to the soil. You can put them in the driveway and run over them first, although this is not recommended unless you have a tractor or large truck. It's difficult to agree with an American book which suggests making oyster shells into earrings, though a British writer, praising the Portuguese oyster in the 1920s, claimed a double advantage for it — that after eating the oyster you could use the elongated shell for a shoehorn.

Ever inventive, children in the oyster town of Whitstable on the Kent coast used to build 'grottos' out of empty oyster shells in the streets and light them with candle ends around August 1st, begging change from passers-by to buy more candles (likely story). Apparently this was in celebration of the feast of St James, whose remains, so the legend goes, were being transported by ship from the Holy Land to Spain when a knight and his horse fell overboard. The horse was never recovered but the astonished knight, after some days, was miraculously (this was attributed to the saint's intervention) fished unharmed from the sea and his clothes, just as miraculously, were completely covered with oysters.

> Secret, and self-contained, and solitary as an oyster
> Charles Dickens, *A Christmas Carol*

As pervasive a notion of the oyster's character as this is, it is not true. In fact the nature of an oyster is quite the opposite — gregarious, open as much as 90 per cent of the time while feeding, and completely dependent on the environment that surrounds it. It is the shell — its formation and the fact that it entirely encloses the oyster — which has intrigued artists, writers and philosophers, and led to these misguided images. Aristotle compared the soul fettered to the body as an oyster to its shell. Nietzsche was hardly complimentary in his likening of the oyster to a poet: 'And they may well have come from the sea. Certainly pearls are found in them; they are that much more similar to hard shellfish. And instead of a soul I often found salted slime in them' (*Thus Spoke Zarathustra*). One scientist has even written an entire paper on the surface of oyster shell as a complete miniature world unto itself (Korringa, 'The shell of the *Ostrea edulis* as a habitat', 1951).

Since at least 30 000 BC human beings all over the world have been fascinated by molluscs, using them in trade, either for their contents as nourishment or for their empty shells, which were the first coins, the first jewels, and some of the first implements. Archaeologists examining traces of exterior charring on shells from several sites have concluded that they were used as cooking vessels. Around the Mediterranean the first decorative motifs used on ceramics were made by pressing shells onto wet clay.

Human beings are not alone in their particular passion for shells. In Australia, the *Polypus cyaneus* octopus collects oysters with its eight suckered tentacles and drags home the helpless creatures where it arranges them in a circle to build a cosy, fortified nest. Sometimes these can be seen at low tide reaching a height of almost a metre. Unfortunately, the oysters, torn from their own homes and piled in a heap, smother from the weight of those on top and suffocate from the silt on the bottom. The octopus, like man, doesn't seem to care much, but eats what it wants while constantly enlarging and admiring its beautiful collection.

A WORD

In the garden there were snatches of music
Wordless, melancholy.
The sharp fresh odours of the sea
Rose from oysters on cracked ice ...

Akhmatova, from 'Evening'

If it is true, as Alice Kaplan says in *French Lessons*, 'that language speaks about itself through [objects]' then in literature the oyster is frequently called upon to provide images of delicacy, beauty, solitude and luxury. Is there anything as visually perfect as the clear glassiness of ice surmounted by the grey and white of oysters with their black lace edges touched by the thin yellow of cut lemons? 'The Oyster!' Cruikshank waxed lyrically: 'The mere writing of the word creates sensations of succulence—gastronomical pleasures, nutritive food, easy digestion, palatable indulgence—then go to sleep in peace! True, true oh oyster! Thou art the best beloved of the loved!' (from *Oyster: Where, How and When to Find, Breed, Cook and Eat it*, 1861.)

Italian:	*ostrica*
Spanish:	*ostra*
Portuguese:	*ostra*
Swedish:	*ostron*
German:	*auster*

And in French, as recently as the Renaissance when the circumflex accent came into use, oyster (*l'huitre*) was spelled with an 's'—*uistre*.

An international language, the shape and size of the oyster is so well known it has been incorporated into language as a standard comparison, for example, 'oyster light', 'oyster steak', 'oyster white', 'oyster satin', the 'oyster' meat of a chicken or other fowl and, of course, 'oyster crackers'. There are references to oysters in no less than seven of Shakespeare's plays. Philpots called it a 'classical character'. Australian writers in this regard have been no different: at least two recent novels have been titled *Oyster*—although, in keeping with the prevalent notions, one is about a secret cult figure and one about a spy. A popular, glossy lifestyle magazine is called 'Oyster', because, I'm told, when the new editors canvassed people for ideas about a title, food words kept coming up, 'oyster' in particular. They finally decided on the famous mollusc, as much for its sensuous sounding name as for its connotations of richness (pearls) and the idea that 'the world is your oyster', all of which was intended to herald a new magazine meant to be 'the natural aphrodisiac for contemporary hormones'.

That saying—which, by the way, is actually 'The world's mine oyster, which with sword will open' and comes from Shakespeare's *Merry Wives of Windsor*—more or less means that the world, like an oyster, can be opened by a sword; neither of which is as easy as it sounds. As we no longer brandish swords about, you can't help wonder what people mean when they use the phrase—the closed but entirely self-sufficient oyster? If you can afford oysters the world is yours? You enjoy life (that is the world) as you do an oyster? It doesn't entirely make sense but I guess like many other clichés is based on mistaken ideas. Another suggestion is the expression implies that, once some difficult thing has been accomplished—once a (metaphoric) shell of some kind has been opened—the world (oyster) is there for your tasting. On the other hand, a less frequently used example of the oyster as metaphor is as 'something from which advantage, delight, profit etc. may be derived' (Collins Dictionary). And Darby Ross (manager, Marine Farming branch of Tasmanian Department of Primary Industries, Water and Environment) is pretty right when he sees the oyster as a perfect image for the state: clean, fresh, delicious and desirable.

Funnily enough, while oceans have been written about the oyster and writer after writer has used it for their own allusions and images, English poets, at least traditional ones, have had some difficulty. This may be because although the French contains at least thirteen different words that rhyme with *huître*, English seems to have only three: clositer, roister and moister. I have to hand it to them for their inventiveness, but generally every one of the pre-twentieth-century poems which mentions 'oyster' falls back on these standards in endless but somewhat shallow variations. (Modern poets haven't had the same problem obviously.)

The Oyster

The oyster, about as big as a fair-sized pebble, is rougher, less evenly coloured, brightly whitish. It is a world stubbornly closed. Yet it can be opened: one must hold it in a cloth, use a dull jagged knife, and try more than once. Avid fingers get cut, nails get chipped: a rough job. The repeated pryings mark its cover with white rings, like haloes. Inside one finds a whole world, to eat and drink; under a *firmament* (properly speaking) of nacre, the skies above collapse on the skies below, forming nothing but a puddle, a viscous, greenish blob that ebbs and flows on sight and smell, fringed with blackish lace along the edge. Once in a rare while a globule pearls in its nacre throat, with which one instantly seeks to adorn oneself.

Francis Ponge, *Taking the Side of Things*

Pearl of any price

Until the sixteenth century, European scholars apparently believed that dewdrops impregnated oysters, which then delivered pearls according to the size of the drops. At least in art, literature and folklore, some of the fascination with oysters has, I suspect, to do with the notion that besides being delicious, eating an oyster may produce a pearl for you. Sadly, your chances of finding a natural pearl are one in 10000. There even seems to be some disagreement as to whether 'true' or edible oysters are capable of such a feat. Our esteemed Professor Yonge states categorically: 'The pearl producing oyster is related to the mussel, *not* the edible oyster'. And yet all the information I have found on pearl-producing oysters puts them among the genus *Pinctada* or *Pynctata*, which he classes as among the true oysters.

It seems the confusion may arise over the definition of the word 'pearl' since, according to another source, pearls can be produced in almost all molluscs—oysters, abalone, sea-pen (*Pinna*), and some freshwater mussels. But the oysters 'that are desirable as human food' do not produce pearls, nor do clams, scallops or mussels, 'since their shells have no nacre layer'. What this means is that although edible oysters do produce 'pearls', these do not have any lustre or the delicate play of surface colour called 'orient'—so, to most of us, they are not pearls at all but simply round chalky bits of waste. I have seen one from a Sydney Rock that was as big as a marble, but it wasn't very pretty.

Until a world slump in commodity prices in 1922, the manufacture of shell buttons had been a profitable industry, especially around the Red Sea. In 1959, a United Nations initiative encouraged farmers to try again, and as a result we have seen 'pearl' or shell buttons replacing plastic on even modest items of clothing. Even so, the pearl and pearl-shell markets have, in the past, been less commercially valuable than the food oyster market, in part because they are more restricted geographically and also because, until recently, they have shown much less potential for farming. The genus *Pinctada* is the oyster most found in tropical seas, since it prefers saline conditions far above those tolerated by 'true' oysters. It also tends to be found singly or scattered rather than in huge groups or beds, and at greater depths, which makes cultivation more difficult. Therefore it shouldn't be surprising to find that pearl oysters are fished off the coast of Venezuela and in Tahiti. In Western Australia, with a lucrative industry centred in Broome, the pearl-producing oyster is the silver or golden lip *Pinctada maxima*. In Japan, the largest producer of pearls, it is the *Pinctada martensii*.

Mikimoto, who is credited with beginning the cultured-pearl industry in 1883 (though there are some that would like to accord Saville-Kent that honour for the experiments he was doing in Western Australia), vowed he would 'adorn the necks of women the world over with his pearls'. And to a certain extent he has succeeded, although when he revealed his first pearls in Paris they were deemed fakes until a court case confirmed they were made from the same organic substance as a natural pearl. The ruling was that they should be called 'cultured' pearls to distinguish them from the natural ones which are designated by the word 'pearl' alone.

The culturing of pearls is different from finding or diving for the rare natural pearl. To make a cultured pearl, a suitable irritant—mud pellets, nacre beads, and even, as in China at one time, small leaden images of the Buddha—is surgically inserted into the tissues of the mollusc, after the valves are carefully pried apart. Because an oyster is notoriously hard to open, they are often narcotised beforehand by immersion in a menthol-seawater solution till the valves gape. Once recovered from the operation, the animal begins to coat the pellet with the nacreous substance it uses for part of its shell. (In 1897 the French apparently tried to grow pearls in abalone though this proved unsuccessful.) A cultured pearl may be harvested as soon as five months after this operation, or as late as seven years.

As is occurring all over the world, however, the Japanese pearl industry is in danger of going 'belly up' according to Toru Nishii, a grower who has been in the business for forty years. A newspaper report of August 1998 relates that an unknown disease is causing the death of up to 50 per cent of pearl-producing oysters in Japan. A government team recently speculated that it may be an infection of a parasite called 'perkinsus' (related to QX disease) which devastated oysters in the Mississippi River

Delta nearly fifty years ago. But some pearl growers suspect artificial insemination and other scientific tinkering may have inadvertently spawned oysters that are more prone to disease. 'Decades ago, growing pearls was a lot of work, but the oysters seemed healthier and happier', Mr Nishii says. 'Today the environment is terrible. The ocean is polluted and oysters are artificially enlarged so they produce bigger pearls. Something is not quite right.'

In the early days of the industry here, Aboriginal, Malay, Indonesian and Japanese divers risked their lives on the dangerous seabeds of Western Australia and the Northern Territory searching for natural pearls. Then in 1957, according to the *Western Australian News*, the first experiments in cultured pearl production were conducted on Thursday Island by a Canberra-registered company (who brought in Japanese experts) in conjunction with the CSIRO. But it was not until around 1965 that cultured pearl farming, as it is practised today, came about.

The growth rate of Australian pearls tends to be slow but they make up for this in size. In 1919 no cultured pearls were larger than 7 mm. During the 1930s they reached 12 mm. Australian pearls today can grow up to 17 mm. In 1965, the industry produced $2.7 million worth of pearls. Today it is worth around $300 million a year in exports. Production of shell and pearl meat (considered a delicacy in Asia) is also important. There is, at the moment, also research into pearl production being conducted in New South Wales using a native species *Pinctada imbricata*.

MFK Fisher claims to have been the only person she knows to have found a pearl—while eating oysters at

Galatoire's in New Orleans—and for a few seconds sat in 'a reeling dream of riches and royalties' until she recovered, finding it in truth to be 'small, brownish, rough, rather like an abnormally dingy piece of gravel' which she promptly forgot to take home. My daughter, who is the luckiest person on earth in terms of finding things (she is the one who finds twenty-dollar bills in parking lots, the streets of Paris littered with ten-franc coins and wads of lire stuffed in holes of old buildings), discovered a pearl at Greenwell Point, the first time she ever opened an oyster. It was hardly bigger than a pinhead—which we would have missed if Barry Allen hadn't pointed it out—embedded in the biggest feral Pacific I had ever seen that she had been breaking open with a screwdriver, but in fact was white and quite perfect in shape. Sadly, it was dropped and lost forever in the sand and shell bits at the bottom of the punt.

The point is that while almost any oyster will produce a 'pearl', the oysters that we most often eat do not make pearls of any value because the final product, even though it can be sometimes quite large (almost every oyster farmer and opener has a collection in a jar somewhere), is always greyish white and chalky, without any coating of nacre to give it the highly prized orient colour and reflective quality. So don't count on becoming rich by finding a priceless jewel while eating your dozen Sydney Rocks, just enjoy them.

chapter vii

A Gastronomic Nostalgia

HE WAS A BRAVE MAN WHO FIRST ATE AN OYSTER
Jonathan Swift, *Polite Conversation*

PERTH, PORTLAND, PARIS, Hilton Head, Hobart, Padstow, Puilacher, San Francisco, Sydney, Washington, Mèze, Montpellier, Melbourne, Sète, New York, Cowell, Canberra, Cancale, Vancouver, Launceston, New Orleans, Depot Beach: I have eaten oysters of a great many varieties in a great many places, and I seem to remember them all — unlike, say, eating a good steak or warm crusty bread. What is it about the oyster? Savouring your first one is like losing your virginity. No one forgets it. Maybe it is the implicit, inevitable allusion to sexual performance and desire, because the very physical nature of a freshly opened oyster can't help but remind one of the act of making love. Or, it may have to do with the ritual and romance of eating oysters, a delightful sensuality so well conjured up by Akhmatova's 'Evening'.

Perhaps Eleanor Clarke best explains it: 'It is briny first of all, and not in the sense of brine in a barrel, for the preservation of something; there is a shock of freshness to it. Intimations of the ages of man, some piercing intuition of the sea and all its weeds and breezes shiver you a split second from that little stimulus on the palate. You are eating the sea, that's it, only the sensation of a gulp of sea water has been wafted out of it by sorcery, and are on the verge of remembering you don't know what, mermaids or the sudden smell of kelp on the ebb tide or a poem you read once, something connected with the flavour of life itself.'

> Chekhov's body
> was shipped
> from Badeweiler to Moskow
> in a railroad car that said, in large letters
> FOR OYSTERS.
>
> ...
>
> Gorky didn't conceal his chagrin at the mistake.
>
> But what's so bad about oysters?
>
> Poets kept on ice
> (swimming in their liquour
> and bordered by lemon wedges),
> extracted from the shell
> (parsley, garlic, oil, thyme; grill), ...
>
> Miroslav Holub, 'Funerals'

Yes, what *is* so bad about 'for oysters'? Chekhov's was hardly an inappropriate ending for a poet, or anybody else for that matter, and an interesting recipe worth trying. From birth to the grave; life itself, and all its connections with the sea. 'I have often said that there is no true love short of eating and consequent assimilation' mused Samuel Butler in his notebooks:

A Gastronomic Nostalgia

> What ... can awaken less consciousness of warm affection than an oyster? Who would press an oyster to his heart, or pat it, or want to kiss it? Yet nothing short of its complete absorption into our own being can in the least satisfy us. No merely superficial temporary contact of exterior form will serve us. The embrace must be consummate, not achieved by a mocking environment of draped and muffled arms that leaves no lasting trace on organization or consciousness but by an enfolding within the bare and warm bosom of an open mouth—a grinding out of all differences of opinion by the sweet persuasion of the jaws, and the eloquence of a tongue that now convinces all the more powerfully because it is inarticulate and deals with but the one universal language of agglutination. We become one with what we love—not heart to heart—but protoplasm to protoplasm ...

Perhaps it is some kind of primordial memory we all share. After all, our very bodies are three-quarters water ...

One thing we humans don't seem to share with each other, or perhaps we're not *able* to share, is the same tastebuds. At least, we don't often have the same expressions for the same tastes. It's like vision—no one can see *exactly* the way another does, or *know* how another sees. Except for noting the fact that most people tend to find Sydney or Western Rocks have a stronger flavour than Pacific oysters, and flat Natives (particularly the wild ones) with their meaty texture even stronger still, I'm not going to attempt to describe the tastes of different oysters from different localities. An American oyster book which does attempt this contains three pages of fairly useless and wonderfully pretentious descriptions such as:

'slightly salty with a hint of watermelon', 'sweet with a musky almost spinachlike aftertaste', 'fruity overtones' and 'a zesty ocean flavor'. The following descriptions, however, may give an idea of the vast range of possible sensations evoked by eating an oyster, or at least illustrate the incredible variations in the ways we perceive them. In M F K Fisher's words: 'Then an oyster will taste like what the taster expects, which of course depends entirely on the taster.'

After complaining about the paltry number, the Roman poet, Ausonius (who also divides Gaul into three parts but, unlike Caesar, according to the quality of its oysters), describes a hamper sent to him of thirty oysters from the Médoc as 'of substance both full fat and snowy white, and with their sweet juice most delicately mingle some flavour of the sea touched with a fine taste of salt'. Certainly a more lyrical description than the results of an *Australian Gourmet Traveller* tasting which characterised 'mud' oysters (wild Native *angasi*) from Jervis Bay as 'meat and three veg' with 'a thick and—because it's wild—sulphur dioxide smelly shell'. An information sheet from the Freycinet Marine Farm describes the Native *angasi* oysters they grow in Great Oyster Bay as having a 'strong flavour and powerful aftertaste ... recommended for the serious oyster man or woman'.

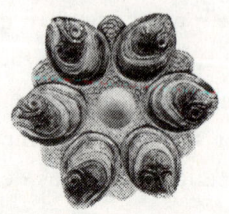

The *Gourmet Traveller* tasters went on to say that the Rocks from Wallis Lake had a 'rich full flavour, a good dose of iodine on the end palate' and those from the Clyde River were 'well-farmed', while Pacifics from southeast Tasmania elicited comments like 'pre-spawning, fat and creamy—a rich and most delicious "unoysterlike" flavour'.

Whereas Toussaint-Samat praised the *plates* refined at Belon as 'most expensive, fragile, iodized and best flavoured of all', his fellow countryman, Guy de Maupassant (in *Bel-Ami*) was able to appreciate oysters from the famous Belgian growing area of Ostende as 'small and rich ... melting between the palate and the tongue like salted sweets'. Naval officer and novelist, Captain Frederick Marryat, having also grown up on *Ostrea edulis* like Toussaint-Samat, writes with typical imperial condescension about American oysters (*Crassostrea virginicus*): 'very plentiful, very large, and, to an English palate, rather insipid. As the Americans assert that the English and French oysters taste of copper, and that therefore they cannot eat them, I presume they do, and that's the reason we do not like American oysters, copper being better than no flavour at all'. MFK Fisher thought 'the greenness and tepid brassiness of those shellfish [*Portuguaises vertes*] were at first a shock' though later said, 'I like the metallic tiny bites of the Olympias'. And according to Waverly Root, 'It is almost the unanimous opinion that *Ostrea* is the best-flavoured oyster in the world ... it sometimes recalls hazelnuts'. French *Ostrea edulis* are also often described as or having a 'nutty' flavour characteristic of oysters finished in the *claires*.

The Dutch researcher, Peter Korringa, had this to say about Sydney Rocks: 'The Australian oyster has a pleasant sweet flavour, especially when full of spawn, a condition which in many other types of oysters gives them an unpleasant oily tang. Also, they do not have the cucumber-like flavour so characteristic of that other *Crassostrea* species, the Portuguese oyster (*Crassostrea angulata*)'. The menu from The Fish House in Perth describes the Rocks from Albany as 'earthy, tannic & creamy', and goes on to say Tasmanian Pacifics are 'plump, sweet & briny', whereas South Australian Pacifics are 'reefy, juicy & briny'.

Clearly the knowledge of where the oyster comes from, and the time and place in which you eat it, all heavily influence your response. For example, according to Waverly Root 'the Romans were always ready to fall for the latest fashion, and decided, each time they discovered a new oyster, that it was better than any they had ever known before. They occupied southern Gaul and told themselves that the finest oysters were those fished between the eastern end of the Pyrenees and Narbonne. They pushed north and promptly promoted the oysters of Bordeaux to first place.' And so on and so on ... I wonder what the results of a blindfold taste test would be? (According to the New South Wales Oyster Farmers' Association, a study was conducted at the University of New South Wales using 4000 oysters given randomly to a panel of 36 people, who were asked to rate them on appearance, odour, flavour, texture and overall acceptability. Apparently the Sydney Rock came out 'way, way ahead'.)

But is there anyone alive who would not at least know *what* they were eating? Perhaps not ... exactly.

'It is open to question', writes Moguin-Tandon in *The World of the Sea*, 'as to whether it is judicious to enter into the details of the anatomical structure of the oyster; for, generally, when we dissect an animal it certainly does not improve our relish in eating it ... we warn the reader, if he is about to indulge in an oyster supper, not to read the description we are giving, lest by any chance it should blunt the edge of his appetite.' Even the most squeamish of readers can be assured, however, that the following few pages will do nothing except further their amazement and delight in this delectable creature.

ALL THE OTHER BITS YOU MAY HAVE WONDERED ABOUT

The actual body of the oyster occupies only a small area, less than a quarter of the shell, while the mantle, the sensitive outer sack, extends far beyond this. The gills, which are relatively enormous, are found in the mantle-cavity just inside from the margin and popularly known as the 'beard'. (This is the part the New South Wales Oyster Farmers' Association recommends that we hide by turning the oyster over. It can be slightly confusing here because the 'fringe'—that darker, lacy area around the edge which is actually the sensory 'tentacled' part of the mantle—is also sometimes called the beard.) Known as *ctendia* (little combs), the gills of molluscs carry on respiration as well as other functions, although the sedentary oyster doesn't need as much oxygen as it is actually capable of producing.

The gills hang down from the roof of the mantle-cavity like the leaves of a book held by its spine, making a series of 'sieves' or latticework—the whole thing creating the feeding surface over which cilia pass currents of water. This ciliary movement is so frantic that if a section of the gills is removed, it literally swims away and continues to 'row itself in a given direction so long as the cilia upon its surface continue their mysterious movements' (Rymer Jones in the *Aquarian Naturalist*, 1858). These cilia are too minute to be seen by the naked eye but are so numerous that they can create relatively strong water currents or move particles at a surprisingly high speed. So rhythmical is the beat of adjacent cilia, that various observers have described the ciliated surface viewed under a microscope, as resembling 'a field of corn blown by the wind', with waves of movement passing continually over it in the same direction.

The stomach, a sort of brownish mass near the centre of the oyster at the hinge end, is sometimes called the 'liver', and many believe this is the part of the animal that becomes fat, so that the oyster is occasionally thought of by some people as a kind of seafood pâté. (Of course it is actually the sexual organ which enlarges.) Apparently it has 'no resemblance whatsoever to the liver in vertebrates' and is what Professor Yonge would prefer us to term the 'digestive diverticula'. He then goes on to describe 'one of the most remarkable structures in the animal kingdom', the crystalline 'style', a kind of rod found in all bivalves, that projects out of a tube or sac and, in a healthy feeding oyster, continually rotates like a digestive eggbeater that keeps

A Gastronomic Nostalgia

everything well mixed and in contact with the walls of the stomach. The style is not something we would ever be able to see. Even zoologists have difficulty, since when the oyster is opened for examination the delicate tissues are pretty much destroyed and the style stops working. But this remarkable little 'wheel mechanism' can be seen through the transparent shells of larvae and early settled spat, rapidly rotating as if life depended on it, as of course it does.

When an oyster has been out of the water, or if its shell has been closed (i.e. when it has not been feeding) for some hours, its metabolic processes are put on hold: it no longer produces the style-substance, and the style dissolves. As a result there will be no normal digestion—the conversion of starches into glucose—or 'fattening' going on. Significantly, one of the things the style contains is a powerful oxidase system which helps to supply oxygen to the tissues. This may begin to explain why, even though an oyster can remain alive and well for many days when closed tightly out of the water, the sooner they are eaten, the fresher, the better and more delicate they taste. On the other hand, old timers in Tasmania, like some gourmands in France, believe that waiting two or three days after harvesting actually improves the flavour of an oyster.

When a good oyster is opened, the mantle, which has retained the sensory function (remember, an oyster has no head ... but yes, it does have a heart, with two auxiliary ones as well) and is chemo-receptive, will instantly withdraw if it is touched with certain substances such as lemon or vinegar. This means that the oyster is still alive and very fresh.

> Oyster, dear to the gourmet, beneficent Oyster, exciting rather than sating, all stomachs digest you, all stomachs bless you!
>
> Seneca

As well as the famous claims made for it as an aphrodisiac, the oyster has long been acknowledged for its therapeutic and nutritional value, even by the usually grumpy Seneca—thus Vancouver recording in his journal the 'sufficient supply of oysters, not only for our *convalescents...*' According to the New South Wales Oyster Farmers' Association, 'few foods compare with oysters in terms of nutritional value. The oyster is well balanced, easily digestible, nutritious food, rich in vitamins such as B1, B2, and C'. My research suggests vitamin A, rather than C, and the oyster is now credited with containing omega–3 as well. Probably most of the economists studying the problem of food for a growing world population would agree; oysters were, at many times in human history, an important source of nutrition for the poor. Oysters are considered to be one of the best-known stimulants to the appetite and very good for digestion, supposedly because of the high sodium-chloride content of the meat, and especially the liquid. Apparently, they are among the lowest of seafood in cholesterol, one quarter that of squid or prawns and equal to that of most fish, with levels well below the levels in red meats and duck. On top of all that, 100 oysters apparently contain fewer calories than 100 grams of steak; there are approximately 20 kilojules per oyster, or one gram of fat in a dozen. And for those of you who worry about such things, Pacific oysters have lower amounts of fat and cholesterol than Sydney Rocks, and Native *angasi* lower still.

Although the following example of Brillat-Savarin's 'science' from 1825 does not recognise the nutritional facts, the oyster's lack of calories and easy digestion are supported by his observations about oyster-eating. While praising the effects of the mollusc on appetite and digestion (he seems to rate truffles higher as an aphrodisiac, at least for the 'ladies'), he states categorically that 'shellfish, and especially oysters, provide little nourishing substance; and this is the reason they can be eaten immediately before a meal without any harmful effects'. He then adds in his own inimitable way:

> In the old days, a meal of any note usually began with oysters, and there were always a good many guests who did not stop before they had swallowed a gross (twelve dozen, a hundred and forty-four). Wishing to know the weight of this advance-guard, I investigated the matter, and found that a dozen oysters, water included, weighed four ounces, and a gross, therefore, three pounds. Now I am convinced that the same individuals, who were not prevented by the oysters from eating a copious meal, would have been completely sated if they had eaten a like quantity of meat, even if it had only been chicken.'

It will never be certain whether the attribution of the aphrodisiac qualities of oysters came about as a result of the increased nutrition and vitamins (and therefore stamina) they provided the eater, or because as a food it could be consumed in large quantities and still not cause the would-be lover to fall asleep due to a heavy stomach.

One theory is that oysters are high in zinc, a mineral thought to have some effect on sexual performance. What is true is that people believed it—and do, even to this day. The New South Wales Oyster Farmers' again: 'Folk lore indicates that New South Wales Rock Oysters have significant aphrodisiac effects. Whether this is fact or fiction is for you to determine.'

Although the great Casanova apparently consumed at least fifty oysters a day with his evening punch, most of the outrageous feats of oyster consumption we hear about usually feature not an extraordinary lover but an old or very fat man, often of the clergy. Instead it was as a restorative and 'health food' that oysters were taken by many. We are told, for example, that St Everond, eating raw oysters in the eighth century, far ahead of his time, still consumed several dozen for breakfast each day at the age of eighty-eight. Henry IV supposedly ate 300 or so in order to work up an appetite for dinner, and Louis XIV swallowed dozens daily. The fifteenth-century essayist Montaigne, moderate in all things himself, tells of a doctor whose self-prescribed dose was thirty to forty dozen, while Marshal Junot was reputed to have eaten 300, never fewer, every morning, probably along with his calisthenics, to keep himself fit. Napoleon apparently *degusted* many dozens of oysters before every battle—no doubt one of the secrets of his success. Describing a shore dinner in Bordeaux, Montaigne further enthuses: 'They brought us oysters in baskets ... They are so agreeable, and of so high an order of taste, that it is like smelling violets to eat them; moreover they are so

A Gastronomic Nostalgia

healthy, a valet gobbled up more than a hundred without any disturbance.'

In November 1840, returning to his base camp (now Eyre's Waterhole at Streaky Bay, South Australia), Edward John Eyre noted in his journal that:

> Around the camp were immense piles of oyster shells pretty plainly indicating the feasting of my men during my absence, while their strong and healthy appearance showed how well such fare had agreed with them.

And yet curiously, oysters, as water creatures without scales or fins, are among the shellfish prohibited to Jews, for whom they are considered 'unclean'. One commonsense theory for this is that given the climate of the southern and eastern Mediterranean, shellfish and crustaceans, which go bad quickly, were dangerous to eat unless freshly caught and that this prohibition was to protect health. They were not eaten by the Egyptians either and it is believed that many Jewish dietary customs originally came from Egypt.

Another explanation is more original and may be just as sensible: they simply didn't have any oysters to eat! This theory claims that the natural oyster beds which edged much of the Mediterranean simply stopped so abruptly after Greece that the ancient Assyrians and Babylonians had never heard of them. According to the food writer Waverly Root, the oyster 'is not mentioned in the Bible, probably not because it was, according to the definition of Leviticus, unclean, but because it was unknown'. He then quotes from *Antony and Cleopatra*: 'The firm Roman to great

Egypt sends/ His treasure of an oyster' and concludes 'Italy had oysters, Egypt had none'. One also has to wonder how much of a coded sexual message Shakespeare might have meant this to be.

※

> ... and indeed I am convinced that the angels eat, for the sheer pleasure of eating
>
> Gaulish monk

According to Toussaint-Samat's *History of Food*, the first mention of the way to eat a fresh *raw* oyster is in *Le cuisinier françois* published in 1664: 'You must open them, and choose the best, leaving them in their shells to eat fresh'. Apparently this was unusual for the time, since he continues:

> And when you find any that are a little tainted, add to them a little fresh butter and some breadcrumbs and a little nutmeg, and put on the gridiron; when they are cooked, heat the fire shovel until it is red-hot and pass it over them until they take colour; make sure you do it in such a way that they are not too dry, and then serve them.

Not a recipe whose main ingredient is recommended, but it certainly testifies to our ancestors' ability to eat almost anything and survive. *Le cuisinier françois* also has recipes for roasted oysters and oyster fritters. These are typical of the dishes found in cookery books from the fourteenth to the sixteenth century, which contain nothing about raw oysters. 'Perhaps', says Toussaint-Samat with a typical French shrug, 'transport systems still left something to be desired'. A common way to cook them was as a 'civey' (meatless stew), one author recommending 'they should be very well-washed' and 'scalded' first. In medieval life, obviously, cooking was mostly a way of attempting to sterilise, or at least neutralise harmful bacteria, and cover any unpleasantness caused by the food not being quite fresh. *L'ouverture de cuisine* (1604), for example, gives a recipe for 'oyster pie', in which it is recommended to 'wash the oysters in a little white [antiseptic?] wine'. Toussaint-Samat remarks that it would have been *'excellent*, if it included anything to thicken the sauce'.

Food critic and writer John Newton has supplied the following recipe, from Anne Blencowe's *Receipt Book* (1694), for an Oyster Pie. He suggests using Sydney Rocks or Natives:

Oyster Pie

Take a quart [a bit over a litre] of oysters and take off ye black fins [this would be the edge of the mantle or the beard, and not necessary with our smaller oysters] and wash 'em clean and blanch 'em and Drayn the liquor from them; then take a quarter pound of fresh butter and a minced anchovie and two spoonfulls of Grated bread, a spoonfull of minced Parsly, and a little pepper, and a little grated Nuttmeg, no salt (for ye anchovie is salt enough). Squese these into a lump, then line your Patepan with a good cold crust, but not flacky, and put one half of your mix's butter and anchovie etc, at the bottom; then lay your oysters, two or three thick at the most; then put to 'em ye other half of ye mixed butter and anchovie etc and pick some grayns of Lemon on ye top (and some youlks of hard egg if you like 'em). Put 2 or 3 spoonfulls of ye oyster liquor and close it with ye Crust which should be a good deal higher than ye oyster to keep in the liquor. Bake it, and when it comes out of the oven, cut up the Lid, and have ready a little oyster liquor and Lemon juce stew's together, and pour it in and cut ye Lid in Pieces and lay around it.

Other recipes 'modern chefs would not scorn to use', from Massialot in his 1691 *Cuisinier royal et bourgeois,* are for duck with oysters and an oyster and truffle sauce. And surprisingly similar to the *Le cuisinier françois* recipe for reject oysters, though not I think for the same reasons, is this one from 1936 for grilled oysters:

Surely, this recipe would not have the approval of the S.P.C.A. But it is probable that oysters possess a sensitivity analogous to that of the French tax-payer, so that they are incapable of very characteristic reactions. That, then is why there is little reason for weeping tenderly at the idea that these molluscs must be placed on the grill.

As they submit to the same end that overtook Saint Lawrence, the oysters open. It is exactly like the purse of the government pensioner as Income Tax Day rolls around: one does the only possible thing in the presence of bad luck.

Take advantage of their being open to pop in a little melted butter, some pepper, and some bread crumbs. Then close them up again: They will be too weak to resist you. Let them cook a little. And serve them very hot.

Some people like this very much.

Paul Reboux, *Plats du Jour*

Minus the butter, etc, and extra cooking, just throwing oysters on the barbeque *au naturel* ('You may consider that your fastidious taste is marvellously respected if they are washed first') is a fast and simple way of getting them open if you are too hungry to wait—the lids will gape after a few minutes or so, depending on how hot the fire is. (In America, the oysters are put on the barbecue plate, hosed down and then covered with a wet hessian bag—this takes longer.) A traditional recipe for roast oyster sauce provides an appropriate accompaniment for such a primitive repast:

Roast Oyster Sauce
2 tbls butter
juice of $^1/_2$ onion
juice of 1 lemon
Tabasco sauce to taste

Melt butter; mix in other ingredients, pour over oysters; serve hot!

Although cooked oysters were an important part of every chef's repertoire, by the seventeenth century, the eating of raw oysters had become quite the rage, so much so that Menon (*La cuisinière bourgeoise*, 1774) begins by saying that 'oysters are usually eaten raw with pepper'. But, he then goes on as an afterthought, 'They may also be served in their shells, cooked on the gridiron ... and when they begin to open of their own accord they are done. They are called soused oysters'. He adds, 'Oysters also serve to make ragoûts to eat with various kinds of meat ... heat them without boiling and serve them with whatever you think'.

One of the earliest recipes for oysters *is* a civey:

Civey of Oysters

Scald and wash the oysters very well, cook them in a broth and drain them, and fry them with onion cooked in oil; then take grated bread or coarse breadcrumbs, and put to soak in a purée of peas or in the boiled liquid of the oysters and some plain wine, and strain it; then take cinnamon, cloves, long pepper, grain of Paradise and saffron for colour, bray them and moisten with verjuice and vinegar and set aside; then bray your grated bread or breadcrumbs with the purée or the liquid of the oyster.

Le Ménagier de Paris, c. 1393

'Grain of Paradise' and all that 'braying' aside, I think I'll stick to fresh raw oysters on the half shell sprinkled with a little lemon juice.

Perhaps you might care to try

Apparently, the American Indians (who are credited with the first oyster stews) ate only cooked oysters. According to Cook's observation, the first Australians also enjoyed oysters roasted. The Chinese usually dried them or made them into sauce.

There seems to be generally two kinds of oyster-eater: those who will eat them if and only *if* they are cooked; and purists who find the idea of cooking an oyster difficult to come at, since one fresh out of the shell is so utterly delicious by itself. A variation on this type are the people who eat oysters only natural but *must* have them accompanied by the mandatory cream seafood sauce and buttered brown bread or it just *isn't* eating oysters. (I agree with John Newton when he remarks: 'if pink sauce is served, you are quite justified to throw it at the waiter'.) MFK Fisher describes a third category, who I'm sure exist though I'm not sure I've met one: 'those loose-minded sports who will eat anything, hot, cold, thin, thick, dead or alive, as long as it is *oyster*'. (Come to think of it, I do know a few ...)

> ... the true connoisseurs, however, swallow without lemon, vinegar, pepper or anything else
>
> Alexandre Dumas

Samuel Johnson, who was also against cooking oysters, described a dish of scalloped oysters as 'children's ears in sawdust' but the reminder that in Australia perfectly good fresh oysters already open — 'seconds' — can be had cheaply in a bottle which will keep in the fridge for up to two weeks, means you can have oysters more often. To borrow the words of Paul Reboux: 'I understand that you haven't much sympathy for hot oysters. But ... perhaps you could bring yourself to try the recipe[s] that follow'.

MFK Fisher's account of a 'thin young-old man' making oyster stew in Doylestown, Pennsylvania made me realise what I might have been missing. The main complication of this dish for those of us with ordinary kitchens is that it requires *three* small copper saucepans; you could manage with what you've got, but no doubt it won't be quite the same.

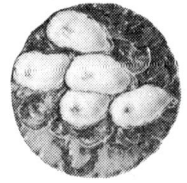

Oyster Stew

In the first pan put a knob of fresh [unsalted] butter.

In the second, oysters fresh from their shells (you could use bottled instead).

In the third, a cup of milk heated through.

As soon as the butter had frothed and settled he poured it quickly over the oysters and started skimming them around in the pan ... In about one minute ... he whiffed them past his questioning nose and then into the hot milk, which was just on the point of steaming. He put in red pepper and salt in a flash, and before I realized it the oyster stew I had so long talked about and waited for was under my nose, and the young-old man stood watching me.

Serve with a few drops of sherry *in the stew.*

Steamed oysters Chinese style may be a gentle way to coax an absolutely-no-way-am-I-going-to-eat-that-disgusting-thing sort of person into trying one.

Steamed Oysters

Scrub shells of Pacific oysters if not clean. Place cupped side down in Chinese steaming basket or stainless steel steamer. Cover with lid and steam until oyster shells are just open. While oysters are still hot (they will be only slightly cooked), remove lids carefully, you may need to use a tea towel to hold them. Sever muscle so that the oyster is free in the half shell. Try not to lose too much of the liquor in the process. Arrange oysters in their shells on large warm platter. Sprinkle with a little light soy sauce and finely slivered spring onions. Serve immediately.

A Gastronomic Nostalgia

Dressings for oysters on the half shell (cooked or raw) can be easily concocted with different variations of Asian herbs — such as fresh coriander, chilli, etc. — and sauces, so popular in Australia. It may be a handy way to blend oysters into an Asian meal, or an option when faced with a styrofoam tray of pre-opened oysters, or for those poor unfortunates who have had so many oysters that they need a change for a jaded palate.

Coral and Jade

For one dozen open oysters: 1 tsp finely chopped fresh coriander, 2 young spring onions slivered, ¼ red capsicum finely julienned. 2 tbs dry sherry, 3 tsps white vinegar (I recommend chinese rice vinegar), 1tbs light soy, 1 clove garlic crushed, 1 tsp finely grated ginger, 1 tsp Sambal Oelek, 1 tsp sugar.

Place vegetables in separate bowls of iced water. Combine all other ingredients except oysters. Just before serving, spoon dressing over chilled oysters, garnish with capsicum and spring onion.

A Thai version

Combine finely chopped red chilli, small clove garlic, and a quarter of a red capsicum with the juice of 2 lemons, 1 tbs of fish sauce and 2 tsp palm sugar. Spoon sauce over oysters. Garnish with lemon grass, slices of Spanish onion and lime leaves.

A Japanese version

For two dozen Pacific oysters. Peel a nob of fresh ginger, 1 cucumber, 1 carrot, ½ daikon radish. Cut into fine matchsticks about the length of oyster shell. Marinate in rice vinegar in fridge for at least an hour. Drain excess vinegar, scatter vegetables over open oysters.

For the epitome of New Year's Eve luxury—called 'Oysters Siegersdorf' (possibly because of the famous Barossa Riesling of the same name)—oysters natural with a sliver of smoked salmon and a half a teaspoon of black caviar, garnished with a feather of fresh dill.

Although oysters are a usual addition to seafood gumbo, it's not often you come across a gumbo made only of oysters. Both MFK Fisher and H Bolitho (*The Glorious Oyster*) give recipes for one. Here is a version which is cooked slightly differently depending on whether you have filé powder or not:

Oyster Gumbo

Clean and open 2 doz oysters removing from shells (or use bottled) reserving liquid. Sauté one finely diced onion in olive oil until cooked and very slightly browned (do not brown if you are using saffron). Blend in a tbs of flour, one red chilli finely chopped or chilli powder (then add a bay leaf if you are using saffron) and cook on low heat checking not to burn. (This is the all important 'roux' which should finish being the colour of brick.) Add oyster liquid, some water stirring to blend and cover the pan to cook for 15 minutes stirring occasionally. Add oysters. When oysters are just cooked (do not boil) stir through 1 tbs Louisiana filé powder if you have it or saffron to taste and let cook for another minute. Serve spooned over white rice.

Michael Klausen, executive chef for The Boathouse and The Bayswater Brasserie, shared this recipe with a session of the Sydney Seafood School:

Poached oyster tart with
poached egg and asparagus (serves six)
30 pacific oysters (choose ones with plenty of juice)
6 eschalots finely diced
4 tbs finely chopped chives
18 thick spears of asparagus peeled
150 g butter cut into small cubes
100 ml verjuice
200 ml Riesling
6 tart shells (10 cm) prebaked
6 eggs
white vinegar
salt and pepper

Drain juice from oysters into small saucepan. Cut asparagus into 3 cm long pieces and cook in boiling salted water until just tender. Keep warm. Combine the wine, verjuice and eschalots in small saucepan bring to boil and reduce to about 90 ml. Strain and set aside. Bring 6 tbs of the reduction to the boil and add enough cold butter whisking it over the boiling reduction until it achieves a sauce consistency (i.e. coats the back of a spoon). Season well with salt, pepper and chives. Set aside and keep warm. Heat the tart shells on tray in oven until warm through. Bring a small pan of water to the boil with a little vinegar in it. Slide the eggs in one at a time and poach until white is set. Set aside and keep warm. Poach oysters in their juice until just set (a couple of minutes). Drain well. Add a little liquid from oyster poaching to the sauce and stir through. Arrange 3 asparagus spears and 6 oysters around each warm tartlet shell. Place poached egg in the middle and top with warm sauce.

The famous Oysters Rockefeller was created by Jules Alciatore in 1899 for Antoine's in New Orleans. The cookbook (published 1980) from the restaurant mentions the dish but does not divulge the recipe, which got its name because it contains 'such rich ingredients that the name of the multimillionaire was borrowed to indicate their value'. The sauce is made up of eighteen different components but not, some aficionados argue, spinach. According to MFK Fisher, the only good Oysters Rockefeller are found at Antoine's; Gay Bilson's experience of the dish (only just acceptable) that she had at the Oyster Bar at Grand Central Station seems to bear this out. The following recipe (no resemblance to the New York one), developed for a special dinner at her Berowra Waters Inn does not claim to be authentic but 'one of the great dishes if made exactly as described':

Oysters Rockefeller

These amounts will make approximately 500 ml of purée which keeps well refrigerated. It also freezes well.

Oysters, freshly opened and unwashed (5–6 per serve as a first course)
300 g unsalted butter
750 g (English) spinach leaves (no stems), roughly chopped

25 g parsley, roughly chopped
75 g celery, chopped fine
50 g shallots, chopped
15 g French tarragon leaves
1 teaspoon Tabasco
1 teaspoon salt (adjust to taste)
50 ml Pernod in a plastic spray bottle
1 cup fresh, very fine breadcrumbs
rock salt

Melt the butter in a big pan and sauté the shallots and celery until translucent.

Add the spinach, parsley and tarragon and cook until the spinach leaves are wilted but have not lost their bright green colour. Toss all the while.

Purée this mixture in a blender until very smooth.

Add the second group of ingredients, adjusting the amount of breadcrumbs to make a mixture which will hold well when coating the oysters. It should be neither too thick nor too thin. Add salt to taste.

Coat each oyster so that the spinach mixture covers it entirely and has the appearance of a smooth mound (about 150 g of spinach mixture coats 6 Pacific oysters).

Pile rock salt onto an oven tray and place the oysters on this tray, burying the shells down into the salt. This not only makes them stable but protects the oysters from the high heat needed to cook the spinach mixture.

Bake in a very hot oven (at least 220°C) for about 8 minutes. The spinach should keep its shape and be piping hot (without having formed an ugly crust on top) but the oyster should still be creamy, and only warm.

To serve, place on a plate which has a bed of rock salt on it and spray with Pernod.

All the rest—Kilpatrick, etc.—can be found in ordinary cookery books. I will, however, mention an Australian standby, which at one time, was on the menu of every good restaurant and now hardly ever makes an appearance except in people's memories. A version of this recipe actually appears in Philpots, so it is probably an English classic and a good example of our early culinary inheritance.

Carpetbag Steak

Take a thick piece of rump or fillet steak, make a thin slit in the side with a sharp knife (being careful not to cut all the way to the edges of the steak) creating a 'pocket'. Salt and pepper the cavity. Stuff with raw shelled oysters (bottled seconds can be used) along with some butter. Secure with toothpick. Grill or barbecue steak to your liking.

I have friends—fortunately for them they happen to be oyster farmers—who also do a variation of this by stuffing fish (usually blackfish) with oysters. They swear it is absolutely delicious.

Another popular British recipe which intrigues me—not so much for the end result but for its name—is called Angels on Horseback (in French—*Brochettes d'Huitres à L'Anglaise*):

Depending on their size, take a dozen shelled (or two dozen bottled oysters) and wrap with thin bacon (in some recipes it is recommended this be cooked enough to reduce fat but not enough to make it crispy) and thread on a skewer or secure with toothpicks. Grill until bacon is cooked and serve with buttered toast points and lemon wedges. (The *Larousse Gastronomique* also recommends a grinding of white pepper.)

A Gastronomic Nostalgia

The combination of pork with oysters is not uncommon: in the oyster-growing area of Arcachon, near Bordeaux, a regional speciality is local oysters served with chipolata — fresh salty sausages which are either grilled or fried.

At one time the oysters themselves were very often fried. One recipe in a book by a British writer says that 'though it may be considered sacrilegious by connoisseurs', in Australia and New Zealand 'oysters were removed from their shells, rolled in flour and plunged into moderately boiling fat, to which several sprigs of parsley were added at the same time and then served straight from the pan with slices of lemon'. I wonder if this was the same 'Fried Oysters' listed on the early David Jones menus?

Finally, here is a recipe for oysters mornay which truthfully I would have scoffed at a year ago, though I have since been converted. Not being an oyster farmer, when cooking it myself I add mushrooms to stretch the dish (apparently artichoke hearts are also good). It's based on Barry Allen's recipe, so I'll call it Barry's Oyster Mornay:

Clean mushrooms (any kind or combination is fine) and cut in half if large. Sauté in butter and remove to casserole or baking dish. Using same pan make a little roux with more butter and some flour (here's the secret—*not too much flour*), add cream and stir over low heat until thickened. Add cheese (tasty or mozzarella and Parmesan if you want). Add cayenne (and optional herbs—I used a sparing amount of chives, tarragon and fresh thyme). Take a bottle of opened oysters, drain liquid reserving a little to be used to adjust sauce if necessary. Add oysters to casserole with mushrooms, pour over mornay sauce, cover with fresh breadcrumbs, a sprinkle of cheese and the herbs if you are using them. Bake in a moderate oven until bubbling and golden on top.

Serves two as a main meal with salad or four as an entrée.

In America, oysters on the half shell are always served with Tabasco, that ubiquitous condiment in the familiar little green and red bottle that can be found in everybody's kitchen. I didn't know until recently that it was actually invented to go with oysters. The story is that a veteran of the Mexican–American War returned home to New Orleans with some red pepper (chilli) seeds in his pocket and planted them. His friend Edmund McIlhenny used the peppers to make a hot sauce particularly suited to accompany oysters (remember early gourmands recommended a dash of black pepper) and started marketing it as Tabasco in 1868. Tabasco now makes a green variation of the traditional sauce based on jalapeños, and many Australian oyster connoisseurs think this the better choice if one has to have one's oysters hot. Another typical American accompaniment is a version of seafood sauce made with tomato ketchup, horseradish, Worcestershire sauce and a drop of lemon juice. Sometimes at oyster bars you will find the horseradish and Worcestershire on their own and often there will be a fresh salsa of some kind, as well as the *de riguer* bowl of oyster crackers.

In France, oysters *naturel* are brought to you with buttered rye bread, lemon quarters and mignonette sauce, which is basically a dressing made of wine or champagne vinegar and chopped shallots (and sometimes freshly ground white pepper) which you can spoon over your oysters. One recipe says the 'classic' mignonette is made with white-wine vinegar, but I have had it in a restaurant in Montpellier made with a strawberry vinegar with no evidence of shallots.

Australians generally serve oysters natural with lemon quarters (MFK Fisher recommends putting the juice of the lemon on the bread, not the oysters) and frequently a small dish of that pink seafood sauce. But there are many ways to serve an oyster, as can be seen by the inventiveness of our restaurateurs and chefs.

THE WAY THEY LOOK

> Trash is always abundantly decorated; the luxury object is well-made, neat and clean, pure and healthy, and its bareness reveals the quality of its manufacture.
>
> Le Corbusier, *The Decorative Art of Today*

Reading this I can't help thinking immediately of an oyster. Another French writer, Roland Barthes, likening a tray of Japanese food to a painting, considers the 'rawness' of Japanese food 'essentially visual'. So too the rawness of an oyster, glistening on the half shell, as if on its own individually designed porcelain plate. If more than one is arranged on a platter of ice a composition develops, becoming more complicated, more orchestrated, but still retaining the simplicity and harmony of natural things which have not been interfered with by human beings through processing or chopping up, cooking or saucing.

Elements of texture and subtle tones combine, size and shape interact, but the thing remains itself, pure, the smell only its own, the taste without distraction.

Still-life painting is a reflection of a society's view of itself and its attitudes towards things—their possession, acquisition and value or meaning. These have changed significantly through the centuries as the 'process of selection [in a still life] is traditionally influenced by the role certain objects play in the context of a given society... their choice is dictated by their place, be it passive or aggressive in a historical or cultural fabric' (M Rowell in *Objects of Desire*). While once, the representation of objects—including oysters—was usually symbolic of *vanitas*, later, in the hands of the Dutch genre painters, it became an exhibition of material possessions, almost as if these could be increased by being reflected in a hundred mirrors.

In the late nineteenth and early twentieth century, modern painters such as Manet, Braque, and Rousseau used oysters, among other similar subjects, to express a celebration of life and the senses, as well as a means of developing or exhibiting a particular style. Even Turner, in an early work, carefully paints oysters lying on a beach with uncharacteristic detail. Then there is Matisse's *Nature Morte aux Huîtres* in which the 'cooler yellow of the lemons' is in contrast to the 'harsh geometry' of the dark blue tablecloth, 'where the oysters are handled with poetic lushness'. Titles like 'Plate of Oysters', 'The Oyster-Eater', 'The Oyster Luncheon' abound in the catalogues. Many of the world's artists have worked at depicting the beauty of the oyster—an intriguing study in texture and light on surfaces: rough and uneven as well as smooth, lustrous and wet—and its allusions to sensuality, pleasure, luxury and the mystery of the sea.

By mid-century, however, still-life had come more and more to work at a subversion of the object, often as a social comment, a parody, a joke or an attempt to jolt the viewers' routine reactions and expectations. I can't help remembering the impact of a large pot—complete with lid—piled full of glazed black mussels in the Hirshorn Gallery, Washington, DC. One can think of hundreds of ways the image of an oyster could be used to shock or amuse. And given that the 'immediacy and cultural resonance of food' (according to the Museum of Contemporary Art's catalogue for the 1998 'Eat' exhibition) 'allows some of the traditional boundaries of art to be broken down', one would think that the oyster might be a recurrent image in Australian art. But perhaps there is

still a respect, a kind of reluctance to use this most delectable and much enjoyed food in such a way. Or perhaps it's just 'already been done'.

Yet oysters have always been an important subject in Aboriginal ceremonial objects and painting: 'Centre is a great tongue of rock. There are oysters all around ...' The National Gallery holds bark paintings with such titles as 'Oyster Dreaming', 'Oysters, rangga and lizzard' and 'Oyster Beds and Bundarrarr [waterlilly]'. But so far I have come across only one painting containing the beautiful mollusc by a white Australian artist—a Brett Whiteley entitled 'Magnolias'. Archibald winner Garry Shead has, however, done a nude on the *inside* of an oyster shell.

I once asked an artist friend why few Australian artists painted still-lifes any more. She seemed unable to speak, looking at me in amazement. I quickly added, 'What about platefuls of oysters for example, like the French?' Her answer was quick and to the point: 'They have no form, of course.' Strangely, this is the very thing that the Japanese artist Hokusai, drawing them from every angle, so delighted in.

At the moment it seems that if oysters are represented at all it is not so much for themselves as a 'signature' in a portrait of a well-known chef. And lately, a whole new business of photographing them, usually glistening on a bed of ice, has taken off for use in food magazines, wine and even chocolate advertisements.

Interestingly, one of the most successful Australian paintings, even though it doesn't actually depict oysters,

A Gastronomic Nostalgia

is in a sense an indirect celebration of the delectable mollusc and the elegance associated with them. One can easily imagine the graceful diners of 'The Lacquer Room' by Grace Cossington Smith, as having just finished, or waiting for, their plate of fresh oysters *naturel*. This picture (in the Art Gallery of New South Wales) is named in fact, after the newly opened David Jones tearooms, described contemporaneously in *The Australian Caterer* (March 1928) as the 'latest in restaurant appointments' with its 'almond green chairs and dainty glass topped tables'. The equally touted adjoining restaurant listed at the top of its à la carte menu 'oysters on shell, large' at 3/6.

The Oyster King as he came to be called, Peter Samios, after immigrating to Australia from Greece around 1912, opened a fish and oyster shop in George Street opposite the railway. Years later, at the David Jones oyster bar (which became the Seafood Café in the new Market Street Food Hall in 1953) the King opened over 750 000 oysters a year. 'Large oysters Natural' went for 3/9; 'a large Mornay' or 'Fried' for 5/-. 'Cocktail sauce' was an extra 6d.

> Every morning at 9 o'clock a fresh load of oysters several feet high awaits him for opening. As DJ's only full-time oyster opener he opens and plates approximately 200 dozen a day for service over the counter in the new Seafood Café ... Although the long hours on his feet do not worry him, he says his arms grow weary toward the end of a busy day's oyster opening. PS: Peter has never yet struck a pearl!
>
> *The David Jones Store News*, July 1953

The tradition of serving oysters at DJ's began in 1914 and they are still available at the oyster bar in the food hall at Elizabeth Street today, although sadly no longer opened on the spot by the likes of the Oyster King.

While it may seem to some watching the number of oyster bars springing up recently all over Australia that we are experiencing a new phenomenon, I suspect that there is something cyclical about it. We get tired of the trends and food fads, the complicated entrée lists 'two pages' long, and become re-interested in oysters, searching for and demanding them fresh and freshly opened. It's simple and real and unchangeable, as the history of the world's unchallenged delight in the oyster confirms.

THE RITUALS OF DINNER

> Mastication, digestion are all transformations of the processes of growing, gathering, slaughtering, refining and cooking food, as is the labour that goes into its presentation and the event which culminates in all the mores of the table. What is remarkable about the traditions surrounding food are the ways in which every culture follows means, some elaborate, others strict, of justifying how an item of food has come into being ... 'the rituals of dinner'.
>
> Adam Geczy, 'The Rhetoric of Restaurants'

There are many ways of presenting oysters natural. During the Victorian age there was such a craze for them that special plates with oyster-sized and sometimes oyster-shaped depressions (usually six), were manufactured in Europe and the United States in an unbelievable variety,

A Gastronomic Nostalgia

from the exquisiteness of Lalique to the downright kitsch. Apparently a perfect hostess was expected to have exactly the right equipment and tableware to present each and every kind of food.

When serving oysters at home, we always follow a certain ritual, placing a quantity of ice (if it's a special occasion, the ice may be cracked) on a large platter upon which we then sit the oysters, which have usually been opened then and there, in their half shell (neither turned over, nor rinsed) with a few lemon wedges. Some antique silver oyster forks from France add a little elegance. Perhaps to our guests' surprise there is no seafood sauce, no bread and butter, but always a decent white wine or champagne. So far no one has complained.

Another way, which sets off the beauty of the oyster as an object and shows the subtlety of its colours, is using a large, round, metal tray, with a sprinkle of very coarse sea salt, on which the oysters are placed with a few lemon wedges. Using a bed of sea or rock salt is also the traditional way of serving Oysters Rockefeller to keep the shells upright, not spilling the oyster and its mixture of secret ingredients; the salt does not react with the high oven/grilling temperatures. Placing open oysters on salt is a very common way of serving them in the United States, although I think chilling them on ice brings out their flavour and enhances their sea-brine freshness.

A restaurant in Perth serves oysters in a very different way—a glass bowl filled with coarse sea salt that has been mixed with tiny shells and bits of seaweed. The opened oysters, with their lids replaced, are then piled on top with a garnish of lime wedges. It is pretty, though not completely practical since the oysters are a little more fiddly to get at. Replacing the lids and piling oysters is often done in France, frequently on a bed of seaweed or with a few strands of it for decoration. Another French device which is popular in Australia and also used in England, is the *plateau de fruits de mer*, or oyster tray. The practical purpose of this metal contraption—some of which remind me of a woman's whalebone underskirt or perhaps a barrel with most of its stays missing—seems mainly, especially if it is tiered, to be able to present a very large amount of seafood without taking up much space on the table. With a more modest dozen, it serves to raise the plate of oysters to lip level (so as not to spill the liquor?) and provide a little bowl in the middle for the mignonette sauce. It may also be a way of making sure everyone else in the restaurant can see you are enjoying oysters.

Perhaps one of the most elegant presentations of oysters I have seen is a thick, white serviette/napkin folded twice into a triangle with the most pointed corners folded under to form a kind of chevron or shield shape which is placed on a very large, round, white dinner plate. A generous scoop of crushed ice is then put on top of the napkin, and the oysters arranged in a fan (sometimes in two rows, depending on the number) using the shape of the napkin as a guide, with two lemon wedges at the top. It is a clean and very pure way of showing off the oysters and has the added advantage of soaking up any melted ice water.

The variations are endless, but whatever way you choose to present oysters *naturel* there are really only two hard and fast rules: keep it simple, and make sure the oysters are absolutely fresh. Who was it that said 'the true art of gastronomy is to respect perfection'?

※

Many oyster aficionados believe that an oyster should not be eaten with a fork but raised to chin level in its shell and then, along with all the juices, scooped out with an oyster knife into the mouth. Some recommend tilting back the head and giving the oyster a gentle nudge with the fingers, some just letting it slide in. I've even seen someone employ a car key. I very much prefer using a fork — but not a normal one. The French have a lovely oyster fork, shaped somewhat like a little shovel with tines, which allows you to cut the adductor and scoop out the flesh and juice at the same time. Then one sips whatever liquor might be left in the shell. Failing a *fourchette a huître*, many restaurants provide a slim seafood fork, or an escargot fork. A cake fork is also possible. But not, I would suggest, a large fork and other normal table cutlery — much too unweildy and better to use none at all.

A strange myth which has persisted about the eating of oysters is that one should swallow them or let them slide down the throat whole without chewing. It appears this came to have something to do with the idea of being well bred, especially in the case of 'ladies', who were not supposed to enjoy raw shellfish. But, as Philpots remarks,

> The ancients, our teachers in all arts, but especially in aesthetics, did not bolt the oyster, but masticated it. With true Epicurean tact, they always extracted the full enjoyment out of the good things set before them. Not so we: most of us now bolt them; but this is a mistake, for the oyster has a much finer flavour, and is far more nourishing when well masticated.

It is difficult to understand why anyone would voluntarily eat something without enjoying the full pleasure of it which Frank Moorhouse describes as 'half-having an oyster'. So much of the experience of eating one comes by chewing and savouring the texture, which, like the taste, varies with the kind of oyster. Those molluscs bred and handled properly will always invoke the extraordinary sensation of eating the essence of the sea.

THE OYSTER AND A GLASS

> Some of these nights when twilight lasts until so late, all I want is oysters, six in their crimped shells with pepper and lemon, no other salt than their own, with bread and a glass of iced wine; like Isak Dinesen in her old age, whose doctor ordered her to live on oysters and champagne.
>
> Beverly Farmer, *The Seal Woman*

Perhaps the epitome of luxury and indulgence has always been champagne and oysters. Undoubtedly wine and oysters go together. And good oysters deserve a good wine. A simple principle as to what wine to have is that it should be crisp and delicate so as not to overpower the taste of the oysters, but still with definite flavour. Generally, the wine should have some fruit and complexity but not too much of either, and a dry or acid finish. A chablis style, which in Australia we now generally refer to as Sauvignon Blanc or a Semillon, is always a good choice, as is a dry Riesling. A Chardonnay is also fine as long as it is not too oaked. In France, on the northern *Route de Huître*, Muscadet is often served when tasting oysters, and in the south there is a specially grown oyster wine called *picpoule* or 'wine of the sands'. A Sancerre can also be good. And if you are a red-wine devotee, you might try a light Pinot or, at a pinch, a sparkling burgundy.

In a discussion about the local Native oysters served in a restaurant in Perth, the head waiter, hearing I was writing a book on the subject, earnestly asked me if it was true that oysters go hard in your stomach if you eat them while drinking hard white liquor. Although I had come across lots of strange ideas about oysters, I had never heard of that one. My first thought was: Look out all you shooter drinkers! (A 'shooter' is a shot-glass-sized Bloody Mary containing a raw oyster—both eating and drinking at once.) Much later I discovered a British *Daily Telegraph* report, from the 1940s or 1950s I think, of something similar—an experiment performed by a Doubting Thomas after reading the Scotch Whisky Committee's handbook— which attempted to debunk the belief that drinking whisky with shellfish was injurious to your health. Our sceptic, in true scientific fashion, placed an oyster in each of two wine glasses. In one he poured a little whisky, in the other a little gin. The oyster in the gin quickly dissolved. The oyster in the whisky became 'completely fossilized under his eyes'. He 'therefore doubt[ed] whether the association of whisky and shellfish is as harmless as is claimed'. It seems that at one time a mixture of brandy and water was often had with oysters, but whether this was a good idea is something you'll have to decide for yourself.

Many people, especially in the British Isles, enjoy their oysters with a glass of beer or stout, possibly because when oyster-eating started there, there was no wine to have them with, and later, even if there was, most couldn't afford it. It may also have to do with the fact that the native oysters in Britain are the flat *Ostrea*, which generally have a stronger, meatier taste than species of Crassostreinae. In spite of one critic's opinion that Guinness with oysters is 'not so much a marriage as domestic violence', this combination is a popular (and surprisingly pleasant) choice internationally, so much so that for the last fifty years Guinness has sponsored probably one of the biggest oyster festivals in the world in Galway, Ireland at the end of September each year where more than 100 000 prime Irish oysters are consumed. If you like your beer and prefer it over wine, or as a change, choose a light beer or a smooth, lightly hopped lager to compliment but not dominate the flavour of the oysters.

POVERTY AND OYSTERS

> Of restless nights in one-night cheap hotels
> And sawdust restaurants with oyster-shells
>
> T S Eliot, 'The Love Song of J. Alfred Prufrock'

Jane Grigson writes in her classic *Fish Cookery*, of the *horreur* of her neighbour (she was living in France at the time) when she told him the cost of a dozen oysters in England: 'But Madame, how does the working man pay for his oysters?' *Fish Cookery* was published in 1973 and even things in France have changed since then, but it still serves to illustrate a point. Oysters have gone from being the 'palm and pleasure' on the Emperor's table to sustenance for starving colonists, to entrées at the banquets of kings and millionaires, to poor people's food, and back again. Wars have been fought over oyster rights both on the Thames, between the fishermen of Essex and Kent, and on the Chesapeake between Marylanders and the Virginians. Recently in Australia, a hatchery was actually broken into and subjected to industrial sabotage. It is difficult to think of another edible commodity in the history of human beings which has had such a chequered career and extremes of fortune.

In a suit of 1680, the people of the state of Maryland listed among their grievances 'that their supply of provisions becoming exhausted, it was necessary for them, in order to keep from starvation, to eat oysters taken from along their shores'. I have never had the opportunity to eat as many oysters as I wanted (except perhaps at the New South Wales Oyster Farmers' Association annual luncheon

where we *began* with two dozen each and saw 1700 dozen devoured in about an hour!) nor to get tired of them. This reminds one of Brillat-Savarin's famous anecdote about Monsieur Laperte, who was also extremely fond of oysters and 'used to complain of never having eaten enough of them, or, as he put it, "had his bellyful of them".' 'I decided to provide him with that satisfaction', writes Brillat-Savarin, 'and to that end invited him to dinner':

> He came; I kept him company as far as the third dozen, after which I let him go alone. He went up to thirty-two dozen, taking more than an hour over the task, for the servant was not very skillful at opening them.
>
> Meanwhile, I was inactive, and as that is a distressing condition to be in at the table, I stopped my guest when he was still in full career. 'My dear fellow', I said, 'it is not your fate to eat your bellyful of oysters today; let us have dinner.' We dined: and he acquitted himself with the vigour and appetite of a man who had been fasting.

Alas I have never come across a Brillat-Savarin of my own but I do not think it is because of lack of generosity on my friends' and acquaintances' part (certainly my oyster-farmer friends have tried). Rather it is because, though the oyster is still an affordable luxury for most, it is no longer as cheap as when Sam Weller opined in *Pickwick Papers* that 'poverty and oysters always seem to go together'. Replying to Mr Pickwick's confusion, Sam explains:

> What I mean Sir ... is, that the poorer a place is, the greater the call there seems to be for oysters. Look here, sir; here's a oyster stall to every half-dozen houses—the streets are lined with them. Blessed if I don't think that ven a man's wery poor, he rushes out of his lodgings, and eats oysters in reg'lar desperation ...

In London at the time (1836) about 800 million oysters were consumed a year. The less delectable specimens were hawked for as little as 12 pence a peck (about two gallons dry measure). (Maybe this is where the taste for the combination of beer or stout—poor people's drink—and oysters started?) In the coastal cities of America during the 1850s, oysters could be had for six cents for all you could eat. In 1866 in Hobart, 1000 oysters cost 55 shillings. Thomas Tripcony, from Cornwall, who was one of the first licensees in Queensland, took up oystering in the 1860s around Moreton Bay and sold his produce in Brisbane at 5 shillings (about 50 cents) a bag which contained around 91 kg. Sometimes when things were a bit tougher he would hawk buckets of oysters for a shilling. Early in this century, oysters from the Hawkesbury were peddled around the state in baskets and bottles—1/6 (15 cents) for the 'lady's waist' size and 6d for a half bottle. People even apologised for serving oysters, as in 'Two Pendants for an Ear', a William Carlos Williams poem circa 1949:

> 'Has she eaten anything yet?
> Six oysters—she said
> she wanted some fish and that's
> all we had'.

So what has happened?

As has always been the case, what was scarce was considered a luxury and expensive; what was easily got was cheap. Though oysters were abundant on the shores of the Roman Empire, people were especially mad for the ones that had to be brought with difficulty far distances from the provinces—British natives were especially prized, as well as those famous lake-cultivated 'beautiful eyebrows'. Coastal inhabitants have always eaten oysters along with other shellfish, and as the supply was abundant and became more easily transported to the cities during the Middle Ages, oysters were no longer only a luxury of the king's table—as we can see from the cookery books. Then there comes a point (sooner or later depending on the place) where oysters are fished out, the natural beds depleted and oysters again become an expensive indulgence savoured only by the rich, eventually becoming a sign of respectability and refinement, to be emulated at all costs.

※

Around 1920, we find Queensland Fisheries Inspector J H Stevens writing in his annual report that 'interstate demand has been significantly reduced' due to World War I, 'oysters being looked upon more as a luxury than an ordinary article

A Gastronomic Nostalgia 285

of diet, especially when 1s.6d per plate of twelve oysters is charged ... the growers have reduced the wholesale price per sack in Brisbane by 20% but no corresponding reduction has been made in the prices charged to the public in retail shops'. No doubt World War II also affected the oyster industry and the subsequent supply of oysters—especially in terms of shipping—as it changed so many aspects of the Australian way of life. One perhaps far-fetched but fervently held theory is that the amount of explosives dropped into the world's oceans actually caused a serious decline in the oyster beds themselves. As a labour-intensive industry (but not a primary one), and thought to produce a 'luxury' item, oyster farming suffered from a scarcity of workers during and between the wars. Apparently just before World War II, recruits on R&R stationed near the Great Barrier Reef used their spare time to collect oysters in jam jars they had carefully saved for the purpose. Five or six oysters would usually fill the jar.

The revival of the industry in the 1950s would have been an important source of re-employment but, to quote John Newton, 'it was an article of faith that the Sydney

Rock oyster was "the best in the world" and, in the words of one Australian folk hero, "don't you worry about that". This kind of neglectful respect led to a complacent industry, a degraded ecosystem and — perhaps inevitably — a series of health scares.' What we've seen in the late 80s and 90s has been a renewed interest, coupled with innovations in aquaculture techniques, especially in Tasmania with the Pacific-oyster industry. This has coincided generally with the 'radical rethinking' that has made Australia a producer of fresh regional food that is recognised worldwide.

'The oyster is probably the most famous comestible *arriviste*', according to food writer and broadcaster Alan Saunders, who, as an immigrant to Australia, finds that 'my personal history of oysters echoes that of the chook; they still taste special to me, even though I'm now nearly in a position to test Grimond de la Reymiere's claim that they cease to whet the appetite after the first seven dozen.' Ordinary people can still afford to eat oysters, but not in most restaurants any more, and certainly not if they expect the best quality. We have definitely come to a time when not only demand dictates cost, but handling and middle-men as well. A good example of this is the very popular Roma Restaurant in Fremantle where a dozen oysters still cost 'only' $16; but this is the second most expensive thing (next to crayfish) on the menu — a good fillet steak with spaghetti is only $12.95. On the other hand, if you can open your own, oysters are still quite an affordable luxury, especially if you get them directly from the farmers themselves. Unfortunately, we may see a day — if population/pollution problems are not solved—when there are so few *good* oysters produced, that once again only the very wealthy will be able to afford them.

A WAY OF LIFE

> I don't know anything about oysters beyond their occasionally getting irritated and coming up with a pearl. I haven't eaten any for years but as a child was fond of oyster soup which was like a thick white sauce containing whole oysters and the liquor from them plus lemon juice. I thought it wonderful.
>
> the poet Bruce Beaver, in a letter to the author

Since the moment human beings worked out how to get an oyster open, there have been rituals and customs attendant on its eating, from bashing and slurping al fresco, to the backyard oyster roast, to the more sophisticated degustation described by Brillat-Savarin. Early on, in any major city near an oyster industry, one could buy a bucket of oysters freshly shucked from a vendor on the street (in the seventeenth century during the reign of Louis XIV there were at least 2000 oyster sellers in Paris) or in a house or 'eating establishment' developed especially for the purpose. Dickens noted with delight the number of 'oyster cellars' (850 of them by 1874) in New York and commented, 'pleasant retreats say I!'.

In Australia, it's probable that the first trade in oysters was carried on by convicts who sold or bartered them with the officers and soldiers of the penal colonies. Later oysters were collected and hawked around by cart. Even today there is a clever man who goes around the caravan park at Umina Beach with a little wagon full of fresh oysters which he will open for you if you want. (The normal cost for such an extra service—a cold tinnie and maybe a bit of a yarn if he has the time.) He gets his oysters from his own leases at Brisbane Waters and has been selling them this way for nearly twenty years.

From the 1850s until the 1930s in Australia oyster saloons and kiosks were the main retail outlets for oysters, probably a great relief from a fairly monotonous and limited diet. The proprietors of these establishments (in the early days, very often of British origin) bought the oysters by the sack directly from the oystermen and opened them themselves on the spot, a guarantee of freshness against lack of refrigeration and unreliable transportation.

Descriptions from the 1870s illustrate the features of a well-run oyster saloon and also give some idea of their importance in the social networks of the colonies: 'the rooms are always clean and the supply of oysters obtained daily'; 'those who visit the place will find the proprietor civil and obliging', 'catering to the best people in the colony' or 'working up the best business connection of this kind'. They usually noted that 'the goods [were] the best in the business', 'supplying nothing that will detract from the reputation of a first-class oyster and refreshment room' which was often 'attractively fitted up with shells, ferns, flowers, etc.'

As early as 1849, oysters for 'consumption on the premises' were being advertised in a local newspaper in South Australia, and as late as 1920, a typical advertisement

A Gastronomic Nostalgia

in a Queensland newspaper for Baxter's Oyster Saloon (established in 1862) was still enticing:

> **Visitors to Brisbane** should not fail to give this little old place a call. Famed throughout Australia for its Oysters and Crabs. Situated at the bottom of the hill right near Cabbage Tree creek; it is easily located by the Flag Pole. Crab and Oyster Suppers provided in Private Rooms at short notice The Oysters are always kept in water and taken out as required Boats for Hire [sic]

Besides 'oyster kiosks' in coastal towns, like the J M Phillip's at Redcliffe in Queensland or the Five Ways Oyster Saloon in Woolloongabba, 'oyster bars' and 'parlours' were very popular in cities at the turn of the century (many of the later proprietors were Greek), among them the Cosmopolitan Oyster Parlour on Pitt Street near the corner of King in Sydney and the one located on Angel Place which many people may still remember. In Perth there was the Oyster Bar

on Barrack Street and P Auguste's Oyster Saloon in East Fremantle. Moreton Bay oysters were regularly supplied to Andonicos' Oyster Saloon in Toowoomba. South coast oysters were freshly opened by a Greek from Kithira at the Niagra Café in Bega.

> As I ate the oysters with their strong taste of the sea and their faint metallic taste that the cold white wine washed away, leaving only the sea taste and the succulent texture, and as I drank their cold liquid from each shell and washed it down with the crisp taste of the wine, I lost the empty feeling and began to be happy and make plans.
>
> Ernest Hemmingway, *A Moveable Feast*

I have had the good fortune in my younger days to go to quite a few clambakes, but never to an oyster roast. These were very popular in America and Australia anywhere oysters were available and cheap. Imagine being able to eat as many as you liked straight off the fire on a warm summer night! A friend in his seventies remembers oyster-eating contests in Sydney. I've not been able to find out anything else about them, and I'm left wondering how many oysters the winners would have been expected to consume.

Oysters seem to afford most people both a gastronomic and a sentimental pleasure. It may have something to do with the specialness oysters bring to an occasion: whether they're eaten sitting on a beach or at a sumptuous dinner, we remember it. Brillat-Savarin writes charmingly of a scene from 1801 that could have taken place today:

A Gastronomic Nostalgia

At the appointed hour my two guests appeared, newly shaved and carefully combed and powdered; two little old men, still hale and hearty ... They smiled with pleasure when they saw the table ready, a white cloth, three places laid, and in each place two dozen oysters, with a bright golden lemon in their midst ... A tall bottle of Sauterne stood at each end of the table, carefully wiped except for the corks, which indicated in no uncertain manner that a long time had passed since it had been drawn ... Alas for the countless gay breakfasts of old, when oysters were swallowed by the thousand! I saw the end of those breakfasts, for they went out with the abbés, who always ate at least a gross of oysters and the chevaliers, who went on eating them forever. I regret them, but philosophically; if time can change governments, what powers it must have over mere customs! ... After the oysters, which proved admirably fresh, came broiled kidneys, a jar of truffled *foie gras* and the fondue.

It's not surprising to find many people of all walks of life and economic circumstances include the eating of oysters in some of their fondest memories—often, in Australia, of a simpler, quieter life, as Bruce Beaver evokes in these lines from *Letters to Live Poets:*

> coarse shell-sanded cloths
> of gold interspersed with porous
> rocks oyster decorated,
> bright water weed-webbed.
>
> The mud flat of Forty Baskets
> grey blue with circular soldier crabs ...

the men and boys wading for oysters,
toes feeling through old, thin canvas shoes
the bladed lip, the corrugated shell ...

Where has it gone?
Nowhere I can't recall
with the help of a little woodsmoke
sifting the evening air.

Sitting next to Mrs Blaiklock, sister-in-law of the late Lady Gallighan, at the far end of the table where we had been relegated by that formidable woman, I enquired what she was ordering for her entree. A dozen Sydney Rock oysters, Mrs Blailock replied. We were at the Australia Club for a literary dinner and I had mixed feelings—they could be wonderful or they could be awful. It was difficult to read the place and I had had some pretty sad, dried-out specimens at a restaurant not too long before. I asked her if she thought they'd be good. Yes, of course, they are always good here, she said. I still wasn't convinced and ordered Tasmanian scallops instead. These were delicious, no mistake, but when I watched the relish with which Mrs Blaiklock enjoyed her oysters I had regrets. Perhaps as compensation for my clearly misguided choice, she told me this charming story:

When she was a young girl her family lived somewhere along the Hawkesbury. On fine Sundays they would row out to Pulpit Rock, anchor the boat and proceed to picnic *à flot* on fresh wild oysters. Her brother would pry the oysters from the rock and pass them to the father who would open them. Their mother sat in command at the

A Gastronomic Nostalgia 293

back of the boat slicing loaves of freshly baked bread. Mrs Blailock's job was to butter these loaves ready to receive the oysters, liquor and all. She didn't say what they might have drunk but somehow I imagine a good home-brewed ginger beer.

Bibliography

Australian Dictionary of Biography general ed. Douglas Pike, Carlton: Melbourne University Press, 1969.

Aquaculture in Shallow Seas, Imai, Takeo (ed), Rotterdam, AA Balkema, 1980.

Australian Seafood Handbook, Yearsley, Last, Ward (eds), Hobart: CSIRO Marine Research, 1999.

Barthes, Roland, *The Empire of Signs*, (1970), New York: Hill and Wang, 1982.

Bolitho, Hector, *The Glorious Oyster*, London: Sidgwick & Jackson, 1960.

Brillat-Savarin, Jean-Anthelme, *The Physiology of Taste* (1825), London: Penguin Classics, 1994.

Brooks, William, K, *The Oyster: a popular summary of a scientific study* (1891), Baltimore: John Hopkins University Press, 1996.

Clark, Roy, *The Longshoremen*, London: David & Charles, 1974.

Clarke, Eleanor, *The Oysters of Locmariaquer* (1959), London: Secker & Warburg, 1965.

Collard, AO, *Oyster & Dredgers of Whitstable*, London: Collard, 1902.

Comte, Hubert, *l'Huître*, Paris: éditions volets verts, 1995.

Fisher, MFK, *Consider the Oyster*, (1941), New York: North Point Press, 1988.

Harrison, AJ, *Savant of the Australian Seas: William Saville-Kent and Australian Fisheries*, Hobart: Tasmanian Historical Research Association, 1997.

Harry, Harold, 'Synopsis of the Supraspecific Classification of Living Oysters', *The Verliger*, 28 (2): 121–158, October 1985.

Heasman, M and Lyall, I, 'Problems of producing and marketing the flat oyster *Ostrea angasi* in NSW' Fisheries Research Report Series: No 6, Sydney: NSW Dept of Fisheries, 2000.

Hickman, Neil, 'Flat Oyster Aquaculture; A Summary of Past Research in Victoria', unpublished paper, 1998.

Iversen, ES, *Farming the Edge of the Sea*, London: Fishing News (Books) Ltd, 1968.

The Journals of Cook on his Voyages of Discovery ed. Beaglehole, Vol I, *The Endeavour 1768–1771*; Cambridge University Press, 1955.

Karsnitz, J&V, *Oyster Cans*, Atglen, PA: Schiffer Publishing Ltd, 1993.

Karsnitz, J&V, *Oyster Plates*, Atglen, PA: Schiffer Publishing Ltd, 1993.

Kaplan, Alice, *French Lessons*, Chicago: University of Chicago Press, 1994.

Korringa, P, *Farming the Cupped Oysters of the Genus Crassostrea*, Amsterdam: Elsevier Scientific Publishing Company, 1976.

Larousse Gastronomique (1988), London: Hamlyn, Mandarin Paperback edition, 1990.

Lewis, Alan, *The Japanese Oyster: Amazing Healing Properties from the Sea*, Northhampshire: Thorsen's Publishers Ltd, 1981.

Moorhouse, Frank, 'The Grave Case of Oyster Abuse', *The Sydney Review*, September 1995.

Nell, John, 'Farming the Syney Rock Oyster (*Saccostrea commercialis*) in Australia', *Reviews in Fisheries Science* 1(2):97–120, 1993.

Newton, John, 'The Essence of Oysters', *Australian Gourmet Traveller*, October, 1995.

Newton, John and Greenwood, Helen, *Sydney Sources*, Adelaide: Wakefield Press, 2000.

New South Wales Fisheries 'Oyster Production Data from Oyster Farms in New South Wales', 1998/99.

Oysters, the History of their Growth, Melbourne Oyster Supply Ltd, c. 1957.

Philpots, RM, *Oysters and All About Them*, London: John Richardson & Co, 1890.

Quayle, DB, *Pacific Oyster Culture in British Columbia*, Ottawa: Department of Fisheries and Oceans, 1988.

Root, Waverly, *Food*, New York: Simon & Schuster, 1980.

Ross, Anne and members of the Quandamooka Aboriginal Land Council, 'Aboriginal Approaches to Cultural Heritage Management: A Quandamooka Case Study', Proceedings of the 1995 Australian Archaelogical Association Annual Conference, St Lucia: Anthropolgy Museum, University of Queensland, 1996.

Roughley, TC, *The Story of the Oyster* (Reprinted from the *Australian Museum Magazine*, vol II, 1925), Sydney: Alfred James Kent, Government Printer, 1929.

Rowell, Margit, *Objects of Desire*, New York: Museum of Modern Art, 1997.

Saunders, Alan, *A is for Apple*, Melbourne: William Heinemann Australia, 1995.

Saville-Kent, W, 'Oyster-Culture in Australia', *Australian Association for the Advancement of Science*, Vol 3, 1891.

Saville-Kent, W, *The Great Barrier Reef of Australia: its products and potentialities*, (first published London 1893) facsimile edition Melbourne: John Currey, O'Neil Pty Ltd, 1972.

Smith, GS, *The Queensland Oyster Fishery: an Illustrated History*, Brisbane: Queensland Department of Primary Industries Information Series, 1985.

Sumner, Colin, 'Oysters and Tasmania', part I — *Tasmanian Fisheries Research*, Vol 6, No 2 (1972); part II — *Tasmanian Fisheries Research*, Vol 3, No 2 (1974).

Symons, Michael, *The Shared Table; Ideas for Australian Cuisine*, Canberra: Australian Government Publishing Service, 1993.

Thomson, JM 'The Acclimatization and Growth of the Pacific Oyster (*Gryphae gigas*) in Australia', (1951) and 'The Naturalization of the Pacific Oyster in Australia', *Australian Journal of Marine and Freshwater Research* 10: 144–49 (1958).

Toussaint-Samat, Maguelonne, *History of Food* (1987), Oxford: Blackwell Publishers, 1994.

Trewartha and Bayly, *The World's Your Oyster*, Ceduna, 1993.

Wallace-Carter, Evelyn, *For They Were Fishers: The History of the Fishing Industry in South Australia*, Adelaide: Amphitrite Publishing House, 1987.

Walne, PR, *Culture of Bivalve Molluscs: 50 years' experience at Conwy*, Surrey: Fishing News (Books) Ltd, 1974.

Welsby, Thomas, *The Collected Works of Thomas Welsby*, (1919), Brisbane: Jacaranda Press, 1967.

Williams, L and Warner, K, *Oysters: a connoisseur's guide and cookbook*, Berkeley: Ten Speed Press, 1990.

Wray, Tim, 'Century of Oyster Farming: Batemans Bay', *Australian Oyster Magazine*, November, 1982.

Yonge, CM *Oysters*, London: Collins, 1960.

List of Illustrations

Page 1 Puntload of mangrove sticks being towed to catching area, 1930s (Roy Mills, NSW Fisheries)

Page 23 Working the shell bed, 1930s (Roy Mills, NSW Fisheries)

Page 28 Oyster anatomy. *Top:* left side of oyster with shell removed. *Bottom:* Oyster in left shell, mantle removed to show body. *a.* hinge, *b.* edge of mantle, *c.* adductor, *d.* pericardium, *f.* hinge, *g.* gills, *h.* lips (Brooks, 1891)

Page 36 The different species of oyster cultivated in Australia for food—from left to right Sydney Rock, Pacific, Native *angasi*

Page 51 Stages of larvae development (Brooks, 1891)

Page 57 Midden of Native *angasi* Little Swanport (Gay Bilson)

Page 63 Tonging from a jetty *c.* 1950s (Roy Mills, NSW Fisheries)

Page 65 Oysters growing on catch and grow rock slabs *c.* 1940s (Roy Mills, NSW Fisheries)

Page 70 Culling oysters on shore, Bill Smith and stepsons, Carters Island, Georges River, 1920s (Allen family)

Page 74 Dredgers with the tools of the trade (1909) Photograph courtesy of the State Library of South Australia.

Page 78 Pegstone, Clyde River (TC Roughley standing in the boat in the background, 1930s), (Roy Mills, NSW Fisheries)

Page 83 Mangrove catching sticks stuck vertically in the mud, 1930s (Roy Mills, NSW Fisheries)

Page 85 Different early catching and growing methods: rocks on shelves; mangrove sticks in bundles; maturing oysters on sticks (Roy Mills, NSW Fisheries)

Page 87 Shore depot with frames (using sawn sticks) in foreground, 1950s (Roy Mills, NSW Fisheries)

Page 89 Culling in bottom of large wooden punt, 1930s

Page 92 Truck loaded with oyster frames (caught sticks) ready to move to new estuary, 1950s

Page 100 Shore depot and cutter (Melbourne Oyster Company), Pipe Clay Bay late 1930s (Roy Mills, NSW Fisheries)

Page 107 Oyster trays, Hawkesbury (David Brooks)

Page 111 The Big Oyster, Taree (courtesy of *Manning River Times*)

Page 113 Diving for oysters, Clyde River (courtesy Allan Paxton)

Page 114 Oysters growing on 'ironmongery', Oyster Farmers' Association of NSW (Ted Allen as a boy far left) (Andrew Derwent)

Page 119 Oyster farmers at Lime Burners Creek (courtesy Bicentennial Copying Project, State Library of NSW)

Page 127 Dredging in deep water, Government Printing Office collection, State Library of NSW
Page 130 Oyster grader *c.* 1890–1900s imported from France (David Brooks)
Page 140 'Coathangers' on long line with trays of young oysters (in foreground), Ocean Foods International, (Christine O'Brien)
Page 144 Oyster Fleet, Port Pirie, 1910 (courtesy State Library of South Australia)
Page 149 'B.S.T.' adjustable long line system at low tide, Turner Aquaculture (Gay Bilson)
Page 161 Rubber gloves set out to dry, Andrea Cole's shore depot (Gay Bilson)
Page 165 Handforged tools for culling etc. Allen's shore depot (David Brooks)
Page 175 Oyster Farmers' Association of NSW competition for best unopened dozen oysters [opened winning dozen upper right], 1999 Annual Luncheon (David Brooks)
Page 182 Farmers in wooden punt with bags of oysters, 1940s (Roy Mills, NSW Fisheries)
Page 195 View from inside an oyster grader (courtesy of OYSA)
Page 199 Oyster lease sign, Crookhaven River (David Brooks)
Page 201 Ted Allen with sons Barry and Brian at shore depot, Greenwell Point (David Brooks)
Page 206 Pacific oysters from Franklin Harbour (Gay Bilson)
Page 215 Author's collection of oyster knives (David Brooks)
Page 228 Oyster cans (Jim and Viv Karsnitz)
Page 244 Oyster plate (Jim and Viv Karsnitz)
Page 259 Oyster plate (Jim and Viv Karsnitz)
Page 271 Untitled bark painting by Nanitjawuy featuring Yulungul (the great python). Djarka (goanna) and Wayanaka (oyster beds) (Anthropology Museum, The University of Queensland)
Page 277 Oyster forks (David Brooks)
Page 282 'Knights of the Round Keg' early 1930s (Andrew Derwent)
Page 285 Lily Cups Executive Dinner, 1967 (photograph by Jack Hickson, APA Collection, State Library of New South Wales)
Page 289 Parkes Oyster Refreshment Rooms *c.* 1900 (Clarence River Historical Society)
Page 293 Smith family, oyster farmers Georges River. Harriet Smith (the Allen's maternal grandmother) is the young girl, 1905, Carters Island (Allen family)
Page 296 The Good Life, 1956 (photo Ern McQuillen, courtesy Festival Records)

INDEX

A
à pleine mer flavour 160
Abers Disease 101
Aboriginals 57–59, 117
adductor muscle 37, 95, 224
Adelaide 153
Adjustable Longline System (B.S.T. system) 120, 141, 149
affordability 281–287
age 52
Albany (WA) 69, 134
Albany rock oyster 135–136
algal blooms 104
America *see* United States
American Indians 83
anatomy 25–29, 37–41
  hinge 224–225
  organs 247–249
  shell 202–209
Angels on Horseback (recipe) 266
aphrodisiac qualities 251–252
appearance 202–203, 269–270
appetite stimulation 250
aquaculture 199, 286
Armoricaine oyster 35
auctioning of leases 118
availablility 21–25, 53, 166–172, 176–180

B
'bad' oysters 184
barbecue 257
Batemans Bay (NSW) 126, 129, 130
'beard' 247
beer 280
Belgium 245
Belon oyster 35–36
Biblical prohibitions 253–254
Big Oyster 110
Bilton, Jonathan 134–137
biology *see* anatomy
'bistro' grade 193
Blacklip oyster (*Saccostrea echinata*) 31, 120
blacksick 24, 50
blindfold taste test 246
blooms, algal 104
Bonamiasis 102–103
'bottle' grade 193
breeding 44–50. *see also* spawning
Brittany 33, 35–36, 141, 160
Broome (WA) 237

B.S.T. system 120, 141, 149
buoying 162
buttons 237
buying 172, 174, 184, 185–187, 225

C
calories 250
canning 227–228
carbon-fixing 207
carpetbag steak (recipe) 266
catch muscle 208–209
catching spats 75–87
'catching' sticks 86
Ceduna (SA) 153
chalky deposits 207
chambering 207
champagne 278–279
chewing versus swallowing 278
Chinese 82
cholesterol 250–251
cilia 37, 248
civey of oysters (recipe) 258
classification 29–37, 203
cleaning 216
Clyde River (NSW) 126–131
Coffin Bay (SA) 143
Cole, Andrea 160–162, 165
collecting oysters
  see also dredging
  diving for oysters 112–113
  early Queensland 116–118
  tonging 63
collecting spat 75–87
colour
  body 41–42
  pearls 237
  shell 205
comingling 187
communication 48
conchyolin 205
condition 43, 53–54, 166–167, 169, 180
contests, eating 290
Cook, Captain 58
cooking 254–259
cooking vessels, shells as 232
copper flavour 245
Coral and Jade (recipe) 261
Cossington Smith, Grace 273
Coste, Jean Jacques 71–72, 83
Cowell (SA) 148–151

crabs 209–210
Crassostrea gigas see Pacific oyster
Crassostreinae
  classification 30–32
  cultivation methods 84
  feeding 39
  'R' rule 23
  reproduction 44–47, 48–50, 53
cross-breeding 34
ctendia 247
cultivation
  Aboriginals 58
  ancient world 70–71
  Clyde River (NSW) 126–131
  early Australia 55–56, 64–70
  England 72–73
  France 41–42
  Hawkesbury (NSW) 122–126
  intertidal culture 94–96
  labour 111–112
  modern methods 86–97
  origin of modern methods 70–72
  Queensland 119–120
  single-seed culture 93–94
  South Australia 142–153
  stick and tray 82–93
  subtidal culture 96–97
  Tasmania 156–165
  technological advances 110–111
  unusual methods 112–115
  Western Australia 133–141
cultured pearls 237–239
cupped oysters 36–37
cylinders for cultivation 93–94

D
David Jones oyster bar 273–274
depots 89
depuration 183–184
destruction of beds 60–62
differences between species 29–37
digestibility 250–251
digestive organs 248–249
diseases 98–108
  see also pests
  Bonamiasis 102–103
  pearl oysters 238–239
  QX disease 101–102, 238
  winter mortality 99–100
diving
  for oysters 112–114
  for pearls 239
dredging 62, 113
  England 72–73
  NSW 63
  Queensland 63, 118
  South Australia 144–146
  Tasmania 61–62, 73–74, 145, 157
droppers (lines) 103
Dyke family 154, 159–160, 161, 162, 165

E
eating 241–247, 254, 268–269, 277–278, 290–292. *see also* cooking; restaurants
eggs 46–47, 49, 53
Emu Point (WA) 134
England 72–73, 279–280, 281, 283, 284
environmental degradation 101
European oyster (*Ostrea edulis*) 23–24
eutrophication 43, 104
evolution 26
excretion 41
exhalant chamber 41
explorers' records 58–60
export
  oysters 188
  pearls 239
Eyre, Edward John 60

F
family ownership 201
farming *see* cultivation
fat content 250–251
fattening 55–56, 172–176
favourites, author's 14–15
feeding 37–39, 43
fencing 91
fish predators 210
five-finger starfish 211
fjords 114–115
flat oysters 36–37
flavour 13, 181, 243–246
floods 104–105
foot 27, 30
forks 277
France
  Belon oyster 35–36
  buying oysters 174
  Coste's research 71–72
  cultivation 41–42
  eating oysters 268–269
  serving oysters 276
  spat-catching 80–81
Franklin Harbour (SA) 148–150
freezing 228–229
Frenchman Bay (WA) 136–138
freshness 184, 225

Index

Freycinet Marine Farm (Tas.) 160, 196
frying 267
future developments 110–111

G
gaping 225
genetic engineering 110–111
Georges River (NSW) 66
gills 30, 247–248
goût de terroir 12–13, 41
government leases 118
government regulation 199–200
grades 193–194
Great Oyster Bay (Tas.) 159
Greece, ancient 29
Greek immigrants 128
greysick 24, 50
growth 52
Guinness 280
gumbo (recipe) 262–263
Gwawley Bay, Georges River (NSW) 66

H
habitat 32–35
harvesting 91–92, 169–170, 183–184
hatcheries
  Native *angasi* 189
  South Australia 152–153
  Tasmania 160, 164
  Western Australia 138–141
Hawkesbury River (NSW) 122–126
head 26
health food, oysters as 252–253
heart 249
heat kill 103–104
hermaphoditism 44–45
hessian bags for storage 226
'highway' oyster production 92–93
hinge 224–225
hobby farms 201
holiday season 24–25
Holland 200
Holt, Thomas 66
huîtres vertes 12, 41–42
hybrids 34

I
indigenous oysters 31. *see also* Native oyster
intertidal culture 94–96

J
Japan
  buying oysters 174
  cultivation 95
  pearls 237–239
  spat-catching 79, 82
Japanese oyster (*Crassostrea gigas*) *see* Pacific oyster
jewellery, shells for 230, 232
Jewish dietary customs 253

K
King George Sound, Albany (WA) 69
knives 214–215
Kumamoto oyster 156

L
language 233–234
Larner's Oyster Supply 133–134, 225
larvae *see* spat
laying out 90
lease system 118, 199–200
legends 231
legislation 64, 118, 145–146
life cycle 45–54, 76–78, 87–88
life span 51–52
lime production 64
liquor 278–280
literature, oysters in 233–236
Little Swanport (Tas.) 159, 162, 165
'liver' 248
locomotion 27
Louis XIV 12

M
Macquarie, Governor 59–60
mangrove crab 209
mangrove sticks 83
mantle 205, 247, 249
marketing 185–199
Marteilia sydneyi disease 101
maturity 52
Melbourne Oyster Supply Ltd 189–191
metamorphosis 50–52
metaphor 234–235
microwaving 217
middens 57–58, 159
Milky oyster (*Saccostrea amasa*) 31, 120
modernisation 201
months for oysters *see* 'R' rule; seasons
Moreton Bay (Qld) 119
Moreton Bay Oyster Company 191
mornay oysters (recipe) 267–268
mother-of-pearl 206
movement 27–29
Moxham, Rob 122–126
mud oyster *see* Native oyster
mudworm 65, 99, 118

muscles 208–209
  adductor 37, 95, 224
mussels 123

N

nacre 237, 238, 240
names, scientific 31–32
national parks 119, 124, 126
Native oyster (*Ostrea angasi*)
  buying 225
  classification 31
  diseases 102
  feeding 38
  flavour 244
  habitat 34–35
  marketing 188–189
  season 179
  shell 206–207
  size 176
  South Australia 142–147
  storage 227
  Tasmania 158
  Western Australia 134, 135–136
New South Wales
  cultivation 120–131
  early attempts 66–67
  season 176–180
New Zealand rock oyster (*Saccostrea glomerata*) 32
nomenclature 16, 31–32
Norway 83, 114–115
nutritional value 250

O

oatmeal 55
Ocean Foods International 97, 134–141, 194
octopus 232
'off' oysters 184
omega-3 250
openers 220–222
opening 212–224
opening disease 99–100
organs 247–249
'orient' (pearl colour) 237
Ostrea angasi see Native oyster
Ostrea edulis 23–24, 36
Ostrea ordensis 40
Ostreinae
  classification 30–32
  feeding 38–39
  'R' rule 23
  reproduction 44–45, 48, 49
overcatch 88–89

oxygen requirement 27, 247
oyster bars 273–274, 289
Oyster Bay Oysters Pty Ltd 154, 162
Oyster Farmers' Association 114
Oyster Farmers Coffin Bay (company) 147
oyster knife 214–215
oyster saloons 288–290
Oyster Town (SA) 143
oyster tray 276
Oysterage (company) 129

P

Pacific oyster (*Crassostrea gigas*)
  classification 31
  flavour 181
  introduction 33–34
  as pest 40–41
  'R' rule 23
  season 179–180
  shell 206
  size 176
  South Australia 147–148, 151–152
  Tasmania 154–156, 162–165
  Western Australia 135
packing 183
painting oysters 270–273
parasites 101–103, 238–239
pearl buttons 237
pearl meat 239–240
pearl oyster (Pycnodonteinae) 30
pearling 239
pearls 236–240
pegstone method of spat-catching 78–79
periostracum 205
perkinsus 238–239
Perth 133, 136
pests
  England 73
  mudworm 65, 99, 118
  predators 90–91, 209–211
pests, oysters as 33–34, 40–41
photographing oysters 272
Pinctada 236–237, 239
plankton 38
'plate' grade 193
poached oyster tart (recipe) 263–264
poetry 15, 235–236
pollution 105–108
pork 267
Port Albert (Vic.) 131
Port Lincoln (SA) 143, 144

Index

Port Phillip Bay (Vic.) 132
Port Stephens Fisheries Centre 189
position 26–27
poverty and oysters 281–284
predators 90–91, 209–211
preserving 227–228
prices 189, 195–199, 283, 286
production 198
protection
  early England 72–73
  legislation 64, 118, 145–146
  'R' rule 24, 171
provenance 186–187
purification 183–184
Pycnodonteinae 30

Q

quality
  assessing 174–175
  determining factors 37, 41–43
  purification 183–184
Queensland 116–120
quick muscle 46, 208
QX disease 101

R

'R' rule 21–25, 45, 167, 171
racks 87–91
rafts 97
recipes
  of earlier times 254–258
  modern 260–269
'recruitment' (spat-catching) 75–87
'reefers' 117
refrigeration 22, 168, 226, 229
reproduction 44–50. *see also* spawning
respiration 247
restaurants 172, 220–222, 273–275, 287–290
retail 287–290
rinsing 181, 214, 218, 222–223
ripeness 53, 168, 180
roast oyster sauce (recipe) 257
Rock oyster (*Saccostrea glomerata*)
  flavour 243, 244
  habitat 32–33
  New Zealand Rock oyster 32
  Queensland 119
  season 177–179
  Sydney Rock oyster
    see Sydney Rock oyster
  Western Australia 135–136
Rockefeller oysters (recipe) 264–265
Romans, ancient 22, 71, 83, 284

S

Saccostrea amasa (Milky oyster) 31, 120
Saccostrea echinata (Blacklip oyster) 31, 120
Saccostrea glomerata see Rock oyster
safety 184
salinity 42–43, 100–101, 181–182
saloons 288–290
saltiness 181–182
Samios, Peter 273
sauces 257, 268
Saville-Kent, William 66–69, 131–132, 157–158
schedule, oyster-farmers' 108–110
scientific names 31–32
seasons 21–25, 53–54, 166–167, 171, 176–180
sensory function 249
serving oysters 274–277
set and forget system (stick and tray culture) 82–93, 123
sex change 44–45, 48–49
shape 202–203
shell
  anatomy 203–207
  empty, uses for 29, 230–232
  evolution 26–29
  hinge 224–225
  middens 57–58, 159
  for spat-catching 79–80, 82
shell buttons 237
Shellfish Quality Assurance Program 183
shore depot 91
shucking 212–224
single-seed culture 93–94
size 39–40, 175–176, 193–194
South Australia
  cultivation 142–153
  season 179–180
spat (larvae)
  catching 75–87
  growth 50–52
  hatcheries *see* hatcheries
spawning
  biology of 45–47
  effect on condition 166–169
  number of times 49
  season 53
  spat-catching 76
  species differences 23–24
species 23, 29–37
sperm 46–47

splitting (opening) 212–224
spoilage 22
Stansbury (SA) 196
Stanway cylinder 93–94
starfish 211
steak, carpetbag (recipe) 266
steamed oysters (recipe) 260
stew of oysters (recipe) 260
Stewart Island (New Zealand) mud
 oyster (*Tiostrea chilensi*) 203
stick and tray culture 82–93, 123
stomach 248–249
stone method of spat-catching 78–79, 82
storage 225–229
stress 103
style (organ) 248–249
subtidal culture 96–97
supply companies 189–192
swallowing versus chewing 278
Swan estuary (WA) 68–69
Sydney Fish Markets 185–186, 197
Sydney Rock oyster (*Saccostrea amasa*)
 buying 172
 classification 31–32
 cultivation in NSW 120
 flavour 245–246
 habitat 32–33
 harvesting 169, 170–171
 'R' rule 23
 season 167
 shell 206
 size 176
 South Australia 146–147
 storing 225–226

T

Tabasco sauce 268
Tahiti 237
Tamar River (Tas.) 163
tart (recipe) 263–264
Tasmania
 cultivation 164–165
 season 179–180
taste 12, 181, 243–246
taxonomy 29–32, 37, 203
temperature
 harvesting 171–172
 heat kill 103–104
 quality determinant 42
 for spat-catching 81
 spawning 43–44, 45–46
 storage 228–229
 Western Australia 137–138

texture 175
therapeutic value 250
tides 94–96, 162
tinned oysters 227–228
Tiostrea chilensi 203
tonging 62
tourism 110
toxins 104
transferring 74, 97
transport 22–23, 92–93, 187–188, 226
triploid 111
trompage stage 95
Turner Aquaculture 148–150, 153

U

United States
 cooking 258
 eating oysters 268
 leases 200
 nineteenth century 283
 pollution 107–108
 predators 211
 spat-catching 79–80

V

valves *see* shell
velum 50
Venezuela 237
Victoria
 cultivation 131–133
 season 179
vitamins 250

W

waste expulsion 41
water pollution 105–108
water quality 42–43
'well-flavoured' oysters 14
Western Australia
 cultivation 133–141
 early attempts 67–70
Western Port Bay (Vic.) 131
Western rock oyster 135–136
whelks 82, 210–211
whistling 47–48
wildlife 126–127
wine 278–279
winter mortality 99–100
World War I 284
World War II 285

X

xenomorph 91

Z

Zinc 252

and broken at t
they are viscous

cold

like the at

white